A Daughter of Singapore

Life Lessons of a Homegrown Tour Guide

Thomas W. Paradis with Cathy Ross

Copyright © 2025 by Thomas W. Paradis

All rights reserved. No part of this publication may be reproduced, distributed, or transmitted in any form or by any means, without prior written permission.

Published by Thomas W. Paradis
Indianapolis, IN. USA

Book Layout © 2019 BookDesignTemplates.com
Typeset in Baskerville Old Face

Cover designed and produced by Anna Burrous.
Cover art by Adam Chua, www.caricaturist.sg
Back cover photo: Davide Russo, Creative Commons license

A Daughter of Singapore—1st ed.
ISBN 978-1-7334838-6-5 (paperback)
ISBN 978-1-7334838-7-2 (eBook)

Dedicated to all tour guides in Singapore and beyond

Contents

Author's Notes 7
Preface 9

1. Mama's Corner 14
2. The Busybody 24
3. Life Inside the Teapot 31
4. Errol's World 39
5. A Phantom Grandfather 47
6. The Rich Auntie 59
7. Being Errol's Daughter 71
8. Visiting the Kampong 77
9. Eating Potatoes 83
10. A Catholic in Singapore 91
11. The House of Durians and Incense 103
12. Across the Strait 113
13. Filial Piety at Tiger Balm Gardens 123
14. A New Hope 131
15. The Promoter 137
16. Breaking Out 147
17. The Clubbing Years 159
18. Selling Singapore 167
19. A Coveted License 179
20. A Second Reunion 189
21. Precious Earrings 193
22. Four Cultures and a Wedding 199
23. Into the Suburbs 209

Select Topics: Around Town with Cathy 221

Guiding Behind the Scenes: An Interview 223
Supporting the Troops 241
The Lighters: Cleansing the Singapore River 253
The Hungry Ghost: Cathy and the Paranormal 269
The Backstory of *Crazy Rich Asians* 285

Bibliography 303
Acknowledgements 309

Author's Notes

To protect the trust and identities of individuals mentioned throughout the book, the names of some family members and friends have been replaced with pseudonyms.

Any mention of monetary costs in "dollars" ($) is shorthand for Singapore dollars (S$).

Preface

This is the witty and inspirational early-life memoir of Singapore tour guide, Cathy Ross. As a mixed-race child from a Chinese Catholic family, she lived with her paternal grandmother and was bounced around to various extended family members throughout her youth. She further happened to live amidst Singapore's upheaval from a sleepy, colonial outpost to a bustling, global metropolis that took off during her childhood years. Hers may not be a full-blown "rags to riches" story—after all, she is still seeking the latter. Rather, perhaps her experience is more a "missing parents to middle class" tale, which may be even more relatable to her fellow, first-generation Singaporeans.

In many ways, Cathy's personal story parallels that of Singapore, albeit immensely scaled up. She and her country both experienced growing pains, setbacks, lessons learned, hard-won accomplishments, and steadfast perseverance to reach some version of success. Most important, both Cathy and her national leaders remained staunch optimists, dreaming of a brighter future. Consequently, this book weaves these narratives together to better understand our protagonist, along with the emerging nation in which she grew up.

Just as great ideas can emerge from scribbles on a napkin, the concept for this book was born inside a tour van. Cathy first came to the attention of my wife, Linda, and me during a multi-day visit there in January 2019. Like many visitors, we were primarily there to experience the "highlights reel" of the urban scene, hoping to one day return for a protracted stay. And yes, we had already adored the hit romantic comedy film, *Crazy Rich Asians*, released the previous year. As an American professor of urban geography, I was personally curious to explore the reality on the ground as compared to the glitzy metropolis portrayed on-screen. Was this place little more than a backdrop and playground for the "crazy rich?" I suspected there was much more reality to uncover, as there always is.

For that expedition we splurged on a private tour, without knowing who would greet us on the receiving end. It was to our unequivocal luck and benefit that Cathy was matched with us for the duration of our stay. Better yet, she graciously put up with my endless nerdy questions about urban history and population traits (much of which she knew well). When in teacher mode, she even quizzed us periodically on Singaporean terms, such as *kampong, choping,* and *trishaw.* But she could also pivot quickly to more unusual requests, including strolls through actual public housing estates and their everyday urban neighborhoods.

She further took us to more obscure places not found on a typical itinerary. One amazing stop involved the headquarters for the Urban Redevelopment Authority (URA), the heartbeat for the country's land-use planning and visioning processes. It was here where Cathy launched into a portion of her "maritime tour" as we gaped in awe at a sprawling, interactive 3-D model of the entire island. Equally eye-opening was the expansive sales floor of the Housing and Development Board (HDB), where some 80 percent of all Singaporeans shop for their future homes built within walkable, transit-friendly communities.

If Cathy was still trying to figure me out, she hit it off

instantly with Linda. They both became fast friends and behaved accordingly. Both displayed their gregarious, fun-loving personalities and senses of humor in full force, quickly making them "sisters from another mother." For these reasons, Cathy felt even more comfortable sharing tidbits from her own storied past.

At some point, Cathy made the offhand comment that multiple people had suggested writing a book about her colorful life and rather chaotic upbringing. There was apparently much more to tell than what we were hearing on short notice. We had already enjoyed a sampling of her personal tales, along with her efforts to break into Singapore's emerging tourism industry. She recounted her family's early public housing flats, how she stayed safe from roaming street gangs, and how she avoided the unpredictable rages of an alcoholic father. Somewhere in there was a "rich auntie" and a "phantom grandfather," both of whom seemed to appear at critical times in her life. Oh, and most of her numerous uncles had been to jail, with tattoo-covered bodies and all. Such spotty stories captured our attention, and we wanted to learn more.

Despite all of this, three decades later she had ascended to become one of her nation's most respected and accomplished tour guides. Her success was due less to personal ambition and more to an insatiable desire to learn, experience new things, and to teach others. Of course, all of this was secondary to her unwavering drive to escape the relative poverty of her childhood. More recently she has delivered keynote speeches at regional tour-guiding conferences, and she increasingly appears on professional YouTube videos and even local newscasts. When not formally guiding, she can be found volunteering to teach up-and-coming tour guides the tricks of the trade or giving inspirational talks to school children. We came away with the same underlying question: How did she make it from there to here?

After first mentioning the book idea, Cathy quickly confessed that writing was not her forte, let alone publishing a full memoir. Without thinking twice, I offered to consider taking on the project if she wished to continue. Given my previous academic and travel books, I was certain this could be accomplished in one way or another. Still, I had never written a memoir of someone else, so there would be a serious learning curve on my part as well.

Fast forward about four months, when the *Coronavirus*, or Covid pandemic had shut down much of the world. Cathy found herself suddenly out of work and essentially stuck inside her family's flat for nearly a year. Back in America, my faculty colleagues and I were sequestering in our own homes while stumbling through our spring courses now taught online. The United States endured a lengthy "lockdown" while Singapore wrestled with its equivalent "Circuit Breaker."

It was at some point during this global mess when I contacted Cathy to catch up and to see if she was still interested in teaching me about her past. With few options there for social outlets—her worst possible nightmare—she was more than eager to chat for hours at a time about her personal history. By the time much of the world had reawakened from Covid, Cathy had provided more than 150 pages of recorded interview transcripts.

Nearly three years later and with rough draft in hand, we convened online once again to review my narrative and to make corrections. From opposite sides of the world, Cathy screened every sentence while I read along. When we managed to thread the time zone needle, we made sure the narrative accurately reflected her stories, emotions, memories, and experiences.

In addition to featuring Cathy's own personal tales and lessons, our vision for this book was broader in scope. As geographers teach, "You are where you live." Cathy's life and cultural identity are rooted in the place where she grew up and resides to this day. We can therefore gain a more nuanced understanding of her life by weaving in Singapore's own remarkable stories since gaining independence in 1965. That Cathy is most certainly a daughter of Singapore will become evident soon enough. For readers eager to learn more about this fascinating city-state, Cathy's memories are interlaced with a good amount of Singapore's own storyline.

To avoid interrupting the flow of Cathy's life story, I further provide some specialized chapters about Singapore's history and cultural traditions at the end. Happily, these all still integrate Cathy's own recollections, though more as an informed observer. The exception is the first piece, an extensive conversation with Cathy about tour guiding behind the scenes and her career within Singapore's tourism industry. This is followed by my own chapters on "select topics," including the Hungry Ghost festival, the tradition of *lighter* boats and former river trade, and Singapore's Armed Forces with Cathy's own role to play. The book wraps up appropriately with the irresistible backstory to the 2018 film, *Crazy Rich Asians*, along with Cathy's perspectives on its local impacts.

What follows is a story full of optimism, perseverance, occasional heartbreak, personal growth, forgiveness, silver linings, true grit, and life lessons galore. Not to mention a lot of fun and laughter. We further intend to provide a rare voice to her fellow tour guides everywhere, who essentially serve as on-the-ground ambassadors for their own homes and countries. With tourism now the world's largest industry, millions of travelers rely heavily on guides like Cathy to learn more and to enhance their understanding of local places. And now, let's get on with it. It is my distinct pleasure to introduce you to Singapore tour guide extraordinaire, Cathy Ross!

Chapter 1

Mama's Corner

Only two years after her nation's independence in 1965, Cathy entered the world as one of her city-state's earliest citizens. She would never know any different, having missed earlier eras under the flags of Great Britain, Japan (briefly), and Malaysia (also briefly). Singaporean or not, there was a catch. This fledgling new nation was still a far cry from the glamorous fantasy world of the *Marina Bay Sands* resort, or the *Crazy Rich Asians* feature film. Most of the nation's two million residents still endured some combination of overcrowding, racial strife, and economic struggles. The household into which Cathy appeared was no different. Cramped inside a small public housing flat with mostly absent parents meant she was not exactly poised for future success. Few children were in those days. Cathy and her sister were not technically orphans; both mother and father were still quite alive. But the result was the same. Without their reliable presence, the girls relied instead on the irregular goodwill of extended family members. It is in this way that Cathy's own story begins.

With no other reasonable option, it fell to *Mama*—a well-meaning if cantankerous grandmother—to take in the girls and serve as primary guardian. Mama had begrudgingly agreed to do so only because no one else seemed very interested in the job. On one level, her selfless generosity was a godsend. When not gambling away precious funds to play the numbers, Mama could usually be counted on for providing basic meals and childcare. On less fortunate days, the scrawny sisters might end up in bed with precious little food in their bellies.

Cathy's older sister by two years also had a twin, though she passed at eight months. Nobody, their mother included, knew why the twin had died. The family wrote it off as a mysterious sickness. It did not help that decent medical care for infants was hard to come by.

The girls accordingly relied upon Mama's basic cooking skills and her religious use of equally basic ingredients. Whether Mama knew it or not, the children were never guaranteed a reasonable blend of daily nutrition. What today is known as food insecurity would remain an ongoing concern well into Cathy's teenage years.

One saving grace was Singapore's unique and relentlessly expanding public housing program. The ambitious goal was to provide sanitary and modern high-rise flats to the new nation's impoverished and overcrowded population. It was inside one of these modest, one-bedroom flats where Cathy and her sister could at least call home. Located on the fourth floor of a 12-story residential block, their flat resembled the standard size and layout of hundreds of similar homes perched all around them.

When compared to Mama's earlier life challenges, caring for two toddlers under a stable roof seemed like, well, child's play. Now middle-aged, she had accomplished nothing less than survive the brutal Japanese Occupation of World War II while managing to provide for five children of her own. She was essentially battle tested, which meant that few other challenges in life concerned her much. When it came time to step up, she once again grabbed the wheel and made sure her granddaughters did not need to fend for themselves.

The fourth member of the household was Cathy's kind-hearted if stoic and reserved Uncle Kellard. He turned out to be Mama's more reliable and dependable son. To his credit, Kellard proved to be something of a surrogate father to the girls. Unlike certain siblings, he managed to remain employed much of the time, serving as the family's designated provider. Together with Mama's flat and their uncle's precious income, their household of three generations plodded along through much of Cathy's childhood.

To be fair, the sisters were hardly alone in their predicament. Singapore had suddenly gained its official independence from the federation of Malaysia on 9 August 1965. While one might presume this occurred through the usual, hard-fought revolution, the precise opposite was true. The island of Singapore was unceremoniously booted out of Malaysia after only two years—another story beyond the reach of this one. The bottom line was that Singapore's fledgling leaders were essentially in shock. They had not intended nor planned to suddenly ramp up a new island nation. And problems at home were mounting. Unemployment hovered around 14 percent. Educational opportunities were similarly grim and were reserved for an elite minority. Overcrowding and unsanitary living conditions were rampant, both in the city and within hundreds of farming villages, or *kampongs*, that still dotted the island.

This is why, as Cathy grew more self-aware, she could easily identify with the plight of her own friends and classmates. Many of them claimed to be outcasts or even orphans scraping by with their own unpredictable lives. It was actually quite rare to find a friend who could boast of at least one reliable and available parent at home.

Such economic and social headaches became the highest priority for the newly formed government to puzzle out—and quickly. In the meantime, it was largely up to the kindness and ingenuity of extended family members to creatively provide for children without parents. This was the Singaporean world in which Cathy found herself at the dawn of her newly minted city-state.

At that time, her housing block was located on the edge of Little India along Serangoon Road. During Cathy's youth, the advent of more spacious and even luxurious high-rise housing was still years into the future. At this point the government was in desperation mode, moving its residents from overcrowded conditions into minimalist, standardized housing with modern conveniences. The government's own Housing and Development Board, or HDB, became responsible for the country's ongoing public housing program—or, as locals refer to it, HDB housing.

As for the whereabouts of the girls' parents, each is owed a separate story to gradually unfold. Their Chinese mother, whose Catholic name is Mary, had left the family when Cathy was two years old. And on the rare occasions when their wayward father, Errol appeared, it was always for a short time and typically accompanied by a lingering stench of beer. Arriving unannounced with a new girlfriend or wife in tow was not out of the question.

In his younger days, local women were known to find Errol rather attractive. His handsome physique was aided in no small part by his Scottish lineage through the Ross family, not to mention a dreamy accent to go with it. His name might have conjured romantic images of Scotland, though it was his light-skinned complexion that gave him away as European. Women of Chinese descent called him *Ang Mo Kia*, or the "White boy," with much admiration.

This special distinction was certainly nothing of his own doing, and it was likely more trouble than it was worth. Singapore neighborhoods were—and are—akin to small towns, and Errol soon earned a local reputation as a ladies' man. Beyond that, he imbibed so often that, as Cathy describes, she "believed he was related to the Guinness Brothers." In truth, Guinness beer was too expensive for Errol's budget at the time, so he enjoyed an average of six cans per day of *ABC*, a brand of the Stout company local to Singapore. More completely known as the Archipelago Brewing Company, *ABC Stout* had become locally accepted, both brewed and bottled in Singapore since 1933. A true Guinness beer was considered a treat that few could afford.

Aside from Errol's Scottish background, his mother (Mama) was Chinese. This meant that the "White boy" was more accurately biracial—or Eurasian, as they say in Singapore. Mama was therefore Cathy's paternal grandmother. For those keeping track, this made Cathy and her sister approximately three-quarters Chinese. The sisters still carried the Ross family name and nearly one-quarter Scottish blood, a fact that Cathy would not realize until adulthood.

With such a mixed-race household, it was perhaps inevitable that Cathy became comfortably bilingual from an early age. This would become a vital silver lining in her otherwise unpredictable childhood. Cathy would no doubt find her unique set of language skills to be of high value later in life.

Though certainly not overcrowded by Singaporean standards, their cramped flat was usually bursting at the seams from its four permanent residents and occasional guests. Their home was composed of a single bedroom, a bathroom, and a living room with attached kitchen. This was standard fare for public housing accommodations at the time. A typical nightly arrangement saw Kellard commandeering the sofa in the living room, while the girls shared a bunk bed in the single bedroom. During these earlier years, the sofa was likely employed more for sleeping than sitting.

What about Mama? Their stalwart grandmother was already quite adept with handling cramped spaces. She had endured substandard housing for much of her life, making this latest home luxurious by comparison. Her choice to sleep on the living room floor by the bedroom doorway was therefore a natural one. Cathy referred to this undefined space as "Mama's corner."

The single bathroom was bare of all but the essentials, with its simple shower stall and sink, but no bathtub. Thinking practically, Cathy recalls that bathtubs were "a luxury, and a bloody waste of water." They did enjoy a modern toilet with a convenient flush mechanism, though even this facility featured little more than a hole in the floor for squatting. The legacy of village outhouses carried over a little too closely within Singapore's latest high-rises.

If that were not enough, poor Mama suffered from a troublesome leg condition due simply to the wear and tear of age. Little Cathy was often deployed to gently step on her legs for a cost-free if unpredictable massage. In preparation for her makeshift home therapy, Mama would lie as close to the wall as possible within her "corner," flip over on her side, and instruct Cathy to step on her legs to relieve the pain.

In the absence of a neighborhood massage parlor—such luxury services did not exist at the time—Cathy's efforts proved effective enough to keep their aging parental guardian on her feet. And this was no trivial matter. The girls had little choice but to keep their primary caretaker up and running. The in-home therapy was probably still not enough to fully relieve Mama's aches and pains. An anxious Cathy was always itching to go off and play instead.

Despite close quarters, their scrappy household managed to persist this way for the better part of a decade. As the sisters got older, it helped that the four of them were only together for a few hours on weekdays and for sleeping at night. Uncle Kellard usually ventured out to work very early in the morning and did not return until almost 7:00 in the evening. Once the girls both achieved school age, they departed just as early on weekday mornings for primary school.

Beyond that, Sundays were devoted to their local Catholic church and to an array of Catechism lessons. And little moss grew under Mama's feet. With child-raising responsibilities in mind, she was no stranger to local markets to negotiate the best deals for basic food and necessities. She could haggle with the best of them. With little predictable income, she found ways to stretch what money Kellard was willing or able to hand over. Kellard and Mama therefore doubled as surrogate parents and kept the children fed and clothed as best as they could.

Unfortunately, their scattered efforts were still not enough to guarantee full bellies at night. Even basic food ingredients remained scarce, and Mama typically relied on cooking simple, one-dish meals. As Cathy recalls, this was about all she could handle, anyway. The reliable if tiring combination of cabbage and soup broth became a dependable staple. Any money earmarked for additional food goods was often repurposed for scratch-and-win lottery cards. This meant that "not much was left in her food basket," Cathy laughs, looking back.

On more fortunate days, chunks of potatoes appeared in their soup, and they sometimes enjoyed rice and vegetables on the side. Still, it was Mama's incessant reliance on cabbage that Cathy remembers most. She recalls, "We had cabbage all the time. She didn't have many culinary skills, so her meals were very basic. Sometimes we even put soy sauce on white rice. It still tasted better than her cooking. The one thing she did cook well was her dumplings, and she also taught me to cook them."

Mama's simplicity in the kitchen reflected her own upbringing and steadfast habits. She and her generation had endured the brutal and unforgiving Japanese Occupation. Daily diets consisted of whatever could be acquired during those dark days. This situation improved only gradually as Singapore moved closer to independence in 1965.

For his part, Kellard was on the hook with his own responsibilities. As the family's foremost source of income, he really had little choice if he cared about the well-being of his nieces. Cathy describes his own life as simple and predictable, working primarily to provide a roof over their heads. Kellard supplied the monthly rent much of the time, and his natural generosity was vital to support his piecemeal family. His meagre earnings were always in high demand to cover a range of necessary household expenses. While food was always at the top of a lengthy list, his income was also siphoned off for Mama's insatiable gambling habit. And as for Cathy's father, Errol seemed to conveniently go missing when monthly bills came due.

Given this rocky start, Cathy learned to harbor a deep anxiety over household expenses. She was barely ten when she started to inquire about the monthly rent payment. This was arguably rather young to be concerned with everyday financial obligations typically handled by adults. Cathy's overly developed sense of responsibility seeped into her schooling as well. No surprise, she and her sister found themselves regularly scrounging up their own monthly fees for school. "If such funds for school had already become scarce," Cathy considered, "just how was my family going to manage to pay for a roof over our heads? I just never knew for sure."

A Bit of a Foodie

Much later as an adult, Cathy developed into an unabashed food lover. She is unafraid to try or enjoy practically any culinary delight placed in front of her. This also means it can be difficult to tolerate picky eaters who might refuse certain dishes or ingredients. To someone who remembers being hungry, her frustration in such instances is understandable.

As a generous host to untold numbers of family and friends, Cathy now loves to cook for her own gatherings. To do so she relies less on planning or recipes, and more on her hard-earned wealth of culinary experience. She explains, "It's not like you're doing a roast and throw it in the oven, with potatoes beside it, chop-chop-chop! There is a whole process to cooking." Although requiring little of her guests when in the kitchen, she only hopes they will enjoy their time and be thankful. "Those who say something about ingredients or what they don't like to eat will receive no more food and no more invitation," she says firmly.

Cathy owes her passion for cooking in part to Mama's diligent efforts decades earlier. She adds, "I just added a post on Facebook about my dumplings. So, the beauty of it all, it's really about nostalgia. For important celebrations in the past, this was how my Mama would make them. We didn't buy things off the shelf, and when she and my other aunties prepared meals, they did it from scratch. And a lot of food was made to be given away to the relatives, and so we got to eat it, too. This is why I say, if I could turn back time, I would have loved to spend more time with my Mama and my aunties."

Cathy's reputation for cooking has clearly spread beyond the family. In a likely effort to compensate for her own childhood, her reputation for sharing is now well known. "That's why I feed my kids until they can't eat anymore," she chuckles, then smiles at another thought. "When Russel posted photos of our food at home during the *Circuit Breaker*—that's what they called our lockdown during Covid—his friends were envious and asked if they could stay locked in at our house because 'his mommy seems to be cooking all the time,'" she laughs with a hint of personal pride thrown in.

Should guests expect to find stacks of recipes in Cathy's kitchen, they will be sorely disappointed. Standard recipes play little role in Cathy's cuisine. Such prescribed approaches are too "stuffy and rigid," she says. There are exceptions, of course. Older recipes handed down from earlier generations have survived, such as prawn noodle soup. When Cathy cooks, flavors matter; she eats less to fill up her stomach now and more to enjoy the pleasure of different tastes and ingredients. Said another way, cooking becomes a new adventure each time, which makes her "a bit of a foodie," she chuckles.

She also cooks as if to serve a small army, whether consisting of family members, friends, or both. "It's not the idea of wanting something in return," she explains her philosophy of sharing. "It's the satisfaction of seeing the smile on their faces when they enjoy my dishes." The foodie in her surfaces most often, however, during more relaxed times with friends at a favorite restaurant. Sometimes, she admits, "I don't always want to cook, so I enjoy going out to eat. Cooking can be too much work."

Most important, Cathy thrives on watching her guests devour her culinary creations. Having endured occasional hunger as a child, it is little wonder that Cathy has vowed to always have enough food to share widely. "If you come to my house," she emphasizes, "you will not just sit there; I will be digging into my whole fridge to feed you."

Chapter 2

The Busybody

The most rewarding treats for the girls typically arrived around Chinese New Year. This was when discretionary cash flowed more freely throughout their extended family. Modest gifts of money magically appeared from little-known Chinese relatives on Mama's side of the family. It turns out the sisters were unwittingly benefitting from a Chinese custom involving something called *little red packets*. As tradition would have it, these miniature envelopes held modest gifts of coins that were liberally filtered across the family on such occasions. Both girls learned quickly to save these welcome windfalls for important expenses later.

Within Chinese culture, the custom of giving money to children is known as *hongbao*, a Mandarin term which translates to "red packet" or envelope. For untold generations, these red packets were filled with small amounts of money and usually placed under a child's pillow at night. This may seem suspiciously familiar to the tradition of the Tooth Fairy in Western societies, though the Chinese had other reasons. The most important was to appease any demons or monsters who might be inclined to take their children's souls away. The chance of this frightful occurrence was apparently more likely around the Chinese New Year. Cathy corrects this myth, saying, "In reality, there was a high infant mortality rate, which explains why many children were really taken away."

While numerous Chinese creation myths exist for the origin of *hongbao*, the most common seems to involve a demon named Sui. As the story goes, on the eve of Chinese New Year Sui emerges from his lair and seeks out the bedroom of a home's unsuspecting children. Sui then scrapes his tentacles across the children's foreheads while they sleep, causing them to wake up with screaming headaches.

As the story continues, a set of determined parents once tried to keep their son awake on New Year's Eve to discourage Sui's arrival. Despite their valiant efforts, the boy still succumbed to exhaustion and nodded off to sleep. Now desperate for fallback options, the mother found eight copper coins. This is—perhaps not coincidentally—the same amount as the eight Gods of Chinese folklore known as the *Eight Immortals*. The mother then placed the coins inside a red envelope and slipped the collection under the child's pillow. The hope was that any demons might be satisfied enough to make away with some easy cash instead.

Regardless, Sui showed up later that night, right on cue. As he approached the sleeping boy, however, the coins began to emit a hazy light. As Sui approached closer, the rays from the coins grew ever brighter until Sui could no longer tolerate it. Discouraged, he and his blinded eyes went shrieking into the night. It turned out that the lucky color red, together with the copper coins, worked well to relieve children of their morning headaches. Chinese parents learned to place money inside red envelopes to ward off evil spirits.

Over time the red packets became more of a symbolic gesture of protection and good luck. The practice remains most popular with older generations such as grandparents, who in

Cathy's younger days might give each of them about 20 cents. For wealthier families, the amount approached a full dollar. This was considered a lot of money during those years, especially for Singapore's low-income households.

Armed with extra funds from red packets, the sisters looked forward on rare occasion to a very tasty treat. They and their cousins gravitated to a special new restaurant located not far from their housing block. This was no Chinese tradition, but more a Western cultural intrusion. Singapore's determined leaders were leaping with both feet into the emerging global economy. As one such influence, American fast food had arrived in the namesake of Colonel Sanders and *Kentucky Fried Chicken*, eventually shortened to simply *KFC*.

It mattered little that Cathy had probably never heard of a place called Kentucky. The sisters had saved their money to splurge on a savory American meal, care of the Colonel himself. KFC had been the first—and only—fast-food franchise to arrive in Singapore, and its special recipe of fried chicken quickly won over many Singaporeans. And yet, even these meals proved to be rather skimpy. Cathy's family was only able to afford two pieces of chicken for each of them. And this was without the typical sides which today serve as standard fare. This meant no coleslaw, and no potatoes. Only the fried chicken. Regardless, the treat was consumed with no complaints. Cathy recalls nostalgically, "We were in euphoria. We ate slowly, to savor it, even as kids, trying to prolong the experience. How long could we take to eat it?"

Other forms of fun were found in closer proximity to home. Living within a residential high-rise in Singapore provides—then as now—an instant community only steps away. Their estate's specially designed public spaces provided vital social outlets for Mama and Uncle Kellard—along with plenty of children for Cathy to befriend. The buildings were all lined up along a central outer corridor, not unlike a pedestrian main street. As one might expect, the close proximity to neighbors provided another level of community support. And while some residents were more social than others, everybody near Mama's flat got to know Cathy's family to some degree. As Cathy recalls, "Everybody knew everybody; we had access to every place in the estate, and we never locked the door. I mean, there was nothing really to steal."

Cathy's own floor became a microcosm of Singapore's racial and ethnic diversity. Immediate neighbors consisted of Malays, Indians, Chinese, and the occasional Eurasians like themselves. With so many children of similar age, they all made instant friends regardless of physical appearance. Cathy describes: "Everyone was color blind. In our community we had people of many races and religions, and so dialect or skin color didn't matter. That's how we got along."

More important than ethnic background was a child's eagerness to play *Make Believe* and related games on a moment's notice. And Cathy was emerging as one of her estate's more outgoing, precocious children. How to make new friends was certainly not a concern. For some time, she knew every family and neighbor within the surrounding flats. The neighbors to one side consisted of a Malay family with four or five children, while a Eurasian family inhabited the opposite side—again with two or three children. Most families were low-income like theirs, with any combination of missing parents or related issues.

Notably, precious few toys were available to anyone. As is typical the world over, the kids made do with what they could find to construct their own imaginary worlds. The girls did enjoy the occasional used tea set, complete with cups and saucers and associated items salvaged over the years. Other families threw away such things, and the girls brought them home.

Regardless, there was always plenty to do with so many children around—cool toys or not. With their tea sets and other makeshift items, Cathy and her friends commandeered the outside corridor to play *House*, thereby escaping their own suffocating flats. Of course, she and her peers dreamed of being more like adults. This translated to role-playing with imaginary families composed of whomever they might conjure up. Assigning roles for father, mother, and siblings was most common in such scenarios, whether the children enjoyed these actual family members at home or not.

If boredom set in, additional opportunities were explored around the estate. They sometimes ran around—or through—the entire corridor, concluding their foot races at the estate's designated playground. Adult supervision was questionable, or simply nonexistent. Each one of their respective flats was fair game as well, running in and out as they saw fit—at least until adult neighbors grew tired of the intrusions. Back inside, the home of one child or another might harbor a coveted black and white television for quieter times. Cathy's flat had one as well, and they loved watching TV. Their own unit came care of Uncle Kellard. The TV had shutters that would close to help it blend in with other furniture. Cathy recalls, "Either you owned a TV or a telephone, or sometimes both. Not everyone had a phone, so those who did shared the numbers for the hospital, police, or school to help one another out."

When finally old enough to offer a hand in the kitchen, Cathy often visited neighbors—invited or otherwise—to assist with cooking and preparation duties. This is how she learned her way around a kitchen from a young age, regardless of whose kitchen it might be. One family operated a food stall perched at the corner of the estate, and she became a regular visitor. She often helped peel mountains of onions for the chili they sold, a task which provided mixed rewards. Aside from generating unwanted tears, the onion-peeling sessions served as an outlet for her to chat with the family. No surprise, Cathy was usually the first child to eagerly appear and help. There were no free handouts, however. She still had to purchase whatever they were selling and simply enjoy the benefit of being a part of the operation.

From the earliest age she can recall, Cathy jumped in to "help" anyone who would allow her to do so. These were the first steps, she now believes, on her path to becoming a self-proclaimed "busybody." But her social nature fit right in, as neighborliness was welcome and expected in those years. If a neighbor happened to cook too much food, the leftovers typically went to someone else nearby. People were generous, when possible, regardless of income. It follows that such supportive neighbors doubled as a social safety net when things went wrong.

Even Singapore's earliest public housing estates came complete with numerous community facilities. Built-in kindergartens were among the top priorities to serve resident families. In Singapore this play-filled educational phase required two years. Fortunately, the "kindie" classroom, as Cathy lovingly refers to it, was located right downstairs on the *void deck*. As its name implies, this lower deck of Singaporean high-rise estates was largely left vacant to allow for all sorts of community events. These spaces were often converted into schools, though they also doubled for funeral wakes or communal party rooms. It was not unheard of to find a Malay wedding ceremony taking place adjacent to a Chinese funeral wake.

Singapore's intent to integrate community functions into public housing is largely owed to architect and urban planner Liu Thai Ker. He and his peers had learned important lessons from the mistakes made in the United States and Europe with their own public housing efforts from the 1960s. And Mr. Liu was well positioned to learn from these initial experiments. He first worked in the New York office of the famed modernist architect, I.M. Pei, having earned a master's degree in city planning from Yale University. He made his way to Singapore in 1969, accepting the daunting position as the head of the design and research unit of Singapore's HDB.

Mr. Liu had barely touched down at Changi Airport when he was directed to design the first generation of high-rise housing estates. Singapore's first and long-time prime minister, Lee Kuan Yew, tasked Mr. Liu with determining how best to resettle many Singaporeans into modern high-rise towers by 1982. He further needed to plan entire urban centers, or "new towns," to accompany the necessary housing blocks. Since nobody had yet formed a vision for these new communities, Mr. Liu was pressured to find solutions quickly. He ultimately favored the notion of all-inclusive neighborhoods with their own grocery stores, shops, schools, playgrounds, and community centers. By 1985 this ambitious dream had become reality; virtually every Singaporean now enjoyed decent, clean housing.

It was within one of Mr. Liu's innovative urban communities where Cathy's earliest years were spent. If any child was going to take full advantage of Mr Liu's designs, it was Cathy. Her high-rise estate had doubled as her own personal playground and social outlet. Such was the life of Singapore's first generation—children who for the first time in history would grow up as official "Singaporeans." Though still oblivious to the grander national experiment swirling around her, Cathy would ultimately grow as Singapore grew. It is not an exaggeration to suggest that she was becoming an unwitting daughter of her new nation.

Chapter 3

Life Inside the Teapot

Daytime may have been fair game for outdoor activities, though nighttime was to be feared. Young Cathy and her friends were regularly cautioned to remain indoors when the sun went down. Any number of gruesome Chinese folk tales and ghost stories usually tamed even the most adventurous child. Adults knew that the promise of safety essentially disappeared with sunset. This was bad news indeed for a boisterous, curious youngster like Cathy. The strict rule of her household was that nobody was to set foot outside after the sun disappeared below the horizon.

Nor did the situation improve much during the tropical summer. The idea of summer in Singapore is a joke anyway. The heat and high humidity are virtually unrelenting throughout the year. Wintertime holidays like Christmas and Chinese New Year are reliably warm and humid. Being outdoors is more about sweating than sleigh rides. This is because Singapore finds itself a stone's throw away from the Equator. The result is a rather predictable routine of incessantly muggy weather with sporadic rain showers. The actual season matters little, and the times of sunrise and sunset remain nearly unchanged throughout the year. For a child, these quirks of geography might as well have been rocket science. The big story was that, for about 12 hours each night, Cathy was not going anywhere—summer or not.

Cathy now likens that experience to living inside a teapot. In this metaphor, the lid of the teapot remains open during the daytime, allowing everyone to frolic outside when it is bright and exciting. As the sun sets, however, everyone must return to the teapot before the lid closes for the night. And she was not about to find out what might happen were she not safely contained inside. To hear the adults speak of it, there would be no protection against whatever evil, ghosts, or other ghoulish figures might be lurking. "If you go outside, you will get lost," her Mama would warn, "and the *Karang Guni* will catch you!" This translates roughly to a scavenger who goes through the rubbish to survive. On other nights Mama might warn the girls of the "*Pontiana* that will follow you," referring to a ghost who dies during childbirth and becomes a female Dracula. *Pontiana's* interest was limited, however, as she only attacked pregnant women. Regardless of whichever entity Mama conjured up, it was enough to scare the wits out of young and impressionable minds. To this day, Cathy still enjoys scaring her friends with the threat of *Pontiana*.

These scare tactics represented only a small portion of Mama's repertoire of Chinese and Malay folk tales. She had many to choose from. Every ethnic group claimed its favorite ghoulish stories, and it follows that there are any number of infamous Chinese, Indian, and Malay ghosts to avoid. It is a wonder that anyone's soul survived each night in multicultural Singapore. When standard folk tales failed to hold the desired effect, Mama simply made them up herself. "Because of her sweet innocence, we believed her," Cathy recalls. "We were very easy to manipulate."

Mama was full of insidious threats for whatever the occasion warranted. Cathy remembers, "If we were upset, my Mama would always demand, 'Stop crying, it's bad luck. Cry some more, and you can join the professional mourners at funerals. You will cry away all your good luck!' Then if we didn't eat all our food, she would say, 'Clean your plates when you eat, or your husband's face will have pock marks on it,' or more generally, 'Your husband will have a very rough-looking face.'" Thinking about her husband, Tony, she spends a few seconds contemplating whether this spell had actually come to pass. She adds, "Oh, and if we were rude to older people, Mama said we would be struck down with lightning. If we lied, our tongues would grow longer. And if we ate the seed of the fruit, a tree would grow inside our stomachs. This was when we were smaller. Later we learned that she really was just full of crap," she laughs, concluding with, "What a character she was! She could make you laugh or make you cry."

As children, of course, Mama's stories were enough to keep the girls sufficiently suspicious of what evil incarnate awaited them outdoors. Only during their early teen years did they learn how to avoid Mama's increasingly spotty surveillance to venture outside after hours. And aside from occasional sneakiness, an expanding list of school activities and jobs increasingly kept the sisters out later at night. Until then, however, the teapot was effectively clamped shut for much of the 1970s. Any semblance of outdoor life after sunset was all but out of the question.

Why all the fuss about nighttime? These days, residents and visitors alike are accustomed to a dazzling, shiny, cosmopolitan city that prides itself as one of the world's safest places. It is when the sun disappears that the glittering and entertaining cityscape comes to life. Not so during the 1960s, however, when the emerging city-state was measurably less hospitable. Street and gang violence was commonplace and remained a lingering threat. This was nowhere truer than within lower income, working-class areas like Cathy's neighborhood. She adds, "In those days, the government wasn't able to clamp down on all the gang activity. Every large family had at least one gang member, usually from poor families. My father and his brothers—my uncles—were members, and most ended up in prison at some point. They had huge tattoos all over their bodies. It was common within lower income families."

As the sun went down, parents feared the streets could be consumed at any moment with intermittent gang fights or robberies. At least, this was the conventional wisdom, and not entirely exaggerated. Of course, the sisters were unaware of these pressing social issues. Rather, it was easier to invent fantastical ghost stories to sufficiently scare them silly.

If the persistent threat of territorial street gangs was not enough, political upheaval and racial tensions contributed to anxiety. Singapore saw its first full decade of independence during the 1970s, just as Cathy was moving through her own childhood. As with any bold venture such as this, these formative years were apt to be rather messy. Most poignantly, the so-called Race Riots of 1964 remained fresh in the minds of all Singaporean leaders struggling to find ways to keep the peace. For largely political reasons just prior to independence, the ethnic Chinese and indigenous Malay populations were not getting along so well. In one sense, it was not only Cathy and her peers who were transitioning from toddler into childhood; so too was their newly independent country. Still oblivious to such issues, an ever-wiser Cathy simply wondered why she could not go outside at night—female Dracula or not.

Throughout the 1970s memories of the riots and related tensions remained fresh within Singapore's skittish population. And few families enjoyed the wherewithal to escape to safer neighborhoods. Cathy explains, "There was no extreme wealth around the time of independence; nearly everyone was starting from scratch. Dysfunctional families, low educational levels, and high unemployment were common when I was a child."

And aside from scattered jobs, there were few productive outlets for young men, which naturally led to rampant local gang activity. These gangs apparently held tenuous connections to former Chinese secret societies, and they regularly threatened the peace of everyday life.

Being cooped up inside did little to help Cathy and her Mama get along. Whatever goodwill Mama displayed toward her was taxed by an increasingly stubborn and defiant grandchild. Looking back now, Cathy recognizes how her uncooperative attitude often risked damaging an already shaky relationship.

It did not help that Cathy came to resent Mama for apparently favoring her older sister. There was absolutely nothing Cathy could do right, it seemed, whereas her older sister was continuously praised and doted upon. Few special gifts managed to find their way to the tempestuous younger sibling. This was all very unfair. Looking back now, Cathy suggests she was nothing less than Cinderella reincarnate.

If Mama herself could double as any famous Disney character, Cathy feels it would most certainly have been Cruella De Vil, the villain from the animated film, *101 Dalmations*. Mama often harbored a mean streak and verbally lashed out at Cathy for any number of unknown reasons. If that were not enough to fan the flames, it was Cathy who typically shouldered the lion's share of household chores. Or so it seemed. Such blatant unfairness was simply unacceptable, Cathy felt at the time.

On rare occasions Mama might bring home some modest winnings from playing the numbers. To her credit, these windfalls were usually spent at the market to feed herself and her family. But the temptation to throw some of it back into gambling was often just too overwhelming. Sometimes she invested her winnings in jewelry and related trinkets, a common practice for securing future income. This was also the typical fate of money from red packets, which occasionally appeared for birthdays and the like. It was not lost on Cathy that Mama sometimes lavished her big sister with similar gifts, while the little sister was intentionally bypassed. Cinderella indeed.

A rebellious Cathy typically reacted to such slights in the best way she knew—through defiant outbursts. And the louder the better. She screamed back at Mama in one such instance, "Fine, if you won't buy it for me, when I grow up, I will wear so much gold I won't be able to walk! I'll have bracelets up my arms, chains around my neck, and lots and lots of earrings!" None of this has come to pass, it turns out. Mama usually dismissed these outbursts with a "Yeah, whatever" type of remark, coupled with a wave of her arm. For her part, Cathy does not deny having been a particularly difficult child, often challenging Mama's authority in one way or another.

On the flip side, Cathy recalls how Mama could be "very sweet and cute in various ways." As a wiser adult, Cathy justifies this change of heart because, as she counsels, "to everything there is a balance." Mama was the courageous one, Cathy now realizes, as she had stepped up to assume responsibility for sheltering the girls. Cathy now believes that her love-hate relationship with Mama provided an important opportunity. Mama's tough love ultimately "helped me to toughen up," Cathy states. As such, Cathy will always remain grateful for everything her Mama was able to provide—the lack of gold trinkets to the contrary.

In stark contrast, Uncle Kellard absolutely adored Cathy. While Mama tended to favor the older sister, Cathy could often count on her uncle's steadfast support in whatever drama ensued. Much to her delight, Cathy discovered that her uncle often took her side during any standard sibling argument. He was also the first to lavish genuine praise on Cathy whenever she had accomplished something. "He was always so proud of me, right or wrong," she says fondly.

Kellard could be characterized as a simple, unassuming man with little formal education. He was also more of a recluse, or introvert, quite comfortable with a daily routine of going to work and returning home each night. And he spoke little of work at all, so any intriguing stories were few and far between.

One thing Kellard was not burdened by was the upkeep of an automobile. Private vehicles were still considered a luxury during the 1970s. Rather, a company truck collected him for work each day. For more pleasurable outings he relied on his trusty bicycle to get around the neighborhood.

It so happened that Kellard was also the filial son who reliably looked after his mother. Of her five children, he was the only one to do so. This coincided with the simple fact that he was the only sibling who managed to stay out of prison. Even as the "Goody Two-shoes" of the family, as Cathy lovingly describes him, Kellard was still compelled to decorate much of his body with wildly intricate tattoos.

He did manage to keep a small circle of friends who sometimes visited on weekend nights to play cards. As the group pushed through successive games of gin rummy, the sisters remained on call to serve as their "runners." This required repeated trips downstairs to acquire more snacks and drinks as the night demanded. While barely enduring the group's thick, secondary smoke, Cathy looked forward to the tips they earned for completing such errands. They further enjoyed an extra dollar or two from the winnings. It was such ordinary yet pleasant times that proved most memorable during Cathy's life inside the teapot.

Chapter 4

Errol's World

Singapore's obscure location in Southeast Asia was not enough to escape the horrors of World War II. In fact, the otherwise sleepy entrepot ended up with a target on its back from an expanding Japanese Empire. Few times of the 20th century could have been more precarious for raising a family. But Cathy's Mama found herself precisely in this situation. Already in her mid-thirties at the time of war, she was juggling four young children when the Japanese invaded her island home in February 1942. Cathy's future father, Errol was a mere baby, born the previous July. Although he was the youngest of the four children, he would not be the last. His mother was already pregnant with her fifth child as the Japanese appeared and assumed absolute control. This later arrival eventually became Cathy's youngest uncle, Allan. Born in November 1942, Allan arrived in the midst of the Japanese Occupation. His mother now had five young mouths to feed during Singapore's most devastating and oppressive period in history.

Before reaching Singapore, Japan first invaded Thailand on 8 December 1941. Americans may recognize this as the day immediately following the Empire's brazen attack on Pearl Harbor. Thailand had remained neutral until the onset of the war and ultimately surrendered with little resistance. The

Japanese then utilized the country as a convenient staging ground for their ensuing expansion into British-controlled Malaya and Singapore. Though located at the extreme southern end of the Malay peninsula, Singapore did not escape Japan's wrath. The island was not only definitively conquered, but it was further designated as Japanese headquarters to control the ten Malay states to the north. The main reason was a geographic one. Singapore enjoyed the peninsula's most strategic shipping location and principal port facilities.

As Cathy explains during her military tours for Singapore's Armed Forces, "The Japanese really did not encounter much resistance when they arrived. The British troops in Singapore assumed the Japanese would invade by sea, and so they focused their efforts on defending Fort Siloso along Singapore's southern coast. But the Japanese slashed through the jungles and took the island from the north instead. They conquered Singapore quickly because their scouts had mapped out the Malay peninsula well in advance. From a strategic perspective, the Japanese were smart! They already knew about the existing roads used for moving raw materials like rubber and palm oil through Singapore before it was loaded onto ships and exported."

There remained one unexpected challenge the Japanese had not counted upon. They quickly ended up with something between 50,000 and 100,000 prisoners of war (POWs) who required managing, and quickly. Many of them were marched off to the eastern side of the island where a prison had already been constructed. The place was called Changi, which derives its name from a specific type of tree that once grew on the island (pronounced *Chang-EE*). Changi became a holding area, or staging ground, for sending the POW soldiers north to Burma.

The British barracks were also located at Changi. Together the barracks and prison provided a convenient way for the

Japanese to deal with their sudden POW problem. The prison was new, completed in 1937. The Governor at the time, Shenton Thomas, had commissioned the prison's construction, having no idea that he would be incarcerated there himself only a few years later.

To make matters worse, the POWs were brutally forced to march on their own feet to Changi, walking from the Padang at the center of town. Today the Changi Chapel Museum provides an educational history of the Japanese Occupation and the POW ordeal. This hub of POW activity and imprisonment is better known today as the world-renowned Changi International Airport and home to state-owned Singapore Airlines.

For three years, Chinese families lived in constant fear of random forced searches and indiscriminate violence. In the rare instances when Cathy's mother-in-law recounts the war, she offers tidbits of her own survival stories. She was a child at that time, part of the same wartime generation as Cathy's father and uncles. Just prior to the war's outbreak in the region, one of her wealthier and well-connected relatives had learned that the Japanese were planning to invade Singapore following their takeover of China. These Singaporean families had already been raising funds to assist the Chinese in opposition to the Japanese expansion.

To prepare for the eventual invasion of the island, Singaporeans were encouraged to build underground shelters to hide non-perishable food. *Spam*, Milo (a coco drink), and similar processed foods were some of the common products buried. Wealthier relatives also hid their families within these shelters as the air raids continued. To this day Cathy's mother-in-law despises the thought of *Spam*. This is quite understandable, given her continuous consumption of the infamous product as a child. For her part, Cathy remains more ambivalent about it, simply considering *Spam* a luncheon meat from her own childhood. She does admit to avoiding it as much as possible.

One of Cathy's aunties shared similar wartime stories. For her, it had become standard practice throughout the Occupation to hide with her family in the attic while the Japanese searched house-by-house for resistors. Families especially hid their children, as the soldiers were known to be abusive. During one tense moment in the attic, Cathy's auntie recalls how one of her siblings had dropped something on the floor by mistake and worried that the intruders might hear them. Fortunately, the soldiers heard nothing and eventually left the house. Many others were not so lucky.

Few families or communities in Singapore escaped the wrath of the occupiers. Cathy's own family—and that of her husband—were no exception. During that devastating February of 1942 and pregnant with her fifth child, Mama worked relentlessly just to fend off starvation. She also carried her household's daily supply of water, not having a reliable source in her own home.

At one point Mama seriously considered uprooting her desperate family and taking them northward up the Malay Peninsula. She noticed that others were relocating to Bahau, established by the Japanese as an agricultural settlement for Eurasians and Chinese Catholics. Many who did relocate ended up perishing from disease or malnutrition. Those who survived somehow made their way back to Singapore within a few years. It was probably fortunate, therefore, that she did not take that risk. While Mama rarely spoke of those times to Cathy, she did emphasize the daily scarcity of food and her struggle to nourish her family.

Now as a middle-aged mother herself, Cathy better appreciates how Mama's lingering attitudes influenced her own childhood. Growing up with Mama was an exercise in frugality; meals were simple, nobody wasted food, and thriftiness was the rule. Though two generations removed, Cathy still experienced the residual habits of a wartime family lingering into the 1970s.

Mama's stories and lessons have since trickled into Cathy's local tours. Acutely aware of her own family's hardships, Cathy impresses on her guests the vital roles women played during and after the war. She instructs, "While the front-liners may be the soldiers themselves, it is the women—the mothers, who look after the rest of the families when war breaks out."

Not long after the war, Cathy's grandfather—Errol's father—died young, suddenly leaving their five children to Mama's care. At first the Ross family demanded that Errol's mother relinquish all custody rights of the children. They argued that she would not be capable of looking after and protecting baby Errol and his four siblings on her own. Despite this pressure, she held firm and refused to part with them. A deep sense of responsibility kicked in; she was determined to house and care for all five children and raise them herself.

The exception would be her last child, Allan. She reluctantly gave him up to a pig farmer, who had no children of his own at the time. When the farmer was eventually blessed with his own children, however, Allan was often neglected and forced to fend for himself. He never went to school and remained illiterate into his adult years. Though his artistic skills were noteworthy, he could only write his own name for quite some time.

It is little wonder, then, that Allan later ended up in prison, where he reunited with some of his fellow gang members. With the exception of Kellard, all of Mama's boys eventually entered the street gang culture still variously active into the 1960s. The siblings found themselves on the wrong side of the law too many times to count, easily finding ways to dodge responsibilities and get into trouble.

In hindsight, Cathy notes that Errol had become his mother's favorite child. "My father was essentially her pet," she says somewhat dismissively. Despite their household's challenges after the war, Errol enjoyed a comparatively spoiled upbringing. He had been told repeatedly there was little reason to study or work hard in life. And—better yet—he should "let the women feed you." As Cathy perceives, Errol loyally followed his mother's advice with utmost precision.

Errol's erratic upbringing would have been familiar to many Singaporeans at the time. Cathy explains, "In those days, men were not highly educated, so they took all kinds of questionable jobs to get money, all this illegal stuff. So, you were either an illegal, an alcoholic, or a gambler, or some combination of the three. These were not the kind of permanent jobs you could be proud of," she chuckles, stating the obvious. "My Mama brought up hooligans. She herself got by as a cleaning lady when work was available. Her children were all let loose, so they followed all kinds of gangs and that's how they grew up—instant excitement but no focus. When they were down and out, they started drinking a lot, they stopped thinking and became irresponsible. So, they naturally started to abuse their wives and children. Welcome to my world," she adds sarcastically.

By the time Cathy was old enough to know her Uncle Allan, much of his body's surface area had already filled with tattoos. "He looked like a walking museum," she describes colorfully. "You could see Jesus on his chest, the Virgin Mary on his arm, and any number of other religious figures on just about all corners of his body." This partly reflected the Ross family's Catholic roots, which—as far as tattoos were concerned—doubled as acceptable symbols of gang membership. She continues, "Young men would join these groups because there was no law and order, and no family supervision. This was what life was like in Singapore and how people best handled their lives." It was this risky, chaotic lifestyle into which Cathy and her sister were born.

Although Errol succumbed to similar patterns, he could at least read and write. More impressive, he developed his multilingual abilities and was eventually hired as a translator. Errol later married Cathy's biological mother, Mary, when she was only 17, immediately following her final year in secondary school. It was inevitable that both naïve adolescents were eager to escape their own challenged households. Two daughters of their own were soon to follow. Cathy continues, "By then my mother had learned that she had married a nightmare." Mary was already confronting her new husband's abusive, alcoholic rages. After meeting another, less troubled man, Mary made the bold decision to permanently leave her new home and family. Cathy was only two years old.

Though not exactly one's idea of a model husband, Errol managed to show promise in the job world. With more opportunities came experience, and he eventually worked for various law firms as a linguist. He was hired primarily to translate for those speaking any of Singapore's numerous languages or Chinese dialects. Cathy still admires her father for this positive quality. His own biracial upbringing had provided a strong bilingual foundation. Cathy recalls that, besides English, "he could speak fluent Malay and all the local Chinese dialects. And he could curse in all of them as well!"

To this day, Cathy remains conflicted over how to best interpret her father and their past experiences together. While in no way dismissing his own reckless behaviors, she has attempted to find peace and come to terms with his troubled past. "During the times he decided to be my father," she quips, "he could be fun. We had good times together when I was growing up." Still, she had no choice but to contend with his "two unpredictable personalities," as she describes them. She never knew which one was going to show up—let alone when—at the door to Mama's modest flat.

Chapter 5

A Phantom Grandfather

Fortunately, Uncle Kellard was not Cathy's only staunch supporter. A mysterious older gentleman appeared in her life around age three. This was her "phantom grandfather" as she lovingly referred to him then, as now. Though apparently not related by blood, it was this rather tall, kindly man with a squarish face—and no tattoos of note—who took an active interest in both sisters during their earlier years. As Cathy grew older, she noticed that everyone within her small orbit called him Uncle John, short for Jonathan. To Cathy he simply became *Grandpa*. Since other family members trusted him as well, it was no big leap for Cathy to do likewise. For many years he appeared for regular visits at Mama's flat. As to how this particular gentleman was associated with the family, Cathy had no idea.

Grandpa superbly filled another void in Cathy's life, because her real grandfathers had either passed away or had gone missing. Grandpa earned her trust by simply being available and showing an interest. His occasional and sometimes daily visits to their home continued well into Cathy's teenage years.

Cathy learned to accept anyone associated with the family who was kind and treated her half decently. This is no shocking revelation. Children can generally be won over by any caring adult who simply spends time with them. Likewise, it mattered little to Cathy whether they were bona-fide relatives. She recalls her own thinking at the time, saying "I was always a naturally happy child—except when I was crying. Anyone who was willing to come into my life and give me food or money became my instant friend. It was always easy to make me happy, and I was very appreciative of anyone who paid positive attention to me. I didn't care who they were."

For whatever reason, Grandpa somehow stuck around and provided a valuable sense of stability. He further influenced the decision to send the girls to St. Anthony's Convent Primary and Secondary School—or more simply, convent school, as Cathy calls it. Still a part of Singapore's public school system, St. Anthony's was located at the heart of the city center on Middle Road. Later Cathy would learn that an influential uncle in the Church's administration also had a hand in sending the girls there. Still, to have her phantom grandfather assist in that decision meant he held some serious clout within the family.

Of course, Cathy was much too young to question the influential adults in her life—except, perhaps when she gave Mama a hard time. As for the St. Anthony's decision, Cathy remains grateful to this day. "If it had been left up to my grandmother," Cathy notes, "I would have been sent to a nearby neighborhood school. Grandpa knew I had a better chance of getting a decent education from the nuns and priests," she explains.

It turns out there was a catch with St. Anthony's. With that decision came the obligatory monthly school fees. This was no trivial matter for their frugal household, so Grandpa wisely stepped in to assist with this additional responsibility. Looking back, he was clearly aware that neither Mama nor Kellard could reliably support that endeavor. And their wayward father was not exactly a viable option. Somehow, Grandpa enjoyed access to insider information and was willing to act on it.

Not content to be a supportive advocate, Grandpa also provided modest funds when the household struggled more than usual. This eventually turned into a regular allowance of 25 dollars a month—at least for one period of Cathy's childhood. Though absolutely vital, this was no windfall. It was barely enough to supplement any funds provided by Kellard and Mama. Cathy needed to carefully stretch this allowance for multiple purposes. She therefore credits Grandpa for indirectly teaching her how to budget her precious monthly income.

When Grandpa paid a visit, the sisters could usually look forward to any number of fun outings. Sometimes he took them for ice cream or even to an amusement park on weekends. More important, he was available for them at seemingly all the right times. No complaints were uttered from Cathy's mouth. If someone wanted to pretend to be her grandfather, so be it. Who was she to argue?

One day when Cathy was around ten, Grandpa gave Cathy five dollars in cash. This time there were no strings attached, as the money was not already allocated for necessities. Grateful, she promptly placed the cash in her pocket while leaving for school. During transit, however, she inadvertently pulled something else from the same pocket, causing the money to disappear to who-knows-where. True to the instant emotions of any 10-year-old, panic welled up inside her. What a disaster for a child whose every dollar was a precious gift! Cathy was despondent and wondered what to do. She eventually ran home and cried to Grandpa that she had lost the money. With his serene, comforting voice, he assured her that there was no need to cry; things happen in life, and it was going to be okay. Still, the thought of losing five dollars was intolerable.

Only adding to the mystery of his origins, Grandpa's

influences extended well beyond money. He also became Cathy's most devoted English tutor, helping her develop early reading skills. When she buckled down to tackle her first simple books, it became evident that Grandpa was articulate in his speech and was quite well-read himself. And his coaching efforts were thorough. He instructed her to follow his own pronunciations, to use correct English grammar, and to enunciate clearly.

If Cathy was not practicing with her own books, she knew precisely which one Grandpa would choose—none other than the Holy Bible. Her eyes naturally rolled back in despair with this standard selection. Still, she tolerated the Bible because it meant an enjoyable time with Grandpa and his steadfast personal attention. In those early years, the Bible was, without a doubt, the most prominent book on the shelves of practicing Catholics. Grandpa was no different, often choosing it as the default volume for reading lessons. "So, here comes Adam and Eve again, yada-yada," she now quips, reflecting on their numerous sessions.

Bible or not, his style of reading aloud was mesmerizing. His approach to storytelling was akin to a riveting personal performance. Nearly managing the impossible, Grandpa transformed otherwise tiring Bible stories into magical tales. But the best was yet to come at the end of each session. Cathy picked up where Grandpa left off, offering her own creative versions. She remembers him laughing out loud more than once, enjoying his own education from the lesser-known Book of Cathy.

Most of the time Grandpa was a quiet yet determined individual. He was especially adamant about correcting the way Cathy spoke English. At one point he had outrun his patience with hearing her say "okay" after nearly every sentence. He thus tried a new strategy, charging her five cents for every time she uttered the overused word. In one respect, his creative approach was a clear success, given this direct threat to her own personal income. To this day Cathy rarely uses that word in her everyday speaking. And that's quite okay.

Of course, lessons can occasionally backfire in unexpected ways, as any exasperated parent can attest. In this case Cathy had already developed a fear of public speaking. Grandpa had not helped this issue with his incessant focus on that forbidden word. Now, she worried more than ever that she might accidentally say "okay" whenever she opened her mouth. For some time, this encouraged her own public shyness in a way she would never think possible today. Grandpa's insistence definitely helped Cathy think more about what she was saying. Fortunately, she would grow out of this irrational fear before too long, given more natural inclinations.

Beyond the tutoring, Grandpa's support for sending the sisters to St. Anthony's was prophetic. Cathy came to view convent school as a second home, spending most of her waking hours there. Importantly, the school provided vital direction and creative outlets for Cathy's budding imagination and insatiable curiosity.

The choice of Catholic school made good sense for another reason. Prior to reaching school age, Cathy had become familiar with the Church and its basic teachings and culture. As the mixed-race daughter of Scottish and Chinese parents, she was somewhat uniquely brought up within a Catholic household. The sisters were "cradle Catholics," as Cathy refers to their devotion to this uncommon religion. This unlikely scenario was owed in part to her father and Uncle Kellard, who were themselves brought up within the Church. More surprising was Cathy's Chinese mother, Mary, who had insisted the girls be baptized as soon as they were born. Her mother-in-law, Mama acquiesced, despite her own preference for the

Seventh-day Adventist Church, a protestant denomination which observes Saturday as the seventh day of the week rather than Sunday. Combined with Grandpa's nudging and another uncle's support, the writing was on the wall. The sisters were headed to Catholic school.

For more than a decade, the school provided something of an escape valve for Cathy. Sure, the curriculum was centered around the religious teachings of the Church. Regardless, Cathy gave all this a pass, though it sometimes annoyed her to no end. As she views it now, the important thing was that St. Anthony's offered a quality education as well as a safe place—a true sanctuary—for less fortunate children like her. While she endured years of scrounging for monthly school fees, the cost was comparatively minimal. This contributed to a diverse body of students from all walks of life. In short, Cathy fit right in.

Though thankfully more affordable, being a student there still required an array of additional, hidden costs. The monthly school fees were just the beginning. If the girls actually wanted to attend in person, they needed to get there. This meant a necessary bus pass, or *concession* for Singapore's budding public transportation system. Once purchased, the girls could show their stamps to the driver without paying in cash. Although school buses did exist in those years, their routes were spotty—and expensive. Only wealthier families could afford them.

Added to that were the costs of books and standard school uniforms, sometimes on an annual basis. These obligations compounded on one another and occasionally overwhelmed an already anxious Cathy. Despite occasional benefactors, she regularly wondered where she would find the money. Worrying about such things became embedded within her very being. Whenever immediate family members failed to assist, Cathy relied heavily on Grandpa or on other occasional income sources when possible.

One of her biggest headaches involved school uniforms. Every school in Singapore required them, so St. Anthony's was not off the mark here. In a country desperate to eliminate ethnic violence, Singapore required school uniforms for every child—much as it does today. The problem was that Cathy was physically growing taller each year, as youthful humans tend to do. This only added to her frustration with how often she needed to upsize her outfit. She thus learned to acquire second-hand uniforms that were several sizes too large. In this way she extended their wearable lives and reduced her own costs.

When various school costs arose, Cathy first approached Mama to assist. Even when Mama did comply, however, it was almost always late and well beyond the due date. Sometimes Mama claimed to not have the money on hand, which may or may not have been accurate. Mama's earlier thrill with playing the lottery—with occasional success—gradually evolved into a full-blown addiction. Whether the girls dropped out of school was a distant, secondary concern. The reality was that Mama had agreed to take in the sisters but had not assured their education. Any funds provided by her own children—that is, the girls' uncles and aunties—were often repurposed for gambling.

As Cathy now recalls, Mama and many of her counterparts became enamored with the dream of getting rich quickly. They had survived World War II and the Occupation, and they knew scarcity themselves. Any remaining hopes and dreams were understandably devoted to the rare windfall. Cathy holds no grudges and acknowledges Mama's behavior at that time. Still, her destructive habit did nothing to help Cathy's anxiety. The girls even went without food on numerous occasions as the family's funds disappeared. The daily uncertainty of not having enough money for school, let alone for food at night, proved more stressful than any fear of speaking in public.

When all other options for money were exhausted, the girls sheepishly approached their unpredictable father. Errol could hardly be counted upon to provide funds on a timely basis and was often late like Mama. The real possibility of being humiliated at school was only one of a string of concerns. Only adding to Cathy's horror was the habit of some teachers—usually not the nicer nuns—to announce who had not paid their monthly fees. They had no problem whatsoever using humiliation as a motivator, purposely shaming the poorer students in front of their peers. This was not a time when teachers bent over backwards to make their pupils feel good about themselves. Cathy's own name was called on numerous occasions when her payments were late.

At the time she would have liked nothing better than to "reach up and slap their faces," as she now likes to say with some dramatic flair. To be fair, Cathy realizes she was far from alone in being singled out. A sizable portion of the student body endured financial hardships. Any number of them—wrongly or otherwise—could be the subject of a teacher's wrath from one time to the next. Cathy adds, "This happened nearly every month and year until we graduated."

Decades later, she can now conjure up some sympathy for the teachers, "who were not hired to be debt collectors in addition to their normal teaching duties," she admits. Still, an unpredictable home life had placed adult-level obligations on her and her sister at an unusually young age. Always one to look for silver linings, Cathy believes that her continuous search for more money only encouraged her own resilience and independence in the long run.

Stories From the Bus

Just out of Kindergarten, a jubilant Cathy greatly anticipated her first year in primary school. But now she had to figure out how to get there. Like her sister, Cathy needed to quickly learn to navigate existing public transit options. With Singapore's Mass Rapid Transit, or MRT subway, still well into the future, the young sisters came to rely upon the city's public bus network. Few families owned automobiles, so public transit was the only logical option for moving easily around the city.

In one respect, Cathy was fortunate. For this and many other situations, it was her older sister who often served as the family trailblazer. She was always two years ahead, whether she wanted to be or not. Cathy naturally soaked in vital lessons from her sister's own hard-won experiences, especially traveling together on public buses. There was little choice—their school was located nine stops from home. This was more than a half-hour one way if all went well.

Very little scared Cathy during those years. As the self-proclaimed "busybody" of the family, Cathy loved to talk and experience new things. Still, as she now reflects with some relief, "The road is always paved by the first child." She has her sister to thank for invaluable guidance throughout those years.

Mastering the city bus system further contributed to Cathy's emerging street smarts. Riding the bus provided any number of lessons in handling adversity. Among other issues, those older buses tended to break down. But such experiences led to greater awareness of her real-world surroundings. She explains, "Today's children may be able to get home or to the mall on the bus. But if they end up somewhere else in the city or miss their stop, it is difficult for them to think on their feet and solve the problem. We didn't have any choice and just had to travel, and every time out we were learning something new."

With more confidence on the bus, Cathy expanded outwards on social calls to the homes of various friends. Of course, any number of unplanned things could happen on such non-routine trips. In one early instance she courageously boarded a city bus to play at her friend's house. While the trip there proved largely uneventful, Cathy had spent her last 15 cents to pay the fare back home. This would have been all well and good had the bus not broken down a considerable distance away. Not knowing what to do, she followed everyone off the bus as the driver instructed. Tears welled up as she started to panic. Without obvious options coming to mind, she simply started walking in the direction of home. Her budding street smarts had at least taught her how to orient herself in the proper direction. With tears streaming down her cheeks, she continued to walk, and walk. She trudged some three kilometers, quite a distance for a young child on her own.

Upon her arrival home, her father was actually present to greet her. Better yet, he was sober. In these rare instances when he was physically and emotionally available, he could be a compassionate, loving father. He was rather curious about her sad disposition and ragged condition, so he inquired about what had happened. She had stopped crying much earlier because, as Cathy humorously recalls, "I was all dried out; my tears were all gone."

Still, her father's simple question made her start crying all over again. With his own abrasive brand of kindness, he told her to stop crying because "it was stupid to cry like that." She explained how the bus had broken down and that she did not have money to pay for another fare. Then he explained how the bus system worked. Cathy recalls, "He told me, 'The next time, when a bus breaks down, you should hold onto your bus ticket, and the next bus will take you for free!'" To this she replied in frustration, "But nobody told me that!" He also counseled her to go into one of the nearby shops and ask to borrow the phone, so that she could call home. She admits today that her head was so full of tears, she was not thinking straight. But she was thinking clearly enough to find her own way home—no small accomplishment. Her budding resolve would prove useful with navigating more than bus routes in the years to come.

Chapter 6

The Rich Auntie

Lurking beyond Mama's flat was a mind-numbing array of extended family members. This galaxy of additional relatives entered Cathy's life only gradually, much like a dripping faucet. She never fully sorted out who was related to whom, though she has made impressive progress over the years. It turns out that some of them were keeping a watchful eye on the sisters from behind the scenes. And whether subtly or directly, they sometimes stepped in to assist when things got rough at home.

A few relatives even invited the girls to experience their own homes and lives. During Cathy's primary school years, this meant travel, and in turn, adventure. Even better, such excursions relieved the daily monotony of her home life. It was almost as if a magic portal had opened, providing a window into an alternate universe. Cathy's own extended family consisted of a hodge-podge of uncles, aunties, cousins, half-brothers and sisters, and their own chaotic families and households. And they ran the gamut of lifestyles, from the elite private estate to the last of Singapore's rural villages, or *kampongs*. With each invitation to hit the road, Cathy's response was "Yes, please." She eagerly passed through her own mythical portal to experience a larger world away from home.

Predictably, the girls were swept away to visit relatives most often during school holidays and special occasions. The typical Singaporean school cycle was spread across the entire year, which meant that family gatherings would follow suit. The first day of school officially began on January 2, followed by a one-week break in March. Students then enjoyed a full month off in June, another week in September, and then a six-week break from mid-November to January 1 to close out the year. This is when Cathy found herself visiting an array of distant family members, often without protest. With some exceptions, almost any opportunity to escape the confines of her flat was cause for celebration.

At the wealthier extreme of the family was Auntie Shirley, whom Cathy simply describes now as her "rich auntie." Shirley and her own household may not have qualified as "crazy rich," like Singapore's upper echelon of landed estate owners—and the namesake of the 2018 blockbuster film, *Crazy Rich Asians*. To Cathy's childhood mind, however, Auntie Shirley just had to be loaded with money. As logic would have it, this meant there should be plenty to go around. Shirley's husband, Bill, owned a successful business specializing in insulation products for buildings and roofing. He therefore made a respectable and reliable living, riding the coattails of Singapore's post-war construction boom.

It was no coincidence that Uncle Kellard's day job was provided by Bill's company. At some point early in Cathy's life, Bill had offered Kellard employment in the insulation trade. In this way, Shirley's family was already indirectly supporting Cathy's household, providing Kellard with stable employment and income.

While Cathy often looked forward to visiting her auntie's plush home, her sister was a different matter. She was becoming more of a homebody, satisfied to remain there unless cajoled to do otherwise. And their personal interests diverged further as they got older. Though unintentional, this allowed Cathy to experience new places and meet different people on her own.

Sometimes during her visits to Shirley's place, the whole family would dart off to ritzy social functions or dinner events—but without Cathy. The young visitor was rarely included in such galivanting. Instead, Cathy was placed under the trusty tutelage of Auntie's domestic housekeeper. While other children might feel left out, this was all fine with Cathy. The truth was that such time alone provided a grand opportunity to play *House* in real life! As a junior housekeeper, she stuck by her mentor and started to learn. There was always something in one room or another that required attention. Her rich auntie's place thus served as a sort-of home economics class. In her incessant quest to remain active, Cathy begged the housekeeper to teach her any number of useful skills. Even the drudgery of daily household chores was fair game.

And let's face it, there was little else for a child to do there anyway. The cousins were older, and everyone else was busier with their own lives. Cathy was easily forgotten, and she blended into the background—even when the family stayed at home. And finding a cozy corner to bury herself in storybooks was not an option. There were precious few children's books to be found. She does recall lengthy shelves of encyclopedias, the likes of which were marketed worldwide throughout those decades. The television was likewise off-limits, by some random adult rule. It was clearly not her home to do as she pleased. "It was just a boring place," she states bluntly, adding, "I did not want to sit there and rot in the chair!"

By process of elimination, Cathy volunteered to work. Of course, her definition of working was more innocent through the eyes of a child. She recalls, "Housekeeping was an adventure! There was always something to do." Left with few options, she naturally volunteered for various tasks and chores, tagging along with her de-facto tutor. Cathy assisted—or made valiant attempts—with practically everything, such as making the beds, washing clothes, and cleaning the house. If the housekeeper was busy doing something, Cathy remained steadfastly by her side as an extra hand.

Shirley and Bill's residence was something in itself to behold. The place was jaw-dropping, especially for a child unaccustomed to such opulence. Unlike the vast majority of Singapore's public housing blocks, theirs was a privately owned, semi-detached duplex. Both houses were owned by the family. Each unit included four bedrooms upstairs and a collection of family and dining rooms below, which Cathy perceived as an endless maze. There was always another room or doorway hiding around the corner. This also translated to never-ending housework to relieve the boredom.

She especially came to enjoy the tropical, rainy days that cast a softer, diffuse light over the house. The warm, muggy weather signaled to the housekeeper that it was time to scrub the outdoor flooring and patio spaces. The predicted downpours then arrived, conveniently rinsing the soap away. These simple pleasures were just plain fun for Cathy. For these reasons, Auntie Shirley's home was "where the world came alive."

This was also where Cathy learned to iron at the age of eight, though not without some rough starts. One early attempt did not go so well. She learned the hard way that a hot iron left sitting on a pair of suit trousers was not the best idea. In this case, the housekeeper was not present to witness her mistake. Thinking quickly, Cathy grabbed the smoldering remains and buried the ruined pants in a rarely used closet. It remains unclear as to whether anyone ever found the evidence, let alone connected it to her.

Whenever the chores were done—for Cathy's part, at least—it was time to eat! Unlike at home, acquiring basic foods was no issue here. After her initial shock at all the food, she still recalls, "They didn't even calculate how much we ate or anything. They were very hospitable, and there was plenty of food to go around at mealtime." Following a satisfying day and plenty to eat, Cathy was confident she would finally enjoy a real bed in her own room. Alas, this was too much to hope for, even at her rich auntie's place. Once again, she ended up sleeping on the floor, as the beds were all reserved for family members, not visitors.

A Christmas Gift

Of all the times Cathy looked forward to visiting Auntie Shirley, the most festive was certainly Christmas. Their mammoth tree always stole the show, towering from floor to ceiling with its bedazzling ornaments. To this day, she adores celebrating her own Christmas holidays with family and friends, in no small part due to special childhood memories.

Despite all this, it was all too easy for Cathy to feel lost and nearly forgotten amidst Shirley's festive crowds. Aside from helping to serve food, Cathy could have just as easily been another piece of furniture that nobody really noticed.

Cathy's apparent loneliness must have come to Uncle Bill's attention at one point. No one was more stunned than Cathy when he suggested that Shirley take her on a Christmas shopping trip. The goal was to load up with gifts for the pending holiday. Well, this sounded promising—even if they just really wanted extra hands to carry the bags, which Cathy now suspects was the prime motivation.

In one store, her auntie and uncle were, as Cathy recalls, "buying a truckload of toys and dolls for the children of one of their close friends." To his credit, Bill asked Cathy if she would like to have a doll as well. Before she could pull her jaw off the floor, Shirley interjected and chastised her husband. "No! She doesn't need any dolls. What she needs is clothing!" At this, Cathy fumed. Though usually grateful to receive any clothes that were not hand-me-downs, Cathy's hopes for a real toy had been crushed in sheer disappointment. She says of the incident, "If I could have jumped up there, I would have liked as much to slap her face!" At that time Cathy had never owned a real doll of her own, and she would have been quite satisfied with anything, really. "A Barbie, perhaps, or even Ken! It didn't even need to be a female doll! I would have been perfectly fine with a teddy bear." Apparently, none of that was forthcoming.

In place of an apparently useless doll, her auntie did make good on her statement and purchased two t-shirts for her niece. This was a big deal in its own right; Cathy still remembers the gift to this day. And, as an older and wiser Cathy now relates, there is always payback when the child becomes a parent. In that role, Cathy decided to be more generous to her own children in later years, in part to correct for her auntie's frugality. "I didn't deprive my children, but I didn't spoil them either," she explains, having tried valiantly to strike a decent balance.

After joyfully providing her own children with dolls and toys, Cathy began to understand her auntie's perspective. She invariably found the dolls' heads popped off and their various limbs scattered around the home, not minutes after their arrival. She now readily admits that accumulating too many toys can be a serious waste of money. To this day she believes her auntie was unwittingly teaching her the difference between wants and needs.

It is further likely that Shirley's focus on clothing meant she understood more about Cathy's home life than she had let on. Knowing of their financial hardship, Shirley also provided

Mama with pocket money to keep the household afloat. This was subtly accomplished behind the scenes and out of Cathy's view.

In addition, there were plenty of stingier relatives than Auntie Shirley. Cathy occasionally visited another uncle's modest home, complete with even more cousins to play with. Unlike Shirley, however, this uncle's wife blatantly favored her own children when it came to mealtime. Whenever Cathy stayed over, Auntie prepared food for her own children, but not for her. Any leftovers that came her way after dinner were fair game, but the cousins needed to finish their own meals first.

And while Auntie Shirley could be more generous, Cathy inadvertently got caught up in whatever dieting scheme Shirley was trying next. One reason Cathy preferred to remain with the housekeeper was because she could at least count on some decent lunch. After all, the housekeeper had to eat at some point. But on occasions when Cathy accompanied the family, her auntie and older cousins were typically engaged with yet another diet plan. Even lunch or other vital meals were summarily skipped, meaning that Cathy did not eat, either. She recalls with some lingering bitterness, "Instead, I was forced to follow them around, and they didn't even stop to eat lunch, so poor me, I just felt like dying over and over again." The irony was that she could thus experience hunger pangs with her rich auntie just as she often did at home. At that young age, there was little she could do about it.

Regardless of where she visited, the ripple effect later in life was predictable. She explains, "Since I was so scrawny when I was young, I vowed years ago that I would eat anything and everything I would see for the rest of my life." Given her continuing penchant for cooking and for sharing much of it, this is one vow that she has gratefully been able to keep, with only occasional regrets.

Nor was Cathy always pleased with her opportunities to travel. On one level she welcomed any occasion for family adventures that were—from a child's eye—far from home. As she now recognizes, however, she made these trips with conflicted emotions. Leaving Mama's flat to be dragged along with various adults was not necessarily her choice. Sometimes she even cried at departure time, what with so many friends to play with around home. She explains, "I did cry a lot, yes. I remember I used to cry because I would have to leave Mama's flat to go to someone else's house to stay. So, I guess I was unhappy in a sense, that my sister didn't have to go anywhere. They thought they were being kind by just taking me with them to spend their holidays. So, I did feel lonely, and I cried a lot. They used to call me a crybaby and even said I could qualify to join funerals to be a professional mourner."

Asked whether professional mourners actually exist, Cathy lets out a chuckle and reverts back to teaching mode. "Yes, it's a real thing. For the Chinese, if a person dies and there are not enough descendants or children—that is, a load of people to cry at the funeral—they often hire professional ones to come and be a part of the service. They tell you when to start crying and when to stop. This allows the soul to move on with its journey. That's why when you see a Chinese funeral, you'll see them wailing and wailing away, and calling out to the dead and all that. It's pretty ridiculous, but they actually branded me as a professional mourner. I could cry buckets and buckets of tears. When I tell my student groups this, I say that all of China was flooded because of it, and they all laugh."

Professional mourner or not, it is clearer today that Cathy was not always thrilled with being torn away from the comforts of her home and friends. The silver lining was that she was experiencing more adventures and places than many children her age. As her journeys added up, her eyes were opened to a wide array of households, cultural differences, family habits and traditions, and of course, ever-more children to play with. One might say she was being unintentionally primed for her future career. Whether by personal choice or subject to the whims of adults, Cathy was afoot, moving about her island nation with unlimited curiosity. And even more adventures away from home were yet to come.

The Runner

In addition to playing host, Auntie Shirley was quietly assisting Cathy's Mama as well. Whenever she provided Mama with money for groceries, Mama dutifully headed to the market. This cycle of behavior led Cathy to call Mama "the runner." In return for the cash, Mama insisted on purchasing ingredients for Shirley's meals as well. Quite inadvertently, the pair had developed their own food delivery system. By providing Mama with some cash, Shirley learned that Mama could purchase food for both of them. Upon return, Mama set to work with early preparations for Shirley's family meals. As an added bonus, Mama was allowed to keep the balance of any leftover funds. Shirley then stopped by later to pick up the prepared food.

On those occasions when Mama and granddaughter were getting along, Cathy found herself on the "production line" of Aunt Shirley's meal preparations. Sitting for what felt like hours on end, Cathy dutifully peeled the shells of prawns, plucked beansprouts, and completed any number of related tasks. Unbeknownst to her at the time, she was learning how to cook as well.

As Cathy grew older, she often accompanied Mama on trips to the market. She thereby became a "runner" herself. These outings proved adventurous for their own reasons. One case in point involved their favored method of transport—the *trishaw*, or three-wheeled bicycle. In Singaporean history, Cathy's outings with Mama were timely. They were participating in a distinctly local form of transportation enjoying its last popular decade. First introduced in Singapore in 1914, the trishaw was also known as a "pedal rickshaw," which involved attaching a two-seat bench—covered or not—to the side of a standard bicycle frame. The visual result was like a pedal-driven sidecar. Before they could proliferate on Singapore's streets, however, the British promptly banned them upon their appearance in 1914.

The three-wheeled vehicles staged a comeback during the 1940s and particularly during the Japanese Occupation. Petrol fuel for automobiles became acutely scarce. This situation necessitated more creative ways for people to move around the city, and it was ironically the Japanese who lifted the previous British restriction. Later, its ancestor and competitor, the *rickshaw*—pulled by humans—was banned by colonial authorities in 1947. This only increased the demand for trishaws in later years.

The trishaw had its advantages over the rickshaw, the foremost being that it was a more humane job for their hired drivers. The trishaw was physically less demanding to operate and was decidedly faster than the walking speeds of rickshaws. During their final years in public service, Cathy and Mama made good use of them. After that, the proliferation of auto traffic, roadways, and taxicab businesses eventually led trishaw operators to find other work. Today they are merely seen as a curiosity by tourists, who might pay to take a ride in a refurbished model.

At the other end of the trishaw ride, Mama had certain favored markets to visit. Cathy came to serve as her loyal "bodyguard," transitioning from the role of "little helper" to that of a more responsible caretaker. Mama was already in her 60s, which for a young girl like Cathy seemed very old! Cathy felt more obliged to look after her and assist when needed, including walking closely and holding her hand. These were likely important family bonding times. She later recognized a number of shared personality traits. Both could certainly be difficult, stubborn, and hard-headed, and they demonstrated a natural level of cynicism. But they also enjoyed each other's sense of humor, bantering and arguing with the best of them.

On occasions, the sisters accompanied Mama on a public bus to the market. They effectively became Mama's *advance team*, or protective entourage. Because they could walk faster, the girls typically arrived first at the bus stop. When the bus arrived, they rushed on board to find seats, dutifully reserving a place for their senior companion.

In Singapore this practice of reserving seats or places is known as *choping*, or to *chope*, which means "to reserve." Once considered rude or selfish, choping has gained some level of acceptance given the city's higher population densities. One can experience this practice walking through one of Singapore's bustling malls or food courts, when busy professionals place a business card, a pack of tissue, or even a napkin to reserve their precious seats.

Cathy supports the practice of choping. She knows full well that she would otherwise be walking around in circles while trying to manage her food. Some people even leave small umbrellas or their own lanyards from work to save their places. Fellow Singaporeans can generally be trusted to understand what people are doing, so such items are simply left alone.

Living with Mama provided for other fond memories. "She could be cute, sometimes," Cathy recalls. Her church-going habits provided one case in point. When Cathy was old enough to start questioning people's behaviors, she wondered why

Mama spent so much time at church on Sundays. She left the flat at an ungodly 7:00 am but did not return until after 2:00 in the afternoon. This pattern persisted for years. With curiosity finally getting the better of her, Cathy asked bluntly, "Why does your church service last so long?" Not even the Catholics required Cathy to attend for hours on end. Given that Mama's denomination was Seventh-day Adventist, Cathy never had an opportunity to follow along to see where she went. Instead, the sisters were always expected to attend their own church and Sunday School.

Mama finally explained what was happening. She traveled on a special church shuttle that picked up parishioners around the neighborhood. Upon arrival, she simply remained in place for all successive services—the 8:00, the 9:00 and so forth. Then she boarded the return bus following the very last service. Expressing a combination of surprise and humor, Cathy responded quickly with, "Oh, my God, that means you can go to Heaven right away!" Just as sailors compiled "sea time," Mama had apparently accumulated an impressive amount of "church time." In Cathy's eyes, this promised to allow her entry into Heaven even faster. In any case, one more household mystery was solved. Explanations for other family curiosities would wait until later.

Chapter 7

Being Errol's Daughter

Cathy and her three companions were not always alone in Mama's flat. Sometimes their already cramped space doubled as a holding area for family refugees. A colorful variety of individuals came and went every so often. Their home thus became a fallback—a sort-of halfway house—when someone's life was in transition or took a wrong turn. Whatever the reasons, these visitors were momentarily without direction and had nowhere else to go.

As might be expected, Cathy appreciated some visitors more than others. She even grew fond of some of the more charismatic personalities who came their way. One such individual was her oldest cousin. He had always been up to some kind of mischief. Cathy particularly enjoyed hearing about his time in prison. While some families gather for stories of wisdom from their elders, the sisters gathered around their cousin to hear tantalizing tales from jail.

Beyond their cousin, a collection of other friends and family members ended up in trouble at one time or another. "They're all really nice people," Cathy tries to assure, "but somehow or other they ended up in jail, back in trouble again." She cites how one uncle had been helping the Vietnam refugees, and he went to prison for that as well. A more common reason for short-term incarceration involved various gang activities. One friend told her about his sparse meals while living behind bars. He was forced to eat only sausages or hotdogs for breakfast, lunch, and dinner. Sometimes it was the same sausage cut into three parts, one for each meal of the day. It was understandable why he never wanted to see, smell, or taste another hotdog again.

Another occasional visitor was none other than her own father, Errol. He was usually in transition between one apartment and another. Or more likely, he was desperate enough to ask his mother for money. "Get in line," Cathy now quips in her deadpan humor. He might also stay the night when too intoxicated to return to his flat in one piece.

These occasional transients only aggravated an already cramped household. What seemed like a revolving door to their flat spun even faster after Cathy turned six. Air mattresses were sprawled across the living room, and certain family members—often the sisters—were relegated to sleep on the floor near Mama's corner. "So, whichever adult was the last to return to the flat at night," Cathy explains, "would have a difficult time getting inside, because one or more of us would be sleeping on the other side of the doorway!"

Despite Errol's unpredictable appearances, Cathy retains some fond memories of their times together. These were isolated instances, however, and only when he was sober. As an alcoholic, he quickly transformed into a monster, keeping everyone on edge and sometimes in fear for their own safety.

Cathy especially remembers fun times at the beach, including being bathed there. "If he wasn't intoxicated, he was the nicest man in the world. This was when he decided to be related to me," she only half jokes. The girls also relied on Errol to drive them there. And this was no small deal. It was still a rare privilege in Singapore during the 1970s to own an automobile. For some time, Cathy believed that her father was one such fortunate person. On beach days, Errol appeared in a snazzy car, perhaps a Saab Turbo, to pick them up. Little did Cathy know at the time that her father did not own the car, as it belonged to his American boss instead. Errol somehow managed to borrow the car while the boss' family was on holiday in the United States.

Typically, their trip to the beach was uneventful. But while the girls galloped through the water's edge doing "beachy" things, Errol was knocking back successive beers. The effects of this behavior became more apparent during the ride home, which Cathy simply recalls as "very fast and very scary." Rather than weave slowly around the road as intoxicated drivers are known to do, Cathy says, "our father drove us home like a madman, like a *Formula 1* driver!" Already exhausted, the sisters were usually oblivious of how they made it home, as they quickly fell asleep in the back seat more often than not. When Cathy was wide awake, however, she became alarmed by her father's erratic driving. During one scary instance, she heard another driver shout to Errol, "If you want to die, you should die alone, but don't bring your family along!" Fortunately, most people did not own cars, so the route home was not yet congested with traffic. There was simply less for him to hit. Today Cathy is grateful that such incidents did not lead to more serious problems.

Aside from beach days, Errol's very presence could be troublesome in its own right. The following story provides one poignant case. Cathy was nine or ten when she became engrossed with a creative children's savings program offered by the Post Office. Promoted as something like a "Post Office savings bank," special stamps were sold to students whenever they deposited more money. Each stamp cost five cents, while a full card of stamps was two dollars. In turn, each stamp was placed onto a cumulative card to keep track of how much money had been saved.

For Cathy, the scheme proved irresistible. While learning to manage her own money, she obsessed over the practice and invested whatever she could scrape up. Her sister bought into the program as well. They acquired extra money by foregoing lunch at school and from donations during Uncle Kellard's weekend card games. Even better was the occasional windfall from Auntie Shirley or from little red packets. Money in hand, off Cathy went to the Post Office, a branch of which was located adjacent to their school. It turned into quite a racket. Cathy learned to use their system for her long-term advantage, it was hoped.

Around this time, Errol showed up for one of his random visits to happily announce a new job offer. While other children might shrug off such news, Cathy was greatly relieved. She never entirely knew how their monthly bills might be paid. The catch, Errol said, was that he needed to pay his future boss before he would be given the job. *Say what? Okay, whatever*, Cathy thought briefly. She was not yet able to discern when her father was telling a tall tale.

By then, Errol had gotten wind of his daughters' participation in the stamp program. Not beyond taking advantage of naïve youthfulness, Errol visited the Post Office and withdrew the full balance of their hard-earned savings. He simply appropriated the funds for himself, or "for his liquid diet," as Cathy recalls.

Of course, in the end there was no job offer. But the nearby coffee shop also sold his favorite Stout. As Cathy reflects painfully, "My sister and I were just bleeding to death after that, because I had saved so much money starving myself every other day. And then he just takes our money and spends it on the Guinness Brothers." Later, the girls asked hopefully if he had been given the job, always eager to see him gainfully employed. And, more important, they also wanted their money back. Acting forlorn, he admitted to not having been hired. This news naturally led to the fair question of just when he was planning to return their savings. Cathy remembers him shrugging it off, as if to say, *Yah, right. When the money comes.*

It is difficult for Cathy to not cringe at her youthful gullibility. She further regrets falling into the ongoing trap of trying to please her father. While holding onto serious grudges is not her style, the devastation she felt from losing her hard-earned savings was not easily dismissed.

One important silver lining was undeniable. Errol's behaviors inadvertently discouraged Cathy from drinking alcohol. Aside from her "clubbing" years as a teenager, she now rarely touches the stuff. Cathy explains, "That's why none of us drink to this day. We just don't enjoy drinking because we didn't like seeing him behave like that. So, we never really found a joy in it. Some of us might occasionally have a social drink, some wine, but not like drinking with no sense of responsibility. If you're a responsible person, you will drink just to enjoy yourself, but not have it become your lifestyle."

When asked how she ultimately came to terms with her father, Cathy pauses to collect her thoughts. "Well, there were good days too, and then there were bad days. It wasn't all or nothing. Sure, he could make our lives miserable sometimes, but that doesn't mean I need to disown him. I'm still related to him, you know what I mean? So, there were horrible times, but for how long can I hate a person? He's my father. In one respect, back then with so many broken families, just having a father was like, 'Wow!' Many other children were abandoned completely. If he actually came to visit us, we were impressed and usually happy about it. When he wasn't drinking, he was extremely nice to be with, and very knowledgeable."

Chapter 8

Visiting the Kampong

Soon after the girls' mother left, Errol drifted in and out of various relationships or infatuations. One of them eventually became Cathy's first stepmother, Meiling. Speaking in the Teochew dialect, Meiling still lived in one of Singapore's rural kampongs well outside city limits. How Meiling had met Errol was anyone's guess. No matter, she and Errol then had a daughter of their own, Cecilia.

Cathy sometimes visited the kampong with her father during holidays, offering a taste of farm life that was quickly disappearing. Traditional villages on the island were giving way to the urbanized developments of booming Singapore. At the time of Cathy's visits, the advancing bulldozers were still miles away from Meiling's kampong, called Choa Chu Kang. Much as they had done for generations, Chinese and Malay villagers relied on small-scale peasant farming, in which families produced a wide array of foods to sustain their families. What wasn't needed at home was sold locally, such as vegetables, eggs, and various domesticated animals and poultry.

The village's distance from central Singapore allowed its rural lifestyle to persist into the 1980s. For Cathy, this also made for a rather lengthy—and nauseating—bus ride. In those days the buses were not air conditioned, and diesel fumes poured through the open windows. Combined with a winding route through the rural hills, this was almost too much for Cathy's sensitive stomach to handle.

Upon introduction to her stepmother's home, baby Cecilia instantly became Cathy's new half-sister. For their part, Errol and Meiling were never officially married, though during those decades few couples rarely were. There was little paperwork or official process required for marriage. Errol therefore simply started a new family with Meiling and—sometimes with Cathy in tow—traveled to the village for periodic visits.

Explaining more about marriage practices, Cathy says, "In those days not many people officially registered to get married. If a man and woman moved in together, she simply became his wife. There was no paperwork because many people were still illiterate. It's still surprising to think that this was common practice during those years, but this was still a rural, undeveloped island."

Cathy's multi-day visits to Choa Chu Kang provided little opportunity for father-daughter bonding. With Cathy suitably deposited at Meiling's house, Errol managed to disappear until fetching her again to head home. *Where was he going all the time?* She wondered. No matter, the relative solitude allowed her to absorb the peace and tranquility that came with farm life. A greater contrast could hardly be imagined between this scene and her otherwise bustling, urban home. Her newfound serenity was especially notable during evenings and early mornings. During these times the lush vegetation was often blanketed with dew, given the incessantly high humidity. There was no commotion of traffic or street life to interrupt the peaceful evenings. Better yet, the roaming street gangs and likenesses of the *Kareng Guni* Man were unheard of.

The farmhouse which Meiling called home was wood-framed with a typical zinc-plated roof. Wealthier villagers were sometimes able to replace the traditional thatch roof with a metal one. While the zinc was more fire resistant, the metal also made it hotter inside during the already muggy, oppressive daytimes. Even with this modern upgrade, Cathy recalls, "the roof still leaked like a sieve." She and the family regularly placed numerous buckets under the leaks to catch the rainwater.

Many village homes like this one consisted of little more than a single main room with no indoor plumbing. The toilets were placed rather far away in a separate outhouse, or latrine, a full hundred meters away by Cathy's estimate. This latter fact was a serious price to pay for otherwise enjoyable visits. "Using the outhouse was just a terrible experience," she laments, still conjuring the memory of squatting in that smelly place.

In those days removable metal buckets were placed under the latrines. One unlucky villager was deployed to collect the human waste every day. "If you were the first to go in the morning, you were lucky," Cathy describes, trying to remain polite. "But if you were the fourth or fifth, it was not a pleasant place to be." Countless mosquito bites provided a parting gift from each visit, causing annoying bouts of itching and scratching until soreness set in. Anyone who might be tempted to consider a nostalgic holiday here did not fully comprehend the realities of life in the kampong.

Once back in the house, sleeping presented its own challenges. If Cathy still held out hope for her own bedroom, Meiling's farmhouse was not the place to find one. She relied primarily on an uncomfortable wooden bed not far off the floor. This was a luxury by comparison, as she was sometimes resigned to a homemade mattress instead. Her body's tiny frame was at least able to withstand any hard surface as necessary. Still, sleep never came easily, as any number of issues and distractions could disturb her slumber.

Prior to the bedtime ordeal, she cherished the peaceful evenings as dusk settled in. This is when villagers nursed their wood fires for cooking and other household tasks. They further burned a lot of dried leaves as a valiant attempt to smoke out the mosquitos. For this reason, there was always a pall of smoke in the air. At least this gave the humans a fighting chance against the bloodthirsty insects.

In some ways, the urban concerns of home still managed to follow her to Meiling's place. When Cecilia was still a toddler, Cathy was once again admonished to remain indoors at night. Though safe from urban street gangs and their tattooed bodies, the villages were most definitely haunted by any number of creepy ghosts. Without standard electricity, these rural areas were also measurably darker than Cathy's neighborhood. This only enhanced any concerns about what horrors might be waiting to pounce. More specifically, she was warned about the female vampire, or *Pontiana*, in search of her next prey, along with related paranormal threats. Folk tales of ghosts and spirits came as a regular part of rural village life. Eventually Cathy naturally outgrew these stories as she learned to see through them for what they were. Regardless of what she believed, she was still remaining indoors for the night.

Despite, or because of, these rudimentary conditions, Cathy found plenty of ways to have fun and experience her own little adventures. Notably, she enjoyed a rare chance to connect with nature. At some point she discovered a small pond behind the farmhouse teeming with all sorts of tropical wildlife. Any number of small creatures lived in and around the pond, and Cathy walked among their incessant calls and wails. On one visit she was delighted to discover a family of tadpoles, each of which she christened with its own name. One might imagine how upset she was to find—upon her later return—that they had all disappeared! Devastated, she addressed the water out loud:

"Where did you all go?" She had no idea that they had magically transformed into a species of Singaporean frog. Disappointment turned to relief later that day when someone explained the life cycle of amphibious creatures. Yes, her new friends were alive and well, though in a measurably different form.

Decades later, Cathy would find her stepmother and Cecilia living within their own new HDB flat. Cecilia continued to live with her mother while adjusting to an unfamiliar, urban lifestyle. By then Errol was long gone, which surprised nobody who knew him. A middle-aged Cecilia eventually hired domestic help to care for her aging mother. She had also forged a friendship with their caregiver which continued well after Meiling passed away.

Once off the farm, Cecelia and her village counterparts were compelled to find regular city jobs as hired employees. Meiling found work in a factory, while her daughter eventually took a clerical position.

Today Choa Chu Kang is just another part of Singapore's metropolis, with barely a trace of the old village landscape remaining. Only its former name survives to provide a distant memory. The place is now designated as an official urban planning area and residential town, apparently with the highest population density in Singapore. The budding urban neighborhood was built out by the 1980s, along with the expanding Mass Rapid Transit (MRT) subway system. Cathy and her generation were therefore the last to experience the village lifestyle that once existed here.

For her part, Cathy remains personally grateful for her experiences there, if not entirely for the mosquitos. One might still wonder, what happened to Meiling's unofficial husband? Sometime during the village's conversion to urban housing, Errol "decided he wanted another woman," Cathy says understatedly. To his delight, Errol met a Malay nurse from the Johore state of Malaysia who could not help but fall in love with him. "I wouldn't say now that she fell in 'love' exactly," Cathy reflects, "but she came with him to Singapore and soon discovered to her horror that my father already had three children from his first two wives!" Somehow the woman, named Jessie, managed to brush aside his complicated past, and—in this case—eventually became legally married.

Conveniently for Errol, Meiling and her daughter were all but forgotten. As Cecilia grew older and transitioned into middle age, she had little interest in reuniting with her disloyal father. As Cathy bluntly states, "Cecilia and her mother drifted apart from my father. All Cecilia really remembered was how mean he was to her mother, anyway."

Chapter 9

Eating Potatoes

When Cathy shuffled off to primary school at St. Anthony's, she unknowingly brought with her a priceless skill. That is, she was already bilingual, allowing her to transition with ease into her English-speaking classrooms. Even her intractable father spoke fluent English. His own mother, however—Mama—was Chinese. Because she did not speak English, it was necessary for Cathy and her sister to converse in Mama's specific Teochew dialect.

This is a good place to note that *Chinese* is not technically a language in itself. It is more accurate to speak of Chinese *dialects*, which might as well be considered entirely separate languages. A reasonable comparison would be Europe's Romance languages such as French and Italian, which bear little resemblance to one another. The most common Chinese dialects are subvariants of Mandarin and Cantonese, the latter being the official language of Hong Kong. While Cathy's mother, Mary, spoke basic Cantonese, Mary left the family before Cathy could enjoy a decent chance to practice it.

Also missing from Cathy's household was the common Mandarin, known generally as Standard Chinese. Upon its independence, Singapore recognized Mandarin as one of its four official languages, along with English, Bahasa (Malay), and

Tamil (Indian). The catch was that Chinese Singaporeans seldom spoke Mandarin prior to the 1970s. Much like Cathy's family, they tended to favor one of the more common dialects of southern China such as Cantonese, Hokkien, Teochew, or Hakka. This makes geographic sense because many of Singapore's ethnic Chinese people are descended from that region.

Since the time of Cathy's childhood, the more regional dialects have been discouraged by the government and even prohibited from broadcast media. Instead, national leaders launched an unrelenting *Speak Mandarin Campaign*, which gradually nudged the nation's Chinese population in that direction. To this day some resentment still lingers among senior generations for not recognizing more localized culture and language traditions. As a child, Cathy found herself at the tail end of these popular regional dialects, when their use was more common in homes like hers.

As Cathy explains, "During the 1960s and 1970s, everyone was a linguist, because when we started speaking at a young age, all the different Chinese dialects naturally became a part of our lives." She attributes her current bilingual abilities to her mixed ethnic background. If the adults in her life were less than dependable, her makeshift household still served as an impressive language incubator.

Because Mama spoke Teochew, this became Cathy's first language or so-called "mother tongue" at home. She further missed out on Cantonese, so Cathy found creative ways to teach herself. Over time, she turned to a Hong Kong television series which served as a virtual tutor. Cathy now jokes—with some subtle pride—that she can speak Cantonese better than other family members. "My dialects are so good now," she says, "I can switch quickly to speak Cantonese in the Hong Kong style, the Malaysia style, or the Singapore style."

Aside from its four official languages, Singapore also declared English as the standard teaching language in all schools, both private and public. Prior to that, each school had emphasized its own specialized language, reflecting a specific ethnic community. For its part, St. Anthony's had already taught its classes in English, so the new national mandate for them made little difference. Cathy and her sister fit right in, as they had fortunately picked up English at home as well. Other children of Chinese descent were expected to learn that foreign language from scratch.

When it came to teaching English, the island's convent schools were second to none. They hired well qualified English teachers and maintained high educational standards overall, as compared to the public neighborhood schools at the time. This positive reputation meant that demand for spots within the nation's Catholic schools far exceeded supply. Cathy and her sister were fortunate they had special family members who encouraged that educational path.

Despite the broad appeal of convent schools, some members of the Chinese community voiced another concern. What if their children converted to Catholicism? This was no hypothetical fear, as Cathy recalls, because that is precisely what occasionally happened. For this reason, some of Cathy's classmates may not have begun as Catholics, but they certainly ended up heading in that direction.

During Cathy's youth, students across Singapore were expected to learn a second language to become bilingual. The obvious choice for many students was Bahasa because it was easier to learn. The Malays constitute the island's native, largely Muslim population. As such, they are recognized constitutionally as Singapore's indigenous people, and Bahasa is the country's national language. Even the Singapore National Anthem is sung in Bahasa, even though the country maintains four official languages as noted above.

With Cathy already speaking English, she learned Bahasa as her second language at school. The downside was that she ended up bypassing Mandarin, considered the most common Chinese language outside of Singapore. Although she feels competent with speaking Mandarin, she remains challenged with reading and writing to this day.

This language gap is Cathy's one primary regret from her education. She explains, "If you wanted to learn Mandarin, you needed to hire a tutor, and this costs a lot of money." She further believes her own children were likewise shortchanged in a way. Although their father—Cathy's husband—is Chinese, their children needed to take Mandarin as their second language in school. She laughs, adding that "Mandarin is a difficult language. I could have bought a new house with the money we spent on Mandarin tutors and classes, and even then, they didn't learn it well. I would have loved to learn Mandarin when I was young."

The Case of Singlish

Though Cathy may have missed out on Mandarin, she did pick up on another linguistic curiosity known as *Singlish*. This is short for *Singapore English*, a colloquial version of the English language which primarily emerged from blending English phrases with Bahasa or Chinese dialects.

According to Singapore's National Library Board, Singlish blends informal English words and phrases with elements of numerous other languages traditionally spoken in Singapore. This includes the island's three main Chinese dialects of Hokkien, Cantonese, and Teochew, along with the Indian languages of Tamil and Hindi. These are all stirred in with a sizable helping of the Malay, or Bahasa language to create a vernacular form of English with its own system of rules and grammar. Many Singaporeans have defended this unlikely language combination as a true indicator of their own cultural identity. Everyday Singaporeans can simply "codeswitch," or slip in and out of Singlish on the street, substituting grammatically correct English when necessary.

This is precisely what Cathy enjoys doing as well. She explains, "For me switching is normal, since I was taught proper English by my grandfather who spoke very well. Then it's more about having flexibility to quickly change from one form to the other. When you're bilingual, you can switch and speak in a manner that is required of you in any situation."

Though favoring more formal English in most cases, Cathy leans on various Singlish code words in everyday conversations, such as *lor, meh, lah,* and *leh.* In everyday conversation she ends many of her sentences with the *lah* tag, without thinking twice about it. The use of Singlish is alive and well, Cathy confirms, despite the government's past efforts to the contrary. She explains, "There is even a Singlish book, a Singlish dictionary. So just about everybody speaks that way. I'm not proud of it, but it's fun to listen to, as people use some Chinese words also, like *chiong*. I like to say that I'm a *chiong* person, who jumps right into something without thinking. That's a Singlish word. And I use 'yah lah' a lot. It means 'all right.' It's actually a Malay word. 'Yah' is Malay but is also used by the Chinese, like when they say 'Okay, lah,' or 'Everything is fine.' People also say, 'See you lah,' and 'Don't do like that.' So, Singlish is all about shortcuts and mixing different languages."

In a concerted effort to discredit the use of Singlish, the government launched one of its social campaigns around the early 2000s. State-owned television channels and programs were directed to remove Singlish from their broadcasts as part of a new *Speak Good English* movement. Strangely, the government has come full circle more recently. Leaders have since loosened up on their past strict stances toward the informal language. Singlish still provides an important cultural marker of identity for many Singaporeans and has become a reflection of the country's uniquely multicultural heritage.

Some Singlish phrases are so commonly accepted that they appear in national advertisements or promotions. As the country was slowly lifting its Covid restrictions in 2022, an admittedly cute cartoon video was circulated to educate citizens on the revised rules. In creative Singaporean fashion, the government had labeled its stringent lockdown the *Circuit Breaker*, borrowing the term directly from electronics. As the country's Circuit Breaker was progressively relaxed, the video implored of its viewers, "Don't chiong out!" Cathy explains that "to chiong" is to rush for something. The word is derived from Chinese and is embedded within various English phrases. She continues, "So, the phrase, 'Don't chiong out' means to not rush, or don't go crazy. When approaching a traffic light that's about to turn red, for example, someone in a hurry might drive faster to make it through. This would be to 'chiong.'"

The term also refers to jumping into something headfirst without thinking. Cathy continues, "When someone asks if I can do a certain job, I just 'chiong,' which means I take the challenge and do my best, even without training. It's like blindly doing things, jumping off a cliff. So, during the pandemic, 'Don't chiong out' meant to not go crazy as the country was starting to open up again."

In stark contrast, speaking proper English can indicate someone's Western education and upbringing. Cathy provides one example from her own family. "On my husband's side, they're more Chinese educated, and they tend to lean on Mandarin rather than English. But they do speak Singlish!" She laughs, then explains a common local metaphor. "That's why, when I speak, Tony's family claims humorously that I am 'eating potato.' This means that someone is speaking like a Westerner." This is not necessarily meant to be derogatory. She says, "It just means that you're trying to speak like an educated person from the West, as in 'Oh, you eat potato lah.' The full meaning is that you eat potatoes more than you eat noodles, as you're trying to follow the Western culture."

She continues, "Even the primary school kids will say you are 'eating potato,' because you sound like a Westerner, or a foreigner. Different ethnic groups had to convert directly from their language to learn English. So, because of our different dialects, they are trying to use English the best they can. Naturally they might be envious of those who can speak it well."

One's primary language can even influence TV-watching preferences. Certain channels are associated with specific ethnic groups and their respective languages or dialects. Cathy explains, "If you speak English well, people say you are an 'English channel' person. You watch Channel Five, which is fully spoken in English. And somebody who speaks Chinese is 'Channel 8.'"

Cathy views this unavoidable local diversity in a positive light. She concludes, "This is why I feel that the whole journey in life is based on the activities you learn outside the home. It's the street smarts. That's where you acquire skills, by meeting people, talking to people, and learning manners from people with all sorts of differing backgrounds. But if you're at home all the time, you don't interact with people enough to learn all of this."

Chapter 10

A Catholic in Singapore

Cathy's first days at convent school found her absolutely transfixed. Not only did modern school facilities and new classmates catch her attention, but so did the teachers themselves. Many of her teachers were the very same nuns who lived permanently on campus. She was particularly in awe of their standard white uniforms. Likely yearning in some way for reliable role models, Cathy quickly aspired to become a nun when she grew up. It was so wonderful and inspiring to see all her teachers dressed in their immaculate white habits and veils.

The nuns hailed from various exotic places around Europe and other far-reaching locations. Few were actually Singaporean. They consequently brought their own unique accents and cultures with them into the classrooms. Cathy further noted their disciplined, predictable lifestyle and collective mission to serve the Church. For one thing, they all lived together without returning home to cramped flats at night like she did. They communed together, ate together, and slept together, all of which Cathy viewed as a novelty.

Despite all that, it comes as little surprise that Cathy's fascination with life in the convent inevitably wore off. Their daily routine was, well, too routine. Their strictly disciplined lifestyle did not coincide with her own natural curiosity and outgoing personality. Nor did she have the toleration or the patience for such things. Let's face it, Cathy as a nun would not have been one of humanity's smartest ideas.

Being both Chinese and a practicing Catholic required enough courage already. The Chinese Catholics of Singapore represented a distinct minority in this part of Southeast Asia. According to state government data from 2015, of the roughly 81 percent of permanent Singaporeans who declared a religious affiliation, about 19 percent claimed to be Christians. Of those, only about one-third declared as Catholics.

Devout Catholics in Singapore were occasionally reminded of their minority status, whether they asked for it or not. Even friends and neighbors poorly understood their churchgoing practices and rituals. Cathy's celebration of Holy Communion came as one case in point. As tradition would have it, she wore the expected veil and dress, something she thought little about at the time. Because not many people in her neighborhood were familiar with Catholic ritual, however, she noticed more than an average number of onlookers doing double-takes. Some stared her down with mouths hanging open. A fully visible ghost in daylight would have garnered less attention. As Cathy's entourage walked to find a cab to church, she could hear confused neighbors exclaim, "Oh, my God, how old is she? Don't tell me she's already getting married!" Not one to be embarrassed even then, she found such comments rather amusing. Though quite unaware at the time, her actual wedding day was still a full decade into the future.

False Confessions

Cathy's formative years were essentially shaped and molded at St. Anthony's. Of course, this did not always occur in ways the school leadership intended. Cathy largely forged her own identity there, as the school's campus quickly doubled as an unofficial second home. Because the church and school facilities were combined into a single campus, Cathy spent many of her waking hours at one or the other.

The church itself commanded the central space of the complex, while separate girls' and boys' schools were located to either side. To clarify, the church itself was named St. Joseph's, while the school component was St. Anthony's. As tradition would have it, the girls were taught by the nuns, the boys by the priests. Everyone then came together for Mass and various functions within the central church. Over the years, Cathy and her classmates enjoyed sharing a continuous array of jokes, often at the expense of the teachers. One of countless rumors, for instance, told the story of a secret tunnel under the complex which allowed priests and nuns to mingle out of the public's eye.

Cathy and her sister attended Mass religiously every Sunday, and usually on their own. To recall, Mama had her own church to attend. They typically went with Uncle John—that is, Grandpa, who guided them through many of the Catholic rituals. Together with school on weekdays, Sunday Catechism, the follow-up Mass, and a growing list of extracurricular activities, Cathy spent the better parts of six days a week somewhere on campus.

Of course, with more maturity came Cathy's newfound tendency to question certain timeless traditions. Of all the rituals she was taught to practice, perhaps none confused her more than confession. It seemed she was spending half her waking hours telling some mysterious priest about her daily life. She further questioned the timing of it all. "Why, just at the midpoint of the service, would the priest shift to the confession booth and invite parishioners to queue up?" she wondered. In her more practical mind, confession should be conducted prior to the service, if for no other reason than to avoid unnecessary interruptions.

This line of thinking inevitably led to the question of why confession existed at all. From week to week, she carefully observed the adults expounding upon their lengthy stories of personal sins and crimes. "It was something like watching the modern TV show, *Crime Watch*," Cathy suggests.

When summoned to the confession booth each week, she was forced to get creative, as she usually had no clue what to confess. She could not, for the life of her, determine how she had sinned or behaved poorly the previous week. *What did I do wrong?* she asked herself, eventually declaring, *I really haven't done anything embarrassing!* The only way out of this dilemma was to make up her own stories. Her inventive mind conjured up tales that took on lives of their own. No doubt the priest enjoyed an entertaining earful during the process. She came to the conclusion that, "If so many people are spending all this time confessing their sins, they could better use that time to do positive things for other people. Wouldn't this diminish the need to confess in the first place?" This was—and continues to be—a difficult point to dispute.

Beyond the confession booth, many of Cathy's school lessons were closely tied to the teachings of the Church. Some even required the better part of a school day. "At a convent school," Cathy explains bluntly, "It's God this, God that, everything is about God. You can't escape it. You're taught to pray, and that God is your Savior. So, who do you turn to when you're lonely? God. Who's your best friend? God. Good God Almighty!" By secondary school, this time commitment provided a silver lining. Cathy and her female classmates took the opportunity to size up the good-looking boys who, in turn, might occasionally return their dreamy stares.

Prior to her discovery of boys, Cathy found other creative

ways to entertain herself during church services at St. Joseph's. In one fun, if solitary game, she imagined a lively conversation between the statues of the patron saints. Other statues, she noticed, featured various likenesses of Jesus Christ himself—whether on or off the cross. Cathy's active imagination constructed a mental map of them all, each of which she christened with its own new name. Apparently, her early penchant for naming tadpoles in the kampong was upscaled to the life-size statues of St. Joseph's.

From there it was no great leap to imagine a collective sense of confusion brewing among the renamed statues. They must not have understood why many of their life-sized counterparts looked remarkably like themselves. They consequently engaged in spirited conversation to address this mystery. Recalling her internal dialogue, Cathy pretends, "Hey, your name is Jesus? Well, mine is too! That's amazing. And I think that guy over there is Jesus also! And who's the sad fellow hanging on the cross? That's Jesus too? Wow! Poor guy. Who did that to him?"

She also spent time memorizing the church's interior design and layout. As viewed from above, the church was built in the standard form of a Latin cross, with the altar found at the center of the nave. This was near the intersection of the two transepts, or side wings. One transept displayed an entire row of additional statues. These, Cathy noted, represented important saints, Mother Mary herself, and various companions. Naturally the honorary statue of St. Joseph served as a centerpiece. As for St. Anthony, he had been dubbed the patron saint of all lost items. His own prominent location reduced chances even further that he might go missing himself.

For her own daily ritual, Cathy arrived at school each morning and immediately darted into the church. She was determined to not overlook a single statue, mentally checking each off her list. She greeted them all with a standard "Good morning," and a few related pleasantries, after which she headed next door to school. Then at the sound of the last bell, she repeated the practice and said goodbye to all of them quickly before rushing home.

The statues were undoubtedly pleased, given her diligent effort to recognize each of them in turn. This practice was further assisted with a convenient kneeling stool located at the feet of all the saints. To this day she is grateful for this protection—not spiritual protection, but more so from the hard floor. For all the time she spent there, her knees would have taken a beating.

Though her prayers to the statues were sincere, they were interlaced with the winding narratives of a creative child. Each morning, she moved from one to the other like a receiving line: "Thank you for this wonderful day," she would bid to one. Then the next day, "Good morning, Mother Mary, I'm going to school now, so please let me have a blessed day, and hopefully my teachers won't be such a pain. Please protect me from them."

This conversation ritual was no passing fad. In fact, it persisted for numerous years—some might say religiously. It had become part of her daily, expected routine, providing a comforting stability not always found at home. And quite unlike certain family members, the statues remained reliably in the same place from one day to the next.

In addition to her own daily prayers, Cathy eventually realized that adult parishioners behaved in the same way during Sunday Mass. But strangely, they were repeating precisely the same prayers from one week to the next, often directed to Mother Mary. Cathy further learned from the nuns that every "Hail Mary" uttered would automatically send a rose up to Heaven for Mary herself. Cathy was not so easily swayed, however, asking the obvious follow-up questions: Where exactly were all of Mary's roses piling up? Were they removed each week to make room for more? For all the countless times she muttered "Hail Mary" on her own, she presumed that Mary had already grown an entire rose garden. And, anyhow, just how many roses did Mary really need?

Aside from her unending questions, certain fundamental teachings of the Church managed to hold her attention. Around age seven or eight, Cathy grew fond of books, along with the designer bookmarks that often came with them. This interest was kindled in part by Grandpa who had helped her learn to read. Her newfound enthusiasm led to regular bookstore visits nearby. The Shanghai Bookstore was particularly attractive. It sold colorful stationary, writing implements, and related products of interest for highly creative people.

In one case, she started a collection of bookmarks. Upon shuffling into the store one day, she noticed a beautiful bookmark peeking out enticingly from a notebook. Not having the money for its purchase, however, impulses took over. She grabbed and stashed it, looking around nervously. This was decades prior to video surveillance, so apparently nobody noticed. Having escaped the store, her heart raced as she ran to school.

The thrill and adrenalin were soon replaced with a sense of overbearing guilt. Thinking through her behavior more carefully, she was now certain her life would end as she made the final trip to Hell. By the end of the school day, her guilt was unbearable. She hightailed it back to the bookstore and reinserted the hijacked bookmark precisely where she had found it. Satisfied with her correction, the burden of guilt was immediately lifted.

A more practical matter occupied Cathy's mind around this

time. She was particularly concerned about what might happen if she was forced to leave St. Anthony's for a public neighborhood school. Her main issue, like usual, revolved around costs. If she changed schools for some reason, she would further need to purchase a new school uniform. At St. Anthony's, however, she could reuse her existing uniform for as long as possible. There was no way, she convinced herself, that her family could afford new uniforms on a regular basis.

Regardless of what school she attended, not even Cathy could control her own growth spurts. Because the school did not provide previously worn uniforms to lower-income students, she devised her own creative ways to obtain them. On days when it rained hard, for instance, all drenched students were expected to change out of their wet uniforms to finish the school day. To their credit, the nuns distributed dry uniforms already stored for such purposes, expecting them to be returned the next day. Once again, Cathy worked the system. She kept the borrowed, larger-sized uniform for herself and returned her smaller, tattered outfit instead. She admittedly pulled this trick more than once, depending upon the size and condition of the larger uniform. Even if her success rate was only once every couple of years, that's all she needed. Not only were downpours frequent within Singapore's tropical climate, but nobody really paid attention to precisely which uniforms were being returned.

When not praying for protection from teachers or for new uniforms, Cathy occasionally prayed to her statue friends that certain students would stay home from school. This was more of a practical matter, it turns out, rather than some bizarre childhood vendetta. When one of the school's first nutrition programs kicked in, vanilla milk was provided to the poorer children who had little else to bring. The catch was that Cathy needed a paid subscription to receive the milk. Not having the funds from home, she—once again—learned how to work the system. In the case of absences, extra milk was given to needier children like her. Therefore, the more absences, the more milk would be available.

Beyond the milk, she and her sister sometimes went to school with little or no lunch money. Funds were stretched even further to buy into the infamous Post Office stamp program. To feed themselves they relied instead on a sort-of playground barter system and, better yet, on the occasional kind friend willing to share at recess. In one way or another, the girls found ways to feed themselves.

Acquiring textbooks provided yet another headache. Fortunately, in this case the school offered a donation program for lower-income children. It mattered little if the books were already marked up from prior use. Textbooks tended to remain valid for years, as they were rarely updated or changed out. For her part, Cathy was perfectly happy with the free, used versions. Truth be told, she barely ever opened them, anyway. Eventually Cathy accumulated entire shelves of donated books. Later in life, she launched her own localized campaign to collect books for disadvantaged children. She personally asked friends and family to hand over unused texts so that she could contribute to a local school's donation program.

Whether guided by a compassionate Mother Mary or by her own creative wits, Cathy managed to do what was necessary to survive at convent school. Developing such practical problem-solving skills became a trademark of her early life and would undoubtedly be vital as she grew into adulthood.

The Chiong Factor

Cathy further learned to take advantage of opportunistic school activities, even if some were loathed by her peers. One case involved class trips to the dentist. During Cathy's tenure, Singapore had not yet staffed its schools with on-site dental care as they do today. Instead, a specialized dental facility was dedicated to school children, and all students were required to visit twice each year.

Singapore's school system is now more adequately funded and staffed with professionals. Every contemporary school includes a subsidized office for dental services, and each primary and secondary school employs an in-house dentist. Today this is just one part of the country's subsidized health care, dental, and lunch programs provided to everyone.

For Cathy's classmates, however, no bigger fear existed than their periodic trips to the dentist. On the appointed day, an aging, beat-up bus was assigned to collect everyone at school. At first, an uncertain Cathy observed the bus-boarding ritual from afar. Various bouts of kicking and dragging were commonplace. Normally confident or arrogant students were suddenly reduced to submissive, crying children. It was not uncommon for teachers to physically drag the more hesitant youngsters onto the bus.

In marked contrast, Cathy's first reaction was one of disappointment, though for a very different reason. A consent form signed by the parents was required to board the bus. Cathy's father had, of course, failed to provide one. She was therefore denied the opportunity to join their busload of fun. In her eyes, the dentist provided yet a new adventure, and she was unfairly being singled out. Eventually she did provide the required consent form for future trips, but only after she learned to forge the signature herself.

Upon finally joining her peers to the *Little Shop of Horrors*, Cathy was all smiles. She was perhaps alone in enjoying every minute of the rickety bus ride, and she adored her outings to the dentist overall. Better yet, a fun prize awaited each child as a reward for being so brave. For Cathy, this often meant a small doll. From her perspective, then, there was no downside here. She enjoyed a field trip from school, a clean mouth, and a present to boot! In one way or another, the consent forms kept coming.

Some children, it turns out, did have good reason for their hesitation. As Cathy recalls, the dentists often discovered all sorts of tooth decay, cavities, and related issues. As she describes, "They would just start digging, and they could dig your whole mouth out, because the assistants were not well-trained professionals back then. And who knows what kinds of horror might occur? Perhaps the drill would slip and dig out your tongue instead, or worse yet, drill through your nose or eyeball!" Even Cathy admits that such necessary corrections could be rather painful. Still, she was typically known for being among the bravest children, and she remembers relishing the experience.

Looking back on her natural sense of adventure, Cathy describes herself as a "*chiong* person"—referring to the Singlish term described earlier. A *chiong* person is someone thrown into the deep end of the pool—voluntarily or otherwise—and is expected to bravely perform on the spot. For her part, Cathy often leapt into her next adventures with little advance thinking, for better or worse. But she always managed to survive. This *chiong* factor was ever-present with Cathy from a young age, always curious to know what was around the next corner or—when at school—where her peers were going. Her daring trips to the dentist may have foreshadowed a more courageous future when even greater chances would be taken.

Close Encounter

Not even the *chiong* factor could adequately prepare Cathy for the shock of her young life. On an otherwise ordinary weekday morning, the sisters and their peers were dutifully playing outside St. Anthony's before school began. Meanwhile, a car crept up the driveway and parked nearby. A lone woman emerged and walked closer to where the girls were playing. Still keeping some distance so as not to alarm anyone in charge, the stranger called out for the sisters and motioned for them to approach her. As they did so, Cathy's curiosity peaked as her eyes took in the woman's startling appearance. Her thick, platform shoes and professional outfit with bellbottom pants screamed *money*. Despite all this, Cathy's attention was fixated most on the woman's towering, black hairdo, which was piled up in a beehive the likes of which Cathy had never seen. "This was retro fashion for those days," she recalls of the encounter, adding, "Her outfit was really loud. There was so much acrylic hairspray on her head that it could have easily blown up in flames if she got too close to a match."

Their sudden visitor was clearly joyful and pleased to see the girls. As they stared blankly, the woman asked if they remembered her. Cathy did not, and her sister seemed unsure. Adding to the story, Cathy recalls, "We were minding our own business, and she met us on the school compound. Right away, she said, 'I'm your mother.' I thought, *Really!* We had seen pictures and heard stories, and we were thrilled. We had a brief conversation, and she asked if we would like to meet our new brothers. Then she left." As any excited children might do, they ran home after school and told Mama about their encounter. Little did they know this news would open a whole new can of worms—or more accurately, an older can of difficult memories drudged up from the past.

Chapter 11

The House of Durians and Incense

Just like that, the sisters gained an instant new mother, now suddenly re-entering their lives. Cathy recalls a sense of delight and happiness with the news. After all, she now had another mommy, as Cathy referred to her. Whether she was blood related made little difference at the time.

Looking back, Cathy recounts more of the story. "The thing is, my mother actually looked for us while we were growing up. She used to come to school to peak at her daughters; she claimed she missed us. My sister was apprehensive and didn't know how to react. For me, I don't care. If you give me stuff and attention, I will call you God." She chuckles at how easy it was for adults to earn her trust and gratitude.

Regardless of the girls' differing perspectives on the matter, Mary persisted and returned to school for occasional visits. She was now determined to reunite with her growing daughters. Cathy remained curious, however, as to why her mother relied upon these awkward school visits, when she could simply find them at home. Only much later would Cathy learn that Mary's mother-in-law (Mama), harbored feelings of resentment. Mama was not beyond holding a serious grudge. She had been understandably angry with Mary for abandoning the family and leaving the children to her own care. This did not sit well with someone who had raised and sheltered four of her own children, all the while pushing through a brutal Japanese occupation. And now she was abruptly obligated to oversee two more children.

It is further likely that Mama never fully acknowledged her favorite son's destructive habits. Long after Mary left, Mama's poor impression of her daughter-in-law continued to fester. These feelings occasionally led to badmouthing Mary in front of the girls. With few alternative voices to hear, Mama most certainly influenced their impressions. They held little comprehension of why Mary felt so compelled to leave them in the first place.

Few Options for Young People

Only many years later would Cathy piece together her mother's own story more completely. Mary's life paralleled that of countless working-class Singaporeans during and after World War II. "Only a small percentage of people had completed secondary school around that time," Cathy begins. "My mother's highest education level was primary six. Even though she spoke Cantonese like her family, she still didn't speak it very well. So, a lot of young people in her generation had minimal schooling and often got married early, as teenagers. My own mother was only 17 when they got married, and my father was six years older. And whomever a woman married tended to be abusive more often than not. Because, if you didn't beat up your wife, you were considered less of a man. That was the thinking back then. And those few men who treated their spouses well were laughed at because, well, it was apparent then who was in control of the house and the marriage! It was not cool to be nice to your spouse."

She continues, "That was the mentality; they got married blindly, desperate to get out of the house and out of poverty. That's basically what my mother did. She had no idea that getting married was just a new version of Hell."

Aside from getting married and having children, women like Mary found few alternatives. Employment was generally not one of them. Few people went to college, and the ones who did were typically from privileged families who could send their children to school. And higher education was primarily reserved for men, whereas the women were expected to remain home with the children. If they were being abused, they often hid it from public view; there was nowhere else to go.

Cathy continued to explain the limitations women endured following the war. "I'm sure that if you asked every family in the days of my mother's time, or Mama's time, they would tell you they could not go into the workforce because they didn't have enough education. The only thing to do was get married, and people had many children. And with that, they could not afford to send children to school, especially the girls. If they had any money at all, they sent the boys to school, but the girls would be the last priority. So, they relied on the hope of having their daughters get married, as that would be fewer mouths to feed. This is what my mother did. After finishing primary school, she met my father and married him at the age of 17. By 18 she was already a mother. She had twins, though one died. Now with a child to care for, her life became a living Hell, another story to tell."

Cathy is not exaggerating these challenging social conditions. Upon Singapore's independence, Prime Minister Lee Kuan Yew was well attuned to the lack of educational and employment opportunities for the population at large, and for young women specifically. The government was especially eager to improve the educational attainment of all Singaporeans. The leadership's primary goal was to build a skilled labor force to work in manufacturing plants being courted by the government.

World War II and the Occupation only contributed to the poor education of many Singaporeans. During the war, a large percentage of students simply dropped out of school. Of course, this only created a surplus of uneducated young people with little else to do. A high rate of unemployment only worsened the situation. It was within these less-than-ideal conditions that both of Cathy's parents found themselves.

Cathy adds, "Lee Kuan Yew specifically wanted women to learn new things, to learn skills, to move them into factories, since the country was desperate for workers. That's when women started to find alternatives to their sealed fate based on who they married. If a woman could land a job, she could at least stand on her own if the marriage became a nightmare."

Mary's New Life

After leaving the family, Mary started a new life with another, more compassionate fellow. Mary had met her beau while working as a waitress at a pub, well prior to leaving Errol. As a regular customer, this gentleman was 30 years older than Mary and turned out to be an excellent tipper. They became closer friends, and the tip amounts increased proportionally. By that time, Mary had already lost all respect and affection for Errol. The truth was that she and her husband were already growing apart.

Beyond her budding romance, the tips Mary accumulated provided a substantial secondary income. She was already wise to Errol's insatiable quest for alcohol and the money that paid for it. In response, she learned to be deceptive. What better place to hide her extra income than inside their toilet's flush tank? Had she not hidden the cash, Mary knew the money would disappear to the nearest bar. And she now had not one, but two girls to feed, clothe, and shelter.

Cathy continues the story in her colorful manner. "My mother budgeted her household expenses based on her own personal 'bank' in the bathroom. My father knew something was up, but never figured it out. He only expressed his amazement at how often she had to go to the bathroom and how much time she spent in there."

After enduring Errol's wrath for several years, Mary's situation at home continued to deteriorate. Eventually she felt endangered and became more concerned for the well-being of her children. Finally reaching a tipping point, she made the painful decision to leave her daughters. At the same time, she continued to nurture a budding relationship with her gentleman admirer at the pub.

When the sisters asked their mother years later why she decided to leave, she told them it was the best of two lousy options. Had she stayed, the abusive pattern would persist and likely escalate. She convinced herself that Mama could adequately oversee the girls' needs. Had she taken the girls with her, she was afraid of what Errol might do to all of them. Still only in her early 20s, Mary consequently made the painstaking decision to simply disappear.

As Cathy summarizes, "Alcohol gives people a sense of authority, gives them a high, and they do things without thinking. It numbs the sense of responsibility. My mother decided that enough is enough, and she walked out. She just left us. I asked why she didn't bring us along, and she said she was too afraid. He used to hammer her, beat her to a pulp. So, she told me that she was planning to come back and claim us later. For some time, she was satisfied to sneak visits with us at school."

Not long after leaving Cathy's family, Mary and her gentleman friend, Mike, were wed. They would later have three children of their own. While this scenario paints a rosy picture for Mary, she was burdened by various personal challenges that she could or would not shake. For one, she lacked the self-discipline for effective household budgeting. And the thrill of gambling was too much to resist, so she fell into a similar trap as her mother-in-law. The difference was that Mike served as her safety net, providing a car and some personal independence. She further found herself immersed within a more educated social class. Mike had already spent years building his own career, moving upwards in the employment chain. This allowed him to integrate into one of Singapore's two primary social organizations, namely the Singapore Recreation Club. This particular club was founded by members of the country's Eurasian population because they were not allowed to join the more exclusive Singapore Cricket Club.

The facilities for both clubs strategically faced onto Singapore's primary public space, the *Padang*, a Malay word which translates to "field." It sits in a prominent downtown location overlooking Marina Bay and is commonly deployed for high-profile recreational activities and national events.

Given Mary's new husband and accompanying club membership, her lifestyle and daily routine began to turn around. Mary often became bored at home during the day, so she drove to the club earlier before fetching her husband. To her delight, she discovered a whole room devoted to slot machines, where her gambling habit continued apace.

Once back on stable footing, Mary had decided to visit her daughters at school. She was already raising her second family as well, though she eventually convinced Mama to take the sisters on occasional outings. At some point a joyful Cathy learned the exciting news that she had three new half-brothers to play with. Over the next few years Cathy visited her mother's home numerous times, though not on a regular basis. To say the least, each visit was an experience not easily forgotten.

For his part, Mike worked as a customs officer, which meant he could easily provide for his new family. He owned three houses as well, so the family was quite comfortable. Even Mama showed some subdued respect for how well Mary had wed the second time.

Better yet, it turns out that Cathy's mother could cook really well. This was immensely refreshing compared to her own home. Mary's pattern, if there was one, was to bring the girls home to let the children play before cooking an evening meal. For all these reasons, Cathy decided to release any lingering animosity toward her mother, and to see the brighter side of things. "Who would not want an extra mother who showers you with gifts and attention? She cooked big meals for all of us. There was really no downside here," she states definitively.

So Much Food!

Compared to the kampong where Meiling lived, Mary's home resembled a holiday resort. Cathy's early visits were filled with wonder, especially at the continuous availability of food. Mike turned out to be a kind and generous person, both during and beyond mealtime. Upon returning from the market, Mike presented a healthy variety of food goods and ingredients for their sumptuous meals.

Cathy quickly came to enjoy her mother's home as a happy refuge, even if she did not consciously realize it at the time. And her sense of intuition was sharp for a child. She could keenly judge the personal character of people based on their relative generosity with—and attitude toward—food. On this measure

Cathy's mother and stepfather excelled grandly, as there was always plenty to go around.

One common food item easily eclipsed the rest—namely, an exotic, quirky fruit known as *durian*. Mike brought these home by the basket load, and quite literally. Each basket included 30 durians. Highly popular throughout Southeast Asia, the surprisingly nutritious durian remains, today as in the past, the region's "king of fruits." Its fundamental shortcoming, however, is no small matter. Durian naturally emits a noxious, almost unbearable odor. And its appearance is as strange as its smell, at least to people from outside the region.

If one can crack into a durian's tough, spiky outer shell, a custard-like inner flesh is revealed. Numerous Southeast Asian dishes call for the fruit as an ingredient, and it has further proven its value for medicinal properties. The taste of the inner flesh can be described as simultaneously eating cheese, garlic, almonds, and caramel, though Cathy describes it more simply as a creamy vanilla custard. That is, if one can endure the unbearable odor.

Basically, "the ball of the fruit smells like Hell but tastes like Heaven," Cathy describes bluntly, and "when you eat it your breath smells terrible." The peculiar fruit is notorious enough that certain Asian hotels and stores simply ban it from their premises. They even post signs alerting customers of their anti-durian policies.

Regardless of the fruit's downside, Cathy and her siblings regularly sat in their mother's kitchen to peel and eat them on the spot. This activity became one of Cathy's fondest memories within the family.

A Suspicious Pastime

This idyllic family scene could have easily appeared on a

promotional poster for one of Singapore's social campaigns. That is, were it not for Mike's bizarre religious practice, or whatever one might wish to call it. Stepping away from the enjoyable family dinner, things could get a bit strange within a separate room down the hall.

As a self-proclaimed spiritualist of some kind, their stepfather practiced a set of rituals aligned with his own unique belief system. Even the girls realized these were no standard Catholic practices. Mike devoted one room for his own peculiar form of worship. The space as Cathy remembers it displayed a "dark, spooky interior that included statue upon statue representing all kinds of gods, all of which were focused on a central altar." In many families, such prayer rooms would normally be off limits to visitors, or they would at least be simply ignored when guests were around. In this case, however, Mike occasionally invited—or outright directed—the girls to join him.

Mike's rituals even created their own carbon footprint, of a sort. Aside from the decorative idols, he also used charcoal and burned incense, apparently due to some keen fascination with combustion. "He burned everything," Cathy mused as she relived those days, continuing with her own experiences. "He would make us kneel in front of the altar, and he would pray over us. It seemed like Satan worship; we were in, like, primary two or three, still very young. Because we were very clean Catholics, to suddenly see all these statues and gods was very unsettling." He also burned a *kris*, a form of traditional Malay sword that somewhat resembles a dagger.

It comes as little surprise that the young girls were scared out of their wits. And of course, they reported all of this to Mama, who was, predictably, less than impressed. Mama was already fighting the urge to outwardly condemn her daughter-in-law. This latest revelation did little to help the situation.

To his credit, Mike never tried to convert the sisters to his own belief system. This unfortunately did not dispel their concerns. Cathy recalls how his ritualism caused the sisters to grow apart from their mother once again. "I thank God that I was not taken by my mother when she left my father, because I would not want to live with a stepfather who's so strange," she laughs, now able to safely look back. "But you see, that fear we had was part of his way of worship, which we didn't understand because we were young, and it wasn't the Catholic way. It was even stranger that my mother allowed it to happen in her own home. She should not have allowed him to pray over us. We had our own God; we didn't need his," she says flippantly. "So, then we wanted to visit her less often, not wanting to go to her house anymore."

Given repeated visits to the "spooky room," an uncomfortable Cathy drifted off once again, losing touch with her mother for a second time. It turns out this natural parting of ways was also convenient, as Cathy's unease with her stepfather coincided with an increasingly active lifestyle. With more commitments elsewhere, Cathy gradually faded away from her mother's life once again.

Chapter 12

Across the Strait

Still a child, Cathy endured yet another lengthy and nauseating bus ride with her father. This time the destination was across the Johor Strait into Malaysia, though her motion sickness made these adventurous outings a bit less enjoyable. After collecting herself on the other side of the Johor-Singapore Causeway, she was suitably rewarded with a visit to a family of exceptional kindness. She was still too young to comprehend any possible family connections. All Cathy knew was that she had yet another "mommy" whom she enjoyed visiting in Malaysia.

Little did she know that her "Romeo" father—as she refers to him sarcastically—had also dated and married a Malaysian woman. Named Jessie, she had grown up and lived with her sisters and parents just across the Causeway in Johor Bahru. The curious aspect of this romance was that Jessie had already married Errol in 1971. Cathy was only four years old.

Even stranger, this was technically Errol's first official marriage of the three. It turns out that neither of his first two "marriages" to Mary, and later Meiling, had been officially registered in the same way. Cathy explains, "Marriage in the villages was more of an informal affair during those years. If a couple lived together, they were considered married." Though certainly not the world's only man to marry three times, there remained one unsettling irregularity. Cathy was still happily visiting her first stepmother in the kampong—and with her father, no less—as late as the age of eight. Clearly, Errol had not yet abandoned his second family on the farm. During those years, Meiling apparently had no knowledge he was already secretly married to Jessie across the Strait. This was an odd twist of fate. While Cathy perceived Jessie as her latest and third "mommy"—or second step-mother—it was Jessie who had first legally married her father.

Cathy's two stepmothers therefore overlapped in her life for numerous years. She now realizes that her father consistently fabricated false stories for each of his wives, knowing that they would likely never meet. One wife had already left him, another was from Malaysia, and the third lived in a rural farming village. Regardless, distance alone was not enough to retain his secrets forever. It was perhaps inevitable that the three women would eventually learn of the others' existence. Jessie was reportedly shocked and horrified to discover that—years after moving in with him—Errol already had three daughters from two different relationships! By then, however, Errol's reputation for violent rages was well known among both of Cathy's stepmothers. Accordingly, they made the mutual decision to avoid confronting him directly about his alternative lives.

Of course, Cathy remained oblivious at the time. She was happy enough to travel and see her other mommies and siblings during school holidays. While her sister was usually content to remain at home, Cathy was the natural traveler and—aside from some inconvenient motion sickness—was usually thrilled to accompany her father to visit either of his illicit families.

Living in a suburban town, Jessie worked as a nurse in a private clinic. She had even attracted a doctor as a serious suiter at one point. That is, until she became the latest in a line of women to be swept off her feet by one Errol Ross. "Her life would have been heavenly had she married the doctor instead," laments Cathy. "Poor dear. Welcome to Hell."

Following their wedding in Malaysia, Jessie moved to Singapore to live with her new husband. In return, Cathy and her father visited Jessie's family across the Strait on holidays. Cathy remained perplexed as to why she had three mother figures in her life, but she simply went along with it. Unpacking who was related to whom was the least of her concerns during primary school. One might say her situation resembled the Hollywood musical comedy, *Mamma Mia*, albeit with three mothers instead of the film's three hopeful father figures. And a lot less singing.

As for her journeys to Malaysia, Cathy gradually outgrew her childhood curse of motion sickness. Better still, the newer, modern buses meant cleaner air inside. Even air conditioning now came as a standard feature. "Imagine if I was a tour guide now and I had motion sickness," she muses. "That would be terrible for all the guests on the bus!"

Sometimes Cathy and her father spent a weekend with Jessie and her family. This was usually reward enough for the young traveler, though over time an even more meaningful benefit emerged. She was beginning to forge a cherished and long-lasting relationship with Jessie, which has continued to the present day. To her credit, Jessie treated Cathy as her own daughter, and she even served Cathy the same amount of food as her siblings. Given Cathy's unfortunate track record with stingier relatives, this was no small deal!

With her first trip across the Strait, Cathy instantly gained yet another extended family. It turned out that Jessie had three sisters and three brothers of her own, which translated to six new aunties and uncles for the sisters. When not visiting her "rich auntie" or first stepmother during holidays, Cathy could invariably be found with Jessie's own family in Johor Bahru.

Cathy further learned that Jessie and all her sisters loved to sew. This had led to their collective decision later to attend tailoring school. The young women had also experimented for years with sewing outfits for their extensive doll collections. In their spare time, the sisters had creatively made use of remnant material from other sewing projects. In this way, their dolls benefitted handily with their own personal wardrobes. By the time Cathy first laid eyes on their collection, Jessie and her sisters had accumulated bags full of doll outfits crafted over the years.

At the time of Cathy's debut appearance, of course, Jessie and her sisters had all grown into younger adults. They now juggled any number of jobs and family responsibilities of their own. Despite their coming and going, they all doted on Cathy like a newfound niece. In return Cathy thrived amidst their company and personal attention.

One further surprise awaited Cathy on a later visit, quite beyond the imagination of a girl from a disadvantaged home. Her new aunties must have conspired in advance. They ultimately decided to hand over their entire collection of precious dolls to Cathy. This amazing gift came with bags full of homemade wardrobes to keep them appropriately dressed for the "runway fashion show" as Cathy jokes. At once overwhelmed and ecstatic, Cathy was simply in euphoria as she remembers it, prancing around the room.

This generous gift was simply shocking for a seven-year-old to comprehend. Each doll might have included 20 or 30 outfits—more than Cathy would likely wear throughout her entire childhood. Not just a doll collection, this was a family heirloom being passed down from one generation to the next. Jessie and her sisters had taken the dolls and their varied wardrobes through their own childhoods. And now young Cathy had taken charge of the collection's well-being—most of all to play with, no doubt, or what-have-you.

Predictably, Cathy unleashed her incredible gifts for all to view only minutes after returning home. She was admittedly working with a tough audience; everyone was tired, and her father was at "peak intoxication" as Cathy recalled. Nonetheless, dolls and outfits were instantly sprawled across the main living room for all to see.

Somehow Cathy and the dolls managed to agitate Errol, and he turned his already aggressive attention back to them. With everyone keeping their distance, Errol swept down to the floor, scooped up the entire collection of dolls and outfits, and promptly threw the lot of them into the trash.

This was bad enough, though another problem only made matters worse for Cathy and dolls alike. Retrieving the collection later was not as simple as returning to the trash bin after Errol fell asleep. Every flat in their building relied on a common rubbish chute leading directly to a dumpster on the ground floor. Constantly collecting waste from the entire estate, the dumpster was methodically emptied every day. This all meant that there was no viable way for Cathy to retrieve her dolls, even had the adults in her life made a valiant effort to do so. Or so she thought. They were gone as quickly as they had appeared.

It goes without saying that Cathy's devastation was instant and prolonged. She remained upset and resentful over the incident for some time. She nearly drowned in her own tears, as she likes to recall, and no doubt the entire estate flooded as well. Although Jessie was present to witness the incident, she was more concerned with enflaming Errol's violent outburst than with risking her life over a doll collection.

Even worse, Cathy eventually learned that the dumpster in

question was not actually locked. Any good-faith effort by her family might have allowed them to retrieve much of the collection. As a child, however, she had no idea this was even an option, and nobody bothered to investigate.

Both Jessie and Cathy kept the whole episode a secret from Jessie's sisters for many years. Still, at some point in Cathy's early adult life, the news spilled out. As one might expect, the sisters' collective anger at Errol was profound. The episode only magnified their contempt for him. They further confided that none of them had ever married, specifically due to Errol's abusive behaviors toward their sister.

In the absence of her very temporary doll collection, Cathy and her sister fell back once again on making their own paper dolls. This was a common practice in lower-income households throughout those decades. There is a favored type of cardboard for such things, and it already comes with 2-D outlines of dolls on them, accompanied by numerous cardboard outfits. The "clothes" can be outlined and then attached with a tab to the doll itself. This was their go-to substitute for real dolls. Of course, Cathy's creativity led her to devise entire bedroom sets for her little, flat friends. Beds were crafted out of shoe boxes, for instance, while blankets emerged from discarded fabric material.

With her own childhood incident still in mind, Cathy more recently decided to treat her grandniece with a similar gift. This was not the first or last time to do so; she admittedly adores the child's cute, happy face upon receiving something new. Cathy's own enjoyment with buying gifts was arguably to make amends for her own father's behavior. In this one instance she had found a doll set with approximately 20 outfits included. Even for Cathy, this was an exorbitant present for a younger family member. Of course, Cathy was instantly rewarded with the child's unfettered gratitude and sense of elation. Neither aunt nor grandniece could have been any happier while sharing the moment.

Of course, the best of intentions has a way of being thwarted. Some weeks later the girl's mother mentioned facetiously that Cathy should have also purchased a closet for the doll's outfits. Mom was finding body parts, dresses, and skirts in the microwave, their storeroom, and even dangling from foods in the refrigerator. Cathy rolled her eyes and had a good laugh. *At least the girl was interacting with her gift*, she thought. Regardless of this particular outcome, she prefers offering more creative types of toys and games rather than simple plastic products that rely on short-lived batteries.

All disappointments aside, the lessons of frugality that Cathy endured as a child have translated to sound wisdom as an adult. Whether it be a mean rich auntie on a Christmas shopping trip, or an intoxicated father sweeping away precious toys, the lesson of cherishing what one does have has stayed with her to the present day. This was clearly evident as she reflected on the lessons taught by a former auntie. She begins introspectively, "I can remember my *Kuma*—my father's eldest sister. In Chinese families, the oldest female auntie is known as the *Kuma*. So, one thing she taught me was, if you don't need it, don't buy it. What you don't have, you don't need, and what you don't need, you don't buy. I got much closer to her as she was growing old. So, I would go visit and bring the kids to see her. Then one day I brought her to the supermarket. Now that I'm grown with my own life, it's my time to be filial and buy things for her, you know. She was a wonderful cook, and she had such a hard life. She was also very filial to my Mama and took care of us. She bathed and cooked for us, and she even put us in a cardboard box and pulled us around."

After setting up her story, Cathy explains the lesson she eventually learned. "We were walking through the supermarket, and I asked what she wanted. It was funny—she was still saying, 'Don't spend the money on things you don't need.' This is what I was trying to teach my daughter," Cathy chuckles with a pause. "Because now she can shop online. I don't know how many pairs of sneakers she's bought already. I told her, 'You only have one pair of legs, you know.' I didn't realize this was an important value until I got married. In our day, even food and clothing were hard to come by, let alone toys. Whatever we did acquire, we made the most of it. And sometimes in life, it may be the simplest thing that we get a lot of pleasure from. You might remember that we used to make our own toys and dolls. You don't need a full set of anything. But if everybody thought like me, I think our economy would crash and all the toy shops in the world would close down," she laughs, though clearly frustrated with today's consumer expectations.

She continues, "For instance, our kids, they had a lot of aunties and uncles, so for birthdays they naturally got a lot of presents. But coming from me? No. I would host a party and tell the kids that some of those things I didn't think they needed. I'm not saying they shouldn't have gifts, but they need to cherish what they get. That's how you learn to value what you do have without always wanting more."

As if Cathy's early struggles were not enough, birthday celebrations of any kind were few and far between. "We didn't have birthday parties when I was a child. Mama would cook noodles for us with egg, and this kind of noodle is sweet. In Chinese tradition, you're supposed to slurp it all up without chewing it so that you have a long life. So, if the noodle is a few meters long, I would live forever," she laughs, adding, "But Mama would simply say, 'Shut up and eat it.' That was her version of recognizing a birthday. There were no cakes, no anything at all."

Asked whether any other relatives ever recognized her special day each year, she contemplates, "Maybe not a party, but my mystery grandfather would have celebrated for us. He was full of tricks; he was the one who was part of my life. Or he would get me a present. One year he bought me a beautiful Seiko watch. And I lost it! I was so upset."

With that troubled memory, she explains why she views birthdays with such high regard. "That is why, when I got older and visited my cousins or siblings for their own birthdays, I would make an effort to buy a cake and pay for the whole party. And my mother didn't believe in buying cakes. She had the money but didn't bother. So, I was like, okay, I'll pay for the cake, the barbecue, I'll pay for everything. Because I didn't have birthday parties when I was young. I could not even blow out a candle, let alone have a party. So, my children are very fortunate."

She now reflects on her own priorities of motherhood, adding, "This is why I feel that birthdays should be celebrated, and these things rub off on my children, like Rachel. When it's my birthday now, she'll go through great lengths to celebrate. Girls are good like that. She takes charge and tells the boys what to do," she laughs, thinking principally of her own household. "That's why I'm lucky I have a daughter. If I had all three boys, they would be useless." Cathy belts out another laugh. "It's always the girls who are up to something, they have more feelings and emotions—but they also fight with you the most. This is the life of a mother, I guess!"

Chapter 13

Filial Piety at Tiger Balm Gardens

A predictably queasy Cathy stumbled out from yet another smelly bus, this time somewhere to the west of downtown. At this particular destination, she found a rather scary, almost morbid public attraction with the official name of Haw Par Villa. Known more locally as Tiger Balm Gardens, this was essentially Singapore's first theme park—albeit without modern-day roller coasters and related stomach-churning thrills. In any case, the bus ride to get there served that purpose well enough. By the time Cathy first wandered the property's roaming paths, the public garden had been hosting her fellow Singaporeans for four decades.

Once inside the park, Cathy was invited to experience a creative, manufactured world. Featured prominently was an array of larger-than life sculptures depicting elements of Chinese cultural myths and traditions. These were scattered amidst fishponds, romantic paths, gateways, and whimsical architectural features. By the time Cathy set foot there as a child, Tiger Balm—and the public park themed around it—had become a household name for Singapore residents. And during her handful of visits, she likely saw the place at its peak of popularity during the 1970s. This is when the park was most authentic, as envisioned by its earlier designers.

Aside from its creepiness, the Gardens provided Cathy with poignant lessons on the roles of family and community, and for discerning right from wrong ... Well, maybe not exactly. Cathy may never know what she truly learned from the place. She may have even forged some troubling childhood memories that have still not completely disappeared. Aside from that inconvenient truth, the upside for families was that the park was free of charge. It was common to pack a picnic basket and wander almost aimlessly for the day.

Those not from Singapore or Southeast Asia may be unfamiliar with Tiger Balm. Westerners are more likely to recognize the potent *Vicks VapoRub* topical ointment—if not from their own childhoods, certainly from desperate parenting efforts later. Tiger Balm can be thought of as the competitive cousin to *Vicks*. Its backstory is one of entrepreneurial creativity that produced immense wealth for one family almost overnight.

To best understand the park requires some background on the product and its inventors. The story for purposes here began with a courageous herbalist from rural Fujian Province in China, who fled to Rangoon, Burma after the 1860s. Happily settled, he grew and maintained a booming apothecary business for more than four decades. In 1908 and on his deathbed, he ended up leaving the entire family business to his two surviving sons, Aw Boon Haw ("Gentle Tiger"), and Aw Boon Par ("Gentle Leopard"). He further directed them to keep improving an earlier ointment product from his own special recipes. By this time the Aw family was among the wealthiest in Rangoon.

By 1924 the brothers had finally perfected the formula, and they relocated to Singapore to set up a branch to manufacture their products. Boon Haw excelled at promoting the brand to Chinese communities regionally and around the world. As part of his marketing strategy, Boon Haw decided to name their primary ointment after, well, himself. He dubbed it Tiger Balm.

As part of the family's relentless marketing efforts, Boon Haw developed three mansions and associated parks in Hong Kong, Singapore, and China's Fujian Province with the fundamental intent of promoting Tiger Balm. The parks were all named Tiger Balm Gardens and essentially served as permanent advertising for the company. Singapore's park was constructed in 1937 on a series of four terraces, the highest of which featured Boon Haw's private estate, Haw Par Villa. The lower three terraces were open to the public.

For Cathy's part, her principal memory derives from the park's featured attraction, the *Ten Courts of Hell*. Chinese followers of Buddhism or Taoism generally believe that individuals will eventually be rewarded for whatever good they accomplish in the world. In contrast, they will be judged just as harshly for poor behaviors and decisions. Upon one's death, it is necessary to pass through these ten courts as punishment for any sins that were committed while on the earth plane. Thanks to the Aw family, the *Ten Courts of Hell* could be experienced directly right here on earth in the form of graphic depictions and grotesque displays.

Although taking some liberties with its interpretation, the *Courts* provided a reasonable and dramatic likeness of the myth's main ideas. Regardless, it was enough to scare the living daylights out of any unsuspecting child. This is likely why so many Singaporean parents brought their children to experience this very exhibit, hoping to keep them on a straight, virtuous path in life.

During Cathy's time, visitors entered a dark tunnel into the

Courts and walked through the exhibits sequentially. Each featured its own gruesome statues and pictorial renditions of the punishments that awaited sinful humans. As envisioned by the Aw Family, the *Courts* were not for the weak of stomach. Cathy explains how the exhibit "was where the horror began. Because we were brought in there and told, if you do this, they will pull out your tongue. If you tell lies, they'll slice your throat. So, it was just like living in Hell, and we were so afraid! Because the statues are all gory and scary. But outside once again it was all back to good fun because we could picnic and all that."

If Cathy gained one principal, lasting lesson, it was the notion of *filial piety*. The concept refers generally to garnering an attitude of respect for one's parents and other ancestors. While notions of filial piety are ingrained within religions and cultures worldwide, it is the premier virtue in Chinese cultural tradition. The notion dates all the way back to the specific moral teachings of Confucius.

Most notable are the gruesome punishments awaiting those not paying enough attention to their families. In Court 4, for instance, King Wuguan reserves the right to unleash his trademark grindstone on those not filial to their parents or respectful to siblings. If this experience was not enough, one can be tied to racks in Court 8 to be split open and have intestines removed. On the brighter side, Court 10 is where punishment formally ends. This is perhaps the most vital contrast from the Christian notion of eternal damnation, from which there is no escape. It is in this final court where one is considered redeemed—if somewhat dismembered—and prepared for reincarnation on earth within the perpetual cycle of karma.

"This is why so many Asians believe in ancestral worship," Cathy explains, "and they take their obligations to the older generations extremely seriously." To practice filial piety does not necessarily mean living under the same roof. Rather, it is more about spending quality time with your elders and genuinely caring for their well-being as they age. "I think you start acquiring filial piety when you regularly visit or even live with older people, so that when your parents get older you can adapt to it," Cathy muses, thinking about why she became such a strong advocate for supporting family.

This tradition has started to slip away in modern-day Singapore. Cathy attributes this cultural shift in part to a wealthier population that travels more. Younger professionals marry and relocate overseas, making regular visits with extended family less frequent. For extensive families like Cathy's, however, filial piety is still on clear display. When not leading tours through her favorite city, she is enmeshed in a nearly constant progression of family gatherings and celebrations throughout the year. "I'm a people person," she declares, then emphasizes, "I would die if I had to move away from Singapore to live in a log cabin with only the bears and wildlife as my friends." Playing an active role in one's extended family is precious and necessary, Cathy believes. "Regardless of the monetary wealth in your life, the most important thing you have is the love for the people around you," she counsels. If this is not sound advice for all of us, it is difficult to imagine what is.

Another contributing factor that reduces filial piety is Singapore's increasingly educated population since the 1980s. Prior to that, opportunities for higher education in Singapore were scant and required numerous hoops to jump through. For one thing, children were required to take—and pass—a second language in secondary school, such as Mandarin or Tamil, as described earlier. Universities did not accept students who had not passed their language courses. This policy became a huge bottleneck for families determined to see their children attend university. As an alternative, many of the island's young people ventured overseas to obtain their education. The result was a so-called *brain drain*.

During Cathy's youth only two reputable universities existed on the island: the University of Malaya and the University of Singapore—the latter of which is now the National University of Singapore. Some families still spend "an arm and a leg" to send their children to study overseas, Cathy says, adding "And this is how young people lose a sense of filial piety, because they find and marry their spouse in another country and rarely return to visit their family here at home."

It follows that Cathy and her husband supported whatever colleges their children wished to attend—with the one stipulation that they were on Singapore soil. "There are many more options for higher education than in past decades," she explains, which is testament to the country's rapid development into a high-tech, global metropolis. Higher education of all kinds is valued seriously by Singapore's leaders.

To Cathy's delight, her oldest child, Rachel, attended a local private college. "And so, I told her," Cathy recalls, "that if only my own father had been around and had a stable job when I was a girl! I probably would have studied to be a lawyer or a judge who gets paid bunches of money to talk all day!"

Retaining friends and family within close proximity is vital for Cathy's well-being. It is not by accident that she regularly encounters friends and even distant relatives wherever she goes. Thinking of recent instances, she says, "Not long ago I was giving a talk at a local school. One of the children recognized me, and she told her mother. She happened to be my grandniece. It was because I looked so similar to my sister. Not long after that, I had this boy come up to me and say, 'My mother's sister is related to your cousin.' So, it's very strange, and these kids are so small. This is how we are all related here.

It's like we're all living within a small village right here in the big city."

Even Cathy's children can be amazed with their own family connections. She explains, "One of my uncles passed on last year, and all my cousins, we only meet up at funerals; everybody will see each other in the same place. My daughter was telling me, 'I never knew I was related to so many people!' And I said, 'Precisely, the world is so small!'" she exclaims, adding, "I love how everyone is at arm's length in Singapore. It's nice just to pop in and say 'Hey, how are you?' Just this week, I went to the clinic to see this guy—he's been our family doctor since the kids were babies. While sitting in his office, I said to the nurse outside, 'Send my love to Dr. Teo.' And she told me, why don't you just go to the door and say it to him yourself." And seeing someone she knows—family or otherwise—is always cause for celebration. Cathy explains, "So even my cousins, whenever we meet, we hug each other. My husband doesn't like it; he's Chinese, so the Chinese don't hug anybody, because they're more reserved; but like I care," she smiles.

As for the fate of Tiger Balm Gardens, the estate fell on difficult times by the 1980s. Its dereliction was reflected on the grounds through lackluster upkeep and decreasing visitor numbers. Not only that, but the government's urban development plan was expanding quickly to the far reaches of the island, encroaching upon the property. The entire estate was inevitably subsumed in 1985 under the Land Acquisition Act, Singapore's powerful legislation allowing for eminent domain. The one stipulation from the Aw family, however, was that the name of Haw Par Villa and any family memorials within its boundaries be preserved.

Three years later the estate was leased to a theme park company to redesign and update the property. This led to the opening of Haw Par Villa Dragon World in 1990, which managed to add a boat ride through the *Courts of Hell* exhibit. Now under the arm of the Singapore Tourism Board, numerous management companies for the park have come and gone with questionable success.

Today, urban Singapore laps up against the garden's borders, though Haw Par Villa remains an island of relative tranquility. While Cathy and her counterparts had once endured lengthy bus rides to access the park, Singapore's modern subway system, the MRT, now stops right near the front entrance. Docents now guide visitors around the grounds on educational tours. Opposite the park is the Port Operations Control Center (POCC), where Cathy now meets her guests for occasional tours of the facility. Though consumer tastes and preferences for entertainment have shifted since then, Singaporeans of Cathy's age still talk about Tiger Balm Gardens and their respective experiences there. No surprise, their stories consistently revolve around traumatic encounters within the *Ten Courts of Hell*.

Perhaps due to nostalgia, or to pass down a Singaporean tradition, Cathy brought her own young children there in the midst of the park's management changes. She adds with a hint of fiendishness, "I took them there to scare the wits out of them just like I experienced as a child. Something about payback."

Chapter 14

A New Hope

During an otherwise ordinary evening, Uncle Kellard ushered his mother and two nieces into their living room. He had a special announcement, and this one would be a game-changer. With Cathy now 13, he declared matter-of-factly that they were moving to a new home. He had managed to purchase a more spacious, three-room flat through Singapore's expanding public housing program. The flat was located in a newer estate, he told them, called Ang Mo Kio, which would be a welcome upgrade from their current place. The government continued to subsidize construction of residential towers at a dizzying rate, and Kellard took full advantage. In part he had Auntie Shirley's husband, Bill to thank as well. He was the one who had generously supplied him with a stable job in the insulation business.

At this time the Housing and Development Board (HDB) was encouraging residents to purchase rather than rent their flats. The government believed that owners would be more likely to view their homes as valued, long-term assets. There were catches, however. For one, single, young men were not allowed to purchase their own flats. Rather, the purchase required two adult co-owners and their signatures. Kellard thus used his mother's name as the second homeowner. He ultimately paid $14,000 for the property in the early 1980s.

With his news, Kellard simply assumed the four of them would remain together. In stark contrast with certain siblings, he was not the type to simply abandon his family and run off to a new home. There was really no question of whether they would join him, and so he simply did not ask.

Recalling her initial reaction, Cathy exclaims, "We felt so happy! We were all excited, but we were also relieved. Now that our uncle owned a flat, there was less stress about how we would pay the rent each month. Mama was especially thrilled; she was the one who really had to worry about finding the money for monthly rent."

Once installed in their new place, Kellard finally spread out in a room for himself while the girls continued to bunk together. True to tradition, Mama once again claimed "her corner" on the floor. For Mama, old habits remained difficult to shake. Nonetheless, everyone could now sleep just a little bit easier, in more ways than one.

As Cathy reached her early teens, caretaking roles had essentially reversed. She assumed more responsibility for Mama—that is, when they were not antagonizing one another. For one thing, Cathy had been learning how to give manicures and pedicures. Mama served as a captive yet willing subject on whom to practice. By then her fingernails had long succumbed to occasional fungal infections and related skin issues. This was largely due to having washed so much clothing by hand for several decades. Without electric washing machines, Mama had made use of standard wooden boards, as did much of the world's population. And all of her laundry was supplemented by copious amounts of a magical, yet toxic substance called Clorox. In a valiant effort to preserve her hands and arms, she also resorted to stomping on the clothes inside a pail. This led to a gradual deterioration of her toenails as well.

Cathy thus enjoyed opportunities to "doll up" Mama to make her look pretty. She painted Mama's fingers and toenails as parts of her complimentary manicures and pedicures. While the color fuchsia was Cathy's favorite and most memorable choice, she sometimes applied bright red polish instead. She then completed Mama's outfit with a colorful hat and sunglasses, accompanied by a fresh bouquet of flowers placed in her hands. In this way Cathy had for all intents and purposes transformed Mama into a "life-sized Barbie doll," the likes of which Cathy rarely enjoyed as a child.

Aside from Cathy's fashion expertise, Mama's own colorful outfits were curiosities in themselves. She often dressed in the style of the Peranakans, as she owned a handful of Peranakan-styled outfits known as *sarong kebayas*. The *kebaya* is typically a lightweight, sheer blouse which partially drapes over the *sarong*, or lengthy, tubular dress for the lower garment. Both men and women still wear the sarong in parts of Southeast Asia. For their part, the Peranakans are a mixed-race people typically sharing Malay and Chinese blood through generations of intermarriage. Cathy is quick to point out that Mama was not Peranakan; her own mother had been from Thailand. But the *sarong kebaya* was a popular fashion trend that Mama had bought into during the early 20th century.

The Peranakan culture itself is little known and poorly understood outside the region. Their ethnic community is sometimes referred to as the Straits-born Chinese, whose ancestors settled on the Malay peninsula or in Singapore several centuries ago. It was common for the newly arrived Chinese men to take Malay wives. Their children and successive generations became the Peranakan Chinese. Peranakan cultural traditions representing food, fashion, and architecture remain influential even within today's rapidly globalizing Singapore. Cathy remains enamored with the cultural legacies of the Peranakans, an interest perhaps amplified by her own Mama's adoration of their clothing.

Not long after the move, Cathy gradually discovered a sense of personal independence. In some ways she had experienced the life of an orphan during much of her childhood. Her father was often distant or unavailable, while her mother had disappeared, reappeared, then faded to the background once again. And the truth was that Mama's nurturing skills were hard to come by. Household rules and discipline were practically nonexistent, and Cathy was usually free to do as she wished during the day.

With little supervision to speak of, Cathy increasingly took to the streets. "In those days the parents didn't really micromanage their children," she explains. "We were free to do whatever we wanted, as long as we came back for dinner." Looking back, she now appreciates certain benefits from irresponsible parent figures. She and her peers learned to live on their own, and much sooner than more sheltered teenagers might have done in today's age of abundance.

On the positive side, then, Cathy became "street smart" and learned to navigate the adult world at a youthful age. Moreover, she had mastered the public bus system. This meant that the city had suddenly become her extended playground, allowing her to pop out anywhere she wished. Overall, she matured faster because of the need to handle an inconsistent home life. Reflecting on her household situation around the time of the move, she says, "With this inconsistency we just ate at our own times, and we were exposed to all sorts of adult things; we had to deal with anything as it was evolving around us. My father would often return home intoxicated and violent, and Mama would usually be cursing or yelling at someone. The whole house could be filled with unpredictable drama."

In some ways life was looking up for Cathy. She enjoyed a

more spacious flat and greater personal mobility when she wanted or needed to escape. That said, the hard truth remained largely unchanged. Her immediate family was still not financially sound and was essentially dependent on the good will of others. Acquiring a new dress or pair of shoes was still cause for celebration until she started to earn more money on her own. On the other hand, some fundamental things were changing in their lives. Now settled into her uncle's new flat, for instance, they started eating a wider variety of foods—including more of that sumptuous Kentucky Fried Chicken.

This relatively good fortune did little to expand their wardrobes. The teenage sisters continued to depend generally upon hand-me-downs from cousins. Older cousins predictably outgrew their outfits, and Cathy's aunties typically gave first choice to the sisters. Regardless of its source, Cathy was always grateful for anything, especially to have a pretty dress to wear. Occasionally she inherited a garment that had only been worn a handful of times for special occasions. She explains, "Because they bought so much clothing and so many shoes, they could no longer fit inside their outfits and needed to get rid of things. So, I was open arms, embracing all that was given to me," she laughs, indicating an imaginary hug.

Still, this unpredictable clothing pipeline did not always guarantee proper sizes. "During my sister's Holy Communion," she recalls humorously, "I was told that my dress was too short. But I was living on hand-me-downs, so did I really have a choice about the length of my dress? People can be funny that way." She laughs it off. Whatever nice clothing Cathy did manage to acquire, she learned to make it last. "Everyone still went to church in their Sunday best," she says. "I could make my small wardrobe of dresses last for many Sundays." Certain outfits were squirreled away for special occasions or holidays, only brought out during the likes of Chinese New

Year and Christmas.

On those rare occasions when the sisters received new clothing, it was often due to the capable sewing skills of their mother, Mary, or stepmother, Jessie. For instance, the girls were provided with new pajamas and other outfits, though the design was typically doubled through the use of the same fabric and colors. The girls thus emerged looking like twins. They learned quickly not to complain, however, and they hid their mutual distaste for looking like mirror images of one another. With age and wisdom, Cathy eventually understood that purchasing fabric in bulk was less expensive. She relented that it made good economic sense to have their clothing originate from the same patterns.

Beyond any wardrobe issues, the chance of going to bed hungry was finally relegated to Cathy's childhood past. She was certainly still scrawny for a thirteen-year-old. "Eating really only started when I reached puberty, when food was more in hand," she recollects with a hint of sarcasm. Before that finding food was hit or miss in the fridge or on the table.

Chapter 15

The Promoter

After moving into Kellard's new flat, Cathy learned that her Auntie Jenny—technically her father's cousin—was working for a company that supplied household goods to local retail stores. During a visit Cathy asked her auntie whether the company had any part-time job openings for a 14-year-old teenager. To Cathy's delight, the answer was "yes." Jenny explained there was a part-time job available for a "promoter" to help sell a toilet bowl cleaner called *Solitaire*. Regardless of the product in question, this was all Cathy needed to hear, quickly asking, "When do I start?"

During those years no rules existed to prevent younger teenagers from temporary employment on holidays or weekends. Recognizing Cathy's gregarious personality, Jenny easily recognized her niece's promise as a sales partner to peddle her company's household products.

While not the most glamorous launch into the retailing world, Cathy's mood was upbeat and optimistic. Most important, she quickly envisioned dollar signs dancing in her head. And there would be plenty of those, it turned out. Her generous auntie was offering $15 or $20 per day, which was considered a lot of money for a teenager. She could now enjoy some precious independence and even splurge on some makeup and clothing for herself. Even better, she earned a commission of five cents for every bottle of *Solitaire* she sold.

It was in this way that Cathy took her first leap into Singapore's workforce. Of course, her new job was reserved for school holidays and occasional weekends for the time being. Upon being hired, she found herself in the household goods department of one of Singapore's first department stores, that of *C.K. Tang*. Little did she know that Tang's was ushering in a new era of retailing for Singapore, and that she would happen to be in the right place at the right time to become a part of it all.

During the 1970s, large-scale department stores and shopping malls were still a rare sight in Singapore. Only two existed during Cathy's early teenage years, catering to the city's small proportion of higher-end shoppers. Such operations were even viewed as experiments by the companies that owned them.

It was in this context that entrepreneur Tang Choon Keng arrived in 1923 and eked out a precarious living selling handmade lace and embroidery brought from his home city in China. Later nicknamed the "Tin Trunk Man" or the "Curio King," he had even hired a rickshaw puller to peddle his wares. A decade later, Mr. Tang was able to open his first small store located inside an existing multi-floor building. With ongoing success, he upgraded again and expanded into his own dedicated building at the corner of Jalan Mohamad Sultan and River Valley Road. His operation became one of Singapore's first-generation department stores.

Not one to take the safe bet, Tang's success led him to purchase a risky piece of unbuilt property at the junction of Orchard Road and Scotts Road in 1958. In this case, his family thought he had now completely lost his mind. He was heavily advised against purchasing this desolate lot for numerous reasons, but mostly because the site faced Singapore's Tai San Ting Cemetery across the street. Tang ultimately brushed off his naysayers. He quietly noted that a community of British housewives had little choice but to pass by the site on their way downtown. Believing he had just discovered his future clientele, this is where he built his first full-scale department store. The gamble paid off.

It was in the basement of C.K. Tang's newest store where Cathy became a "product promoter" for her auntie. The building's architecture was unique and memorable. Tang had his retail emporium designed as a model of the Forbidden City in Beijing, complete with a green-tile roof and broad, overhanging eaves that flared upwards at the corners. The themed structure became an instant landmark for the local community and served essentially as a bold advertisement in its own right.

Other than C.K. Tang, no other major retailers had yet located along the future shopping corridor of Orchard Road. As the first arrival, Tang enjoyed a captive audience. During the store's early years, he marketed largely to the local expatriate community and to upscale families, which explained his focus on Eurasian women. Eventually numerous global retailers would follow Tang's lead.

As Cathy explains, this retailing approach came at the expense of a regional tradition destined to disappear. "When I worked there in the early 1980s, the Orchard Road shopping district really didn't exist yet. Instead, average people went to night markets—the *Pasar Malam*. Pasar means 'market,' and Malam means 'night.' A night market is where they sell everything from food and utensils to shoes to any types of crafts and household goods, under a canopy or out in the street. You know, like flea markets. These are prevalent in Southeast Asia, especially in countries with large, lower-income populations—

Thailand, Malaysia, Indonesia—they all have that style of market, but they're at night to avoid the heat of the day. They're not officially legal, but the authorities largely look the other way," she chuckles, adding, "They're not second-hand goods—just things sold on the streets by people who have no money to open their own store. During the daytime they can't operate."

Recalling her own observations as a teenager, she says, "During those years there was a huge car park along Orchard Road, which was open for parking during the day. Then at 6:00 in the evening the car park closed, and the night market took over, with all these hawkers coming in to sell their food. So, if your car was still parked when the hawkers moved in, everybody would just set up shop and your car would become part of their stalls." She laughs at the memory, adding, "It's so funny. This operation lasted until the 1970s. That market was all food vendors. But in the suburbs, they would have these night and weekend markets selling household goods."

Cathy explains more about her role in Tang's new store. "When I was 14, I was hired and worked in the basement. Household departments were always in the basement. So, I worked as a promoter. In those days companies needed somebody to come and sell their product. I also made friends there because other promoters were selling their own products, but they were usually women much older than me. So, I made friends with them as I like to do," she grins. She needed little time to win over the hearts of her senior counterparts.

Asked if there was any minimum age for employment, Cathy explained that such regulations did not yet exist. "The company didn't mind me working because I was mature enough by then. The promoters like me were not paid by the department store; I was paid by my auntie, who worked at her own company. She was not with me there. So, you could sell anything to anybody in that store, and all you needed was a security check before you left for the day. In those days anybody could work, as long as you were proper and mature enough. If you could speak well, that was the most important thing."

Though Cathy was largely unaware at the time, Mama had already provided her with a strong foundation of social skills. Near the top of the list was how to demonstrate appropriate manners in public and how to respect one's elders. "We were just brought up to be well-mannered and respectful," she notes. Most memorably, her Mama's key refrain was, "No big, no small." The Cantonese equivalent of this phrase referred to someone exhibiting poor manners toward others.

Perhaps most important, Cathy and her sister were taught from a young age how to properly greet older people. When walking into someone's home with numerous family members, for instance, it is good manners to address each one individually. To simply acknowledge everyone collectively with a wave and a "Hello, everybody" was unacceptable. Rather, it was imperative to address them by proper family titles, thereby confirming one's specific relationship. The oldest sister of Cathy's father, for instance, would be addressed as *Kuma*, for her eldest auntie as mentioned earlier.

This pivotal training worked to Cathy's benefit from a young age. Upon practicing her newfound skills on various relatives, she realized that good manners produced immediate and positive attention. Her older relatives naturally lavished the young girl with praise for her excellent manners. "And showing respect to your elders also reflects well on your parents," Cathy adds, before correcting herself. "Well, not so much on *our* parents, as they were missing. But I always told my children that you do not have to be smart, but you must have good manners so people would know that you had a proper upbringing." Mama's relentless training had clearly rubbed off and eventually led to higher sales numbers at C.K. Tang.

Cathy's first day at Tang's was a blur, and she recalls little detail. As a self-described *chiong* person as noted earlier, she took a leap with both feet into the world of retail sales. And some aspects of Singapore's lingering street hawker tradition survived into this new department store format. Tang's retail emporium needed—and encouraged—salespeople to promote their goods right out on the floor amidst the passing customers. Nowadays, the opposite is more the rule. Shoppers are encouraged to wander and browse without interruption from seemingly desperate vendors.

It is not difficult to imagine that Cathy's outgoing personality surfaced quickly in this role. Through hard-won trial and error, she learned which sales strategies worked well and which fell flat. With no guidance provided by her auntie, she eventually discovered that the key was to greet customers with a friendly smile and to chat with them for a while to break the ice.

Within only a few weeks, Jenny's protégé had become the main attraction of the toilet cleaner display area. In this sales environment, the nurturing of customer relationships became more important than special price reductions. Cathy learned quickly that making friends was the route to higher sales. Otherwise, the product would remain largely ignored—as would her bank account. She fondly recalls, "I was always so smiley, and women would look over and see the pathetic, skinny girl standing there."

Cathy learned the art of storytelling to promote a product. After becoming more of a fixture in the store on certain days, some of her customers eventually returned to purchase her product and to say hello.

Not one to rest on her laurels, Cathy soon took her sales act to other employees in the store. She struck up conversations and sold them toilet cleaner, too. Recalling the *chiong* factor,

Cathy looks back and explains, "You also find that you learn more when you're thrown into the deep end, with little training. It takes a while to observe and learn how people act and react to what you say."

It did not take long for Cathy to become a leading product promoter at the store. Better yet, she sold a whole lot of toilet-bowl cleaner and earned impressive commissions. As she fine-tuned her stories, she elaborated or improvised depending upon what the situation called for. In one respect, she was learning to build a rapport with the public.

Cathy further learned to draw out her customers' own stories. And she discovered there was plenty to tell. Many seemingly content and successful women required little prodding to talk about themselves and their personal issues. These often revolved around feelings of loneliness, boredom, or lack of excitement in their lives. Some even admitted to using shopping as an excuse to get out of the house.

Upon encountering Cathy for the first time, women quickly felt some level of comfort and were happy to chat. Eventually, she shifted the content of her sales pitch to one that focused more on personal connections. She explains, "You learn to ask how their day is going, what they are buying, and where they are headed next. Show some interest in them and their lives. At this point in the conversation, it's not so much about the product." Only then would Cathy make her pitch, as she emulates: "I would then change the subject and say, 'So, Auntie'—I address them with respect like my Mama taught—'why don't you try this cleaner? I'm sure you'll like it. It works so wonderfully; the dirt just lifts to the surface, and you don't even need to scrub hard. You'll have a very clean toilet, and your whole family will be very happy.' By then they felt bad enough, or impressed enough, that they relented and decided to try a bottle."

Although she only worked part time, Cathy learned to recognize repeat shoppers. It was not lost on her that the same women reappeared numerous times, to the point where she knew some of them by name. They might even stop to provide feedback on Cathy's favorite product. She recalls, "They would walk by and tell me, 'Oh, it's so good!' And I would reply, 'Yes, just like I told you, right?' or something to that effect. Then I would remind them to stop by my station the next time to purchase more for their friends and relatives." Remembering their names was even more valuable for developing a lasting rapport. In some cases, she never even mentioned the product as she conversed with her new friends.

What decidedly did not work, she discovered, was the "hard sell." To purposely interrupt someone walking through the store with little warning could be off-putting and have the opposite effect as originally intended. To this day, Cathy does not appreciate being on the receiving end of this intimidating approach. Little did she realize how valuable her newfound skills would become when later moving into the tourism industry.

While Cathy emerged as the basement's star salesperson, C.K. Tang's own profits and land values skyrocketed throughout the 1970s. This unprecedented success found him and his family making plans to expand yet again. In 1982—not long after Cathy's tenure—Tang had his landmark store demolished. In its place came a world-class 33-floor Dynasty Hotel and expanded retail shopping complex. This new facility better mirrored the contemporary, modern, and city block-sized store designs that were now commonplace elsewhere.

After a half-century of growing his operation, an aging C.K. Tang retired in 1987 and handed over the reins to one of his three sons. With a legacy of ongoing investments and expansions—along with the occasional failed spin-off—the company assured its place as an anchor of the now-famous, upscale Orchard Road shopping district.

Later in life, Cathy occasionally returned to her first site of employment, but more so to seek out the store's "budget corner" of discounted merchandise. For one thing, the embroidered linens that Tang was known for were beautiful and always caught her eye. Still, beneath the tempting fabrics and irresistible deals was something more meaningful that tugged at her. This was, after all, essentially where her life began. Her time at C.K. Tang would help open more adventurous doors as she forged her way into the 1980s.

Chapter 16

Breaking Out

With a year of experience in retail sales, it was time to seek out her own opportunities elsewhere. Cathy's mid-teen years resembled an incessant juggling act. She struggled to find enough time within a 24-hour day for everything spinning around in her life—namely the academic demands of school, an array of extracurricular activities, the separate world of gainful employment, and a rather chaotic home life. Oh yes, and there were Mass and Catechism lessons to attend. Youthful energy propelled her sufficiently at first. Given the lack of adult guidance on balancing one's life, it was Cathy's natural tendency to simply jump in and get involved. Even for someone with such eagerness, however, something would eventually have to give.

Fresh off the sales floor, promising new prospects awaited on the teen job market. She was now 15 and sensed her next taste of freedom. Among other possible ventures, a waitressing job opened at a new place called Shakey's Pizza. Better yet, her good friend, Lin, recommended that they apply together. The American fast-food chain was still a novelty to Singapore in the 1980s when the franchise was brought to Cathy's attention. It had already become a smash hit in the Philippines, which encouraged its corporate overseers to expand elsewhere in the region. Unfortunately, results in Singapore proved lackluster at best. Shakey's lasted only four years within this otherwise booming city-state. The franchise would make a valiant if questionable attempt at a comeback in 2021.

Shakey's short lifespan did not prevent Cathy and Lin from making their own mark. After being quickly hired as they had hoped, the duo became a fixture there only a year after its grand opening. And once again their youthful ages mattered little, given less stringent hiring practices. Cathy elaborates, "In those days it did not matter how old you were; you could just work—as long as you were presentable and mature enough, and you could follow instructions." Speaking for them both, she adds, "The thing was, our parents were not providing on a steady basis, and we needed money. We were happy to have this opportunity at the time."

No surprise, Cathy's bubbling personality proved well suited once again to this new role. And importantly, she and Lin adored the quirky uniforms required for waitressing duties. It was not beyond the two of them to take advantage of their strikingly similar appearances, playing the famous *switcheroo*.

The idea to do so came at the expense of an unsuspecting customer. Cathy had been serving a woman when she accidentally stumbled and sent a full glass of water all over her upper body and onto the floor below. As much in shock as she was wet, the woman quickly became irate. Cathy instantly panicked and froze up. She had simply not been trained to handle such situations professionally. Instinctively, Cathy ran back to the kitchen and told Lin what had happened, and she urged Lin to return in her place for cleanup duty. Given their sister-like resemblance, however, the woman mistook Lin for Cathy and "handed Lin the scolding of her life," says Cathy, laughing at the memory.

Shakey's provided additional opportunities for fun,

especially prior to the advent of rigorous health and safety regulations. Aside from its thin-crust pizza and tasty chicken offerings, the business' signature product was its trademark *mojos*. These came in the form of sliced, fried potatoes, more circular in shape than standard French fries. The two friends became all but addicted. With each food delivery to a table, two or three mojos mysteriously disappeared prior to the food's arrival.

The fun continued at closing time. While other employees desperately avoided the late shift, Cathy and Lin adored working together to close the place at night. This responsibility often took them past 10:00 p.m. One duty involved hosing down the toilets and floors, which became an adventure of its own. No doubt, just as much water ended up on each other as was dedicated to the task at hand.

Should anyone forget, school still required Cathy's attendance during the day. In fact, her plate of scheduled activities only increased as she entered secondary school. To its credit, St. Anthony's offered a wide range of extracurricular activities running the gamut of music, theatre, and sports. She could not sign up for them fast enough.

With her work at Shakey's, the grueling agenda of an active teenager began to take its toll. She was pushing up against her own human limitations, given the combination of work, school, and social life. Reality finally hit home, and it hit back hard. Cathy's engagement with the world became downright exhausting. And yet, her body and mind fought to keep going. Even after the late-night closing ritual, she was dutifully in her seat at school the next morning by 7:20. Arriving on time was one thing; it was the attempt to remain awake that eluded her. Outlasting the school day became an impossible goal. When the need for sleep overcame her, Cathy's head could be found planted down on her desk, snoozing away.

Teachers began to take notice, and some eventually interceded. Cathy's sleeping body was met with any number of reactions depending upon whom she was offending at the time. Certain teachers were naturally more compassionate than others. Cathy's Malay language teacher approached her desk more than once to kindly state the obvious, "Oh you poor dear, you're sleeping." This still signaled to Cathy that her teachers were paying attention. She explained truthfully that she had been working late the night before and had not been home for very long prior to school.

Fortunately, teachers usually empathized with the varied and challenging home lives of their students. To be sure, Cathy was not the only teen juggling work obligations to enhance unstable incomes at home. Most teachers wisely recognized that belittling them was not going to improve the situation.

Meanwhile, when Cathy was snoozing at school and testing her boundaries, her sister was earning a more positive reputation. It turns out she was quietly yet methodically marching up the academic ladder of success, quite under the radar of her own family. She eventually began her own home business, focused on personalized tutoring of younger students. Her first clients consisted of various neighborhood children, most of whom could not afford expensive private tutors. She wisely charged more affordable fees, perhaps as low as $10 or $20 per month for one school subject.

Cathy discovered a secondhand benefit to her sister's tutoring efforts. With every neighborhood child arriving at their door came the promise of a new friend. For Cathy this revolving door of visitors provided just one more opportunity to expand her social network.

In contrast to her sister's academic successes, Cathy became a rather frequent visitor to the school's office for various disciplinary reasons. Her most common transgression—with no surprise to anyone—involved talking too much and at inappropriate times. Earlier in primary school, Cathy's incessant talking had nearly driven certain teachers mad. They did what they could to admonish her, to the point of even taping Cathy's mouth shut for all to see. In one such instance, however, the joke was on the teacher. A defiant and certainly disrespectful Cathy somehow continued to talk through the tape while returning to her desk.

Despite causing occasional headaches, Cathy's fast work with making friends sometimes won over the affections of her teachers as well. With few exceptions they learned to appreciate Cathy's upbeat, expressive personality even if at times they preferred otherwise. She even managed to return to the good graces of the teacher who had taped her mouth shut, recalling, "I still made amends with her, and I actually became good friends with her daughter, Regina. During holidays I often visited Regina's house for sleepovers—it was another way to avoid staying at home. Of course, her mother was my teacher, so we became friends, too. Her name was Phyllis, so I came to know her as Auntie Phil. She was really nice, and I shouldn't have given her such a hard time!"

In more serious cases, a school official might threaten to call Cathy's parents. Rather than cowering in fear at the very sight of the phone dialing, however, her first reaction was usually one of bewilderment. "You want to call my parents? Oh, my God, why?" Cathy recalls her thoughts at the time. "Just tell me what my problem is, and I'll work on it. Why do you have to go to my parents? My father will be drunk or away half the time, my Mama will not care and can't speak English, and my mother is missing. If my father is drunk, he will beat me to a pulp!"

This general approach proved successful more often than not. Quite aware of their students' troubled backgrounds, situations at school tended to be handled with compassion and kindness. Cathy recalls her teachers as caring and nurturing role models more than strict disciplinarians. In one sense, they collectively served as part of Cathy's overall social support system. At the same time, they still managed to provide some much-needed discipline and boundaries.

Convent school provided further outlets to practice Cathy's budding communication skills. Rather than attract negative attention for acting out in class, she joined more sanctioned activities that better rewarded her outgoing personality. This especially meant one thing at St. Anthony's—theatrical productions, and plenty of them. At one point, Cathy found herself playing a role in Shakespeare's *The Merchant of Venice*, which gave her a taste of public performance. Nearly every literary lesson seemed to culminate with some type of theatric event. Costumes and props were provided for added realism.

Cathy credits her evolving public speaking skills to the school's emphasis on theatre. "Tour Guiding is just like acting in plays at school," she explains, adding, "The world is a stage, and you are up there performing. Everybody is watching you and judging you. If you can't do a good show, you just kill the audience," she chuckles. "So, I'm not a scripted person, but after years of experience you basically know how to talk. When somebody asks you a question, you can quickly reply in a nice, gracious way. That is why, with respect to public speaking, a lot of guides are actually afraid to speak unscripted. They can tell their stories and be personal, and all that. But to stand up there to talk and express yourself is different. I don't get nervous anymore. Once I was leading a military tour, and one guy asked me, 'How did you learn how to speak like this?' and I said that I always had an issue when I was young, that I always feared public speaking. That is why I pushed myself, and the school activities helped. We always had a lot of acting classes, plays to put on. So that enabled me to overcome my fear."

These early brushes with acting only fostered Cathy's expanding interest in public performance. She readily signed up for any activity involving drama or theatre production. The school choir pulled her in as well, as did modern ballet dance. At some point she also discovered the school's concert band. This latter opportunity may have pushed her limits, however; she cannot recall ever learning to play an instrument.

Aside from jumping into theatre, Cathy further attempted various sports. The chiong factor kicked in once again, as she was determined to develop an athletic mindset and a body to go with it. The school regularly fielded a variety of sport teams, including swimming. She eventually found herself competing alongside her classmates in 100-meter school competitions, all the while forging a "love-hate" relationship with her coach. For one thing, Cathy was initially challenged with swimming in a straight line. During one instance on the school's designated Sports Day, all competitors maintained their discipline to swim within their own lanes. That is, except for Cathy, who somehow became disoriented and, as she describes, "swam the width of the pool instead of the length, across the ropes. The whistle blew very loudly!" she laughs, recalling that she naturally turned directions in the water without knowing it. Upon blowing his whistle, her swim coach yelled "Ross!" to get her attention. This only aggravated Cathy further, however, as Chinese custom had taught that it was rude to call people by their surnames; to do so was highly insulting.

His gruff coaching style aside, his continuous dose of discipline was priceless—and necessary, as Cathy continued to mature emotionally. Her knowledge of his passing years later deeply saddened her, and she reflected on his "tough love" approach to her education. In some ways he had served as a mentor who genuinely cared about her personal growth and well-being. She even attended his funeral to offer her own round of goodbyes, "flooding his coffin with buckets of tears," as she recalls her emotions at the time. It is difficult to imagine a more poignant gesture of appreciation for a teacher's genuine contributions.

Pushing the Glass Ceiling

Later in secondary school, Cathy somehow turned her attention to the world of tennis. This sport was not exactly a common choice in 1980s Singapore. But Cathy's determination kicked in, and she ultimately practiced and trained enough to earn a place on the school team. She ended up representing St. Anthony's at various singles competitions for two years.

In this case, her personal motivations for learning tennis were not so simple. Now in her mid-teens, Cathy had become more self-conscious of her disadvantaged home life and her related struggles with poverty. It was all too easy to compare herself with wealthier peers. From her perspective, tennis was a privileged, "rich man's" sport that offered a potential way out of her current existence. It follows that she was compelled to try something outside of her own social class—to break the metaphorical *glass ceiling*. This term originated in the United States during the 1970s, referring especially to social barriers that prevented women from entering male-dominated professions. Although Cathy's principal motive was admittedly to just play tennis, it did not escape her that she would need to break out of her own social class to do so.

One further challenge stood in the way of her goal, this time rooted in basic geography. There were simply no public tennis courts nearby on which to practice. In one sense, she was ahead of her time. Decades would pass before tennis became a popular, global pastime, accessible to nearly all who wanted to play. In her case, it became clear that most well-maintained courts were tucked away within the depths of Singapore's exclusive country clubs. Still undaunted, she strove to find a way onto the very same courts as enjoyed her wealthier friends.

Cathy credits her "rich auntie," Shirley, for providing one important nudge. At some point Shirley learned of Cathy's budding interest in the sport, along with her frustrations. Rather than simply encourage Cathy to go find something else to do, Shirley opened up to this adventurous idea. To get her started, she gave Cathy an older wooden tennis racket to practice with at school.

As Cathy recalls, "Auntie's home was like a sports shop," given all the games and gear that littered their home. By the time her first racket became warped and unusable, Cathy had become suitably conditioned through a standard regimen of training. She then became accustomed to the school's larger *Prince* rackets. With their larger heads and equally oversized faces, Cathy felt there was nothing she could not hit! Her first training with these rackets occurred during CCE—that is, her school's co-curricular activity periods devoted to physical education.

By the time she joined the team, her dedication to the sport only intensified. Practices were grueling and were held every other day. This made for lengthy days on school grounds, interspersed with various jobs during weekends and holidays. Asked why she became so driven to play this particular sport, she responds, "I didn't play just because richer people played. It was just that I was attracted to something that I could not otherwise afford. And since the school offered it for free, why not? It just happened to be a rich person's sport." Said another way, Cathy's *chiong* factor had kicked in again, and she was off and running.

It was during her packed schedule of training and competitions when she became more self-conscious of her own biracial background. Still, she fortunately recalls no outwardly racial or class prejudice from others during her tennis years. She explains, "People liked us—Eurasians—we were unique in Singapore. We spoke well. It wasn't like the earlier British colonial times, so we were not looked down upon."

Ultimately her team may not have won many matches over this two-year stretch. But more importantly, Cathy had accomplished the significant goal of participating in a sports culture typically favoring a wealthier class of people. Beyond all the seriousness, of course, it was just good fun all around. Mingling with the handsome boys her age provided an additional benefit.

One additional, and critical, factor contributed to Cathy's rise in tennis. That is, the school's CCE program was still accessible to every student who desired to try something new. Through the 1980s anyone at St. Anthony's could get involved in a sport. The school's numerous CCE classes served as the gateway to such experiences, including the likes of basketball, tennis, swimming, and numerous others. To the school's credit, anybody who showed some combination of promise and determination might earn an invitation to try out for a team. This is precisely how Cathy entered the worlds of swimming and tennis. She thrived in an environment that allowed someone to compete without the expectation of becoming a top athlete.

Times have clearly changed since then. Student access to team sports is no longer a given. Cathy relates a recent story: "When my daughter started secondary school, I naturally suggested that she try tennis. She looked puzzled and said, 'But Mommy, you have to be able to play the sport first before you can take it as a CCE.'" Whatever inclination her daughter might have had to follow in her mother's footsteps essentially died right on the spot. Cathy was shocked to learn how the focus now emphasized competition and athleticism. This realization only enhanced her appreciation for the times when any given youth could pick up a warped, wooden racket and get out on the court.

Chapter 17

The Clubbing Years

With her life entrenched in extracurricular activities, much of Cathy's waking day took place in or around St. Anthony's. A standard day saw her arrive on campus around 7:00 a.m. and not leave until 6:00 that evening. Training and practice required much of her time outside the classroom, whether it be for tennis, swimming, theatre, choir, or any mixture of these as the season demanded. One fringe benefit for Cathy was an ever-growing accumulation of friends from all walks of life. Together they explored their own personal identities and interests.

Eventually, Cathy noticed that her peers were gravitating toward different life paths. Some female friends were more focused on self-image and appearances, conforming to modern social norms for clothing, hair styles, and makeup. "They could have played roles in the movie, *Grease*," Cathy jokes. "They just wanted to look pretty." Granted, Cathy was no stranger to makeup and hair styles herself. That said, looking pretty did not become a top priority in her life.

Other young women were devoting their energies to sports, like her. Her widespread involvement in so many activities allowed her to find acceptance within a diverse set of social cliques and groups. Combined with an outgoing personality, her bilingual skills meant she could hang socially with the best of them. And her interests were as diverse as her friends' hair styles. She could "look pretty" on one day while training as an athlete on another. Her earlier jobs further taught her how to display more professionalism through personal appearance and grooming habits. And given her familiarity with Tang's department store, it comes as little surprise that cosmetics were among Cathy's first discretionary purchases. For this reason, she and her friends often appeared older than they actually were.

On rare occasion Cathy's inescapable desire to fit in socially led to unexpected opportunities. Even mundane things like a simple sandwich could be burned into her long-term memory as an unforgettable treat. She recounts one invitation to a posh corporate clubhouse. "There is this oil refinery in the south of Singapore. It's owned by Shell. I had a friend whose father worked for them, and there's a clubhouse there. I used to think, if only I could have a club sandwich, I would be so happy! My friends told me about all the food there. So, finally my dream came true. I persuaded my friend to invite me over to the clubhouse, because I was always fascinated by her lifestyle. She asked for her father's permission, and he said yes, I could go! I had several sleepless nights just anticipating my visit."

She continues, "Finally, the day came with all the excitement, and we boarded a ferry to an island called Bukom. The clubhouse was on the island. We went for a swim first, then we went to have lunch. Not having any money with me, I had no choice but to just drink water while she had her lunch. I watched her eat something called a 'club' sandwich. She only ate half of it, because it was so big she couldn't finish. So, she asked me if I would like to have the rest. And I was so happy, and hungry! Before eating, I scrutinized it, and it was made up of cucumber, cheese, chicken, egg, and ham. And when I ate it, tears started rolling down from my eyes. So much drama," she chuckles while downplaying her own teenage emotions. She adds, "And after that I told myself, I'm going to eat so many club sandwiches that I will never be hungry again. Well, I took that pledge to heart. Today I tell my guests, 'See what happens when you eat too many sandwiches? You become my size.' And then they all laugh. It's a true story." She now laughs at herself, also recognizing how food insecurity as a child has influenced her adult habits, for better or worse.

Stories like this one inevitably found their way into Cathy's tours. She explains, "When I go to sea with my maritime guests, I see the oil refinery and remember that visit. Not only do I talk about the refinery in technical terms, but I also mention stories of my childhood and all that. These are the things that people will remember. They won't remember the statistics or the features of the island—you know, like how much tonnage of oil they produce—but they *will* remember my club sandwich story!" And sometimes she is surprised by her own memories, adding, "The clubhouse visit, it was a one-time thing. What fascinates me is still having fond memories of what happened there."

While comfortable with pretty much any teenage social scene, Cathy's best friends still usually came from disadvantaged homes. They formed a mutual support network, and their numerous school activities kept most of them away from too much trouble.

Speaking of trouble, with increased personal freedom came a host of less healthy temptations. First, she was finally earning her own money. When not at home, school, or church, many of her waking hours were devoted to employment. By age 15 this independence exposed her to a number of potential vices which posed their own risks. These years saw Cathy earning a lot of "A's" in her classes—that is, "absences," as she jokes with some truth to the matter. Her academic success was hanging by a thread.

It was perhaps inevitable that around age 16 Cathy discovered "clubbing," loosely defined as hanging out with friends at local bars and nightclubs. If there had been any age restrictions at that time, few establishments paid any attention to them. After working late into the evening already, she and her friends went clubbing even later. This led to typical arrivals back home around 1:00 a.m. and beyond. By this late hour she usually found her Mama sound asleep, and—anyway—she was not in the business of keeping track of Cathy's whereabouts by then.

While this uncharacteristic freedom held its benefits, it was left to Cathy's own devices to discover her personal limits. She says, "Had I lived with a father and mother in a more proper home life, with parents who are responsible, they would not be as likely to allow their daughter to go out every night, right? And they would monitor everywhere she goes and what she does. But Mama didn't lose sleep over where I was, and she was sleeping like a dead rock when I got home."

Occasionally Cathy wonders how she made it through those critical years alive. Some of her peers were not so fortunate. She could have succumbed to any number of experiments that can cause one's life to go wildly astray. Some of her peers in surrounding neighborhood schools ultimately dropped out early due to lack of direction or parental boundaries. And based on her own observations, a high percentage of them came from disadvantaged homes.

Although drug addiction was probably no worse for her generation, Cathy encountered more than her share of opportunities to explore the drug scene. "I've been through that period of trying all kinds of alcohol," she recalls. "And I smoked, but I have never done drugs. I never felt the need to take all that stuff. It just makes your mind go numb."

Smoking was another matter. Her first encounter with cigarettes came during her employment at Shakey's. She and Lin naturally became acquainted with the older boys who served as waiters. All of them were smokers, not an uncommon thing in those years. Inevitably, Cathy was encouraged to try a cigarette of her own. Upon inhaling for the first time, the result was immediate. She vomited up her last meal and felt like she was on death's doorstep. Not to be deterred, however, she gradually grew accustomed to the flavor of nicotine. Most of her friends smoked too, as it was the social thing to do.

With newfound spending money, she learned where to buy her cigarettes. And of course, they were made readily accessible to young people; students could purchase them easily right outside the school grounds. Cathy recalls the so-called *wall store* perched across the street from St. Anthony's. She and her friends regularly frequented this outdoor place to purchase cigarettes and related products. This type of mobile convenience store was common across Southeast Asia at the time, consisting of little more than a stand-up wall on the side of the road. These were operated by merchants who could not afford a full interior storefront. And anyway, cigarettes were so inexpensive that even Cathy and her friends could easily afford them on their own meagre incomes.

This is how Cathy's smoking habit began at age 15. Perhaps this was the lesser of two evils, however, as she managed to stay clear of powerful street drugs. She largely credits this decision to her phantom grandfather, Uncle John, who had somehow entered her life.

By the time Cathy was learning to sell toilet cleaner, Grandpa had moved into a senior care facility. She willingly spent as much free time as possible to visit him there. And now she had one more thing to share—her newfound smoking habit.

Eager to continue her relationship with Grandpa, she creatively purchased a variety of cigarette brands for him to try. At one point he commented humorously that never in all his life had he smoked so many different brands. On days with decent weather, she accompanied him outdoors to share a smoke and some good conversation.

When it came to smoking, Grandpa never made a fuss about Cathy's new habit. In fact, he explained how it was customary and expected to smoke socially—for men and women alike. There was no taboo yet, and so he never tried to dissuade Cathy from doing the same.

Although remaining tolerant of Cathy's new leisure activity, an aging Grandpa provided one clear directive: "Go ahead and smoke, but do not take drugs. They will mess up your life." Cathy reflects and understands the psychology of this approach, whether her grandfather had consciously thought about it or not. She explains, "He was basically saying, 'Go ahead and smoke in front of me,' because then it is no longer a novelty to hide it from disapproving adults." In contrast, he placed drugs on a whole new level of concern—well above the threats posed by common cigarettes. For this reason, her grandfather's strict directive on drugs has stayed with her to the current day.

Aside from her Grandpa's sound advice, Cathy was further sheltered at convent school. She never found herself mingling with friends who experimented widely with drugs. Although later she would discover the worlds of alcohol and clubbing, she would eventually abandon both smoking and drinking all but entirely. With age and some hard-earned wisdom, she came out the other side largely unscathed and in more control of her own decisions. She readily admits, "I was naughty—going clubbing, drinking, smoking. But I never crossed my family's red line of drug use."

Cathy's relationship with alcohol had all but vanished by her early 20s. She elaborates, "I don't like the feeling of losing control. And my father was an alcoholic, so now I say, leave me out. I'll have a Coke," she chuckles. If that was not enough motivation, she adds, "And alcohol's so expensive, and you don't feel good after that. I used to drink a lot in my younger days, clubbing and all. And I realized I didn't enjoy it. I would get all red, my makeup wouldn't look good, I started slurring, and I just wanted to puke. How is that any fun?"

As a guiding hand with wise counsel, Grandpa remained an important companion as Cathy grew older. On one Easter Sunday—not long after she had started their cigarette trading ritual—he came to visit for a traditional Easter dinner. As he was eating, his gums started to bleed profusely. He was taken to the doctor where it was announced that he was suffering from advanced-stage gum cancer. He consequently endured radiation treatments for seven weeks, along with a grueling daily commute to receive them.

At some point Grandpa's facility staff asked Cathy if she would be willing to accompany him to his radiation treatments. Though short-staffed, the cancer center operated a van dedicated to transporting cancer patients to and from the hospital. Upon agreeing to do so, the van picked up her grandfather and then detoured to Cathy's estate. She simply boarded there and traveled with him the rest of the way, enjoying more quality time together. And there was no shortage of time during the commute. After collecting Cathy, the van traveled through additional neighborhoods to gather more patients. She accompanied Grandpa every weekday for seven weeks. Upon returning home, she turned around and headed off to work. She had recently turned 17.

Despite this valiant effort to fight the cancer, Grandpa ultimately passed away soon thereafter in September. Cathy was unabashedly heartbroken with the loss of this caring soul. Grandpa had clearly treated her like his own daughter. For this reason, she took his death much harder than she had with others who had passed. Any fond memory she might conjure of her grandfather was reason enough to break down. Perhaps even worse was the timing. She had lost him during her formative teen years, already considered all but apocalyptic for any young adult. For all intents and purposes, she had lost one of the most meaningful people in her life.

Only many years later did Cathy discover why her "phantom grandfather" had shown such an interest in her family. Much was explained when it was revealed that Grandpa was the godfather of her mother, Mary. Cathy explains, "He first knew my mother's mother, so he became my mother's godfather. He drifted away after I was born, but he came back into our lives when my father wasn't being a father. His concern for us led him to step in and help in whatever way he could. I will always be very grateful for that!"

Chapter 18

Selling Singapore

Despite Cathy's active teenage lifestyle, consistent success in the classroom continued to elude her. It became increasingly clear by secondary school that the college track of coursework would not be a realistic option. A combination of insufficient school grades and substandard placement exams meant she would need to find an alternative path. Even after saying her final goodbyes to convent school, the idea of tour guiding, or tourism in whatever form, had not yet entered her mind. Meanwhile, Mama was only growing more frail and less competent to care for herself. It was now Cathy's part-time jobs that brought precious money into their home. This was not one's idea of being set up for future success upon finishing school.

The tables now turned, Cathy often paid for weekly household necessities and even provided Mama with her own allowance. Despite this added responsibility, frugality was already well entrenched in Cathy's blood. Occasional late-night forays with friends did not seriously curtail her staunch determination to save money. With so much time now focused on earning wages, the purchase of frivolities was a rare treat. Even her newfound pastime of clubbing took a back seat to typical 10- to 12-hour workdays, sometimes involving two separate jobs.

One opportunity came at the behest of—once again—her best friend, Lin. Cathy was thus confronted with a serious choice that could very well set up her eventual path in life. Upon Lin's prodding, they both completed applications for employment at a local factory. Cathy thought flippantly, *Sure, why not?* It might even be fun to work together on the factory floor. Still encumbered with hopeful innocence, she romanticized about the two of them wearing dark suits and head gear like astronauts toiling happily along. Disney's *Seven Dwarfs* would not have been so joyful going to work. More practically, the facility was located conveniently within an industrial area near home.

After submitting separate applications, they shared what they had written. One question asked for the applicant's fluency in multiple languages. Fair enough. Hoping to impress the hiring staff, Lin proudly wrote that she could speak and write French almost fluently. At this news, Cathy's jaw hung open in disbelief. And then she lit into her friend. "Why in the world would you admit to knowing French?" Cathy yelled, knowing right away this would be interpreted as code for "overqualified." These jobs did not require a high-school education. As the verbal pummeling continued, Cathy said it would be her fault if they did not get hired together. "What were you thinking—writing that you could speak French?! You dummy!" In the end, Cathy's good sense was prophetic, as Lin was not hired.

Despite this initial drama, Cathy was called back for an in-person interview. Unlike Lin, she was immediately hired. Upon scanning her new schedule, she learned the job required shiftwork over the course of a 24-hour day. For her own first day, Cathy was expected to report promptly at 6:45 a.m. As fate would have it, Cathy overslept and did not wake up until well after 8:00. Of course, this delinquency did not sit well with her supervisor. Before ever setting foot on the factory floor, Cathy was unceremoniously dismissed.

Not surprisingly, Cathy's motivation for the job all but disappeared without her companion. What fun would it be to work in a factory without her "bestie" perched beside her? At least part of her realized this would be no Shakey's Pizza.

Always reflective, Cathy could not help but wonder how this career path might have progressed. One scenario saw her propelled into a management role, given her positive attitude, work ethic, and empathy for fellow employees. Even with less education, Cathy felt she was intelligent enough to one day lead the whole team. Now with more wisdom and maturity, she recognizes that factory work—in management or otherwise—was not her calling. Her dismissal set off a flurry of additional job applications. Without school and sports to keep her occupied, Cathy launched into that frenzied 1980s ritual of scanning newspapers for job ads, circling various prospects, and hoping for more interviews.

After a stint in cosmetics—which had proven quickly to be a bore—Cathy moved from one retail job to another. In one case she was hired as a salesperson at a family-owned cowboy boot shop. Such western-themed apparel was a popular fad at the time, and Cathy took the job to heart. The aging owner, it turned out, needed someone dependable to staff the shop and to assist with sales on the floor. Channeling her past experiences along with a healthy dose of determination, Cathy sold boots with unrelenting vigor. Impressed by her self-initiative, the owner eventually awarded her with more oversight of the shop's operations. He even listened to Cathy's ideas on how to organize and operate the store to attract customers more effectively. It was not long before she was essentially running the place.

Despite her best efforts and new leadership role, the expected raises and promotions failed to materialize. Perhaps worse, Cathy's mind was just not stimulated enough from the day-to-day drudgery. Lengthy downtimes between customers especially tested her patience. It was only a matter of time before she began to wander around the building to make new friends with equally bored employees at other shops. Everybody knew Cathy, as the facility became her own personal playground. In this way, she learned firsthand about the ups and downs of small-scale retailing. She naturally lasted only a few months before growing weary of the whole thing. Neither retailing nor factory work would be in her future, it seemed. If nothing else, she was learning what types of jobs and sectors to avoid while gaining some diverse experiences.

A New Path

One day a girlfriend called with yet another job opportunity. At this point one might have forgiven Cathy for dismissing such ideas outright. She thought, *Oh no, here we go again.* Her girlfriends were running a less than impressive track record with employment advice. But Cathy listened anyway, always curious to hear what might lie ahead. As she recalls, her friend basically said, "Look, this is a part-time job that requires you to be stationed in various hotels selling tour tickets to the tourists who are staying at the hotel." Beyond that, Cathy would confirm flights and book optional tours which were available from a brochure.

Hearing this idea, Cathy's ears perked up with newfound curiosity. Her first instinct was that it would be fun—one of Cathy's standard criteria—which made the decision a no-brainer. She interviewed and took the job selling tour tickets for a travel agency.

At first, she was directed to greet visitors at various hotel desks around the city while selling them tickets for guided tours. Each tour desk was only open for a few hours each day. Because these desks were located prominently within hotel lobbies, Cathy gradually experienced different parts of Singapore's downtown area. Many guests were already staying at these hotels, and Cathy learned to set up day tours for them. In her case there was no need for "hard sells." She explains, "We didn't just run up to guests and throw a brochure in their hands," she laughs. "That would not go over well. Our company already had permanent desks at these hotels. I was a roving person who moved from hotel to hotel for a few hours each time."

While not hiding behind pillars to jump out at guests, the agency was not beyond using more subtle approaches. At any given hotel, Cathy was tasked with calling the guest rooms of the agency's clients. She or her coworkers then invited their guests to visit them in the lobby, especially to confirm flights and related logistics. "This was how we got them motivated to come down to see us," she recalls, smirking. Then she adds for more clarity, "The travel agency pays for the desk space, to staff a person like me to sit there. Our guests can then stop by and book a day tour with us, or they can ask to confirm flights. So, people came to us. But it was very competitive in those days. There were maybe five or six travel agencies selling basically the same packages. These were early years of tourism development, and the tours at the time were very basic."

At peak times her agency claimed 30 or 40 guests staying at any given hotel. Singapore's budding tourism industry at the time relied primarily on the country's existing cultural character and tropical environment. This was a stopover country, where people might stay for a day or two before continuing with their journey elsewhere. Cathy adds, "We had a lot of British and

Australian travelers, for instance, who wanted something to do between flights. So, it wasn't very difficult to sell day tours. It was better still if they came with a truckload of children, because then we had even more tickets to sell," she laughs fiendishly.

With more confidence in her newfound role, Cathy's sales instincts came roaring back. She was particularly motivated with the promise of a small commission for every tour she sold. "I earned something like two dollars for each tour ticket," she explains. "So, as I sat there, the more tickets I sold, the more money I made. Remember, this was back in the 1980s. Travel agents don't operate this way anymore, since almost everyone books hotels and tours online now. That's why I now find a lot of tour guides promoting themselves on various platforms. It's risky for the guides to get paid through the internet, however, so I don't rely on those platforms. I still have to use my big mouth, just like I did when I was selling toilet cleaner!" She laughs, thinking back to her first sales job.

From Cathy's perch at each hotel, she could observe the larger tourism scene flowing around her sales desk. While gawking at the gleaming motor coaches arriving outside, she paid special attention to the stylish tour guides stepping elegantly off their buses. She was particularly fascinated with—once again—the way guides dressed during their tours. In the 1980s many wore professional, standardized outfits, resembling those of flight attendants. Such a dress code commanded respect as well as a sense of identity.

On one particular day, a guide emerged from her motor coach with what Cathy interpreted as an air of confidence and swagger. Cathy noted that the guide knew where people needed to be and was providing direction to those under her care. The guide then made her way quickly into the hotel with a clear sense of purpose.

Experiencing something of an epiphany, Cathy immediately realized, "That's what I want to do!" As Cathy watched other experienced guides attend to the business at hand, she focused especially on their speaking roles. She explains, "What the guides did was very interesting, talking on the microphone. I saw their tours and thought I'd like to do that, too." Still, she knew that such a dream was likely unrealistic given her general lack of education. Achieving the grades of a stellar student had not been in the cards. She adds, "I didn't do so well in secondary school, as I only passed two subjects, English and math, and I kept failing the rest. I had too much going on in my life, so that's why I didn't do well on the exams. Eventually I graduated, but barely, only by scraping through." During her stint at the hotel tour desks, she learned that becoming licensed as an official tour guide would typically require a college degree. This knowledge poured cold water on her dream, and she considered once again how to move forward.

Sometimes her naturally optimistic outlook kicked in when encountering such roadblocks. She wisely kept in mind that when some doors close, others tend to open with unforeseen opportunities. While attending to her desk one day, Cathy was approached by her stressed-out supervisor who was clearly fit to be tied. Pleasantries aside, Cathy was asked if she could temporarily assist with various tasks at the travel agency's office, as they were severely shorthanded. Weekends were particularly understaffed. *Sure, why not?* Cathy thought once again. Her self-proclaimed *chiong* factor kicked in. Here was yet another learning opportunity, with little warning or lead time. And, of course, she would rarely turn down additional income.

Unlike her ill-fated factory job, she arrived to this job on time. Her supervisor hastily showed her around the office with some minimalist training, after which she was quickly anointed as a new office assistant.

While still reliably staffing the hotel desks during the week, Cathy took on this new role on weekends when other employees were less available. Her primary responsibility involved planning the bookings and preparing the visitor manifests for the next day's tours. To do so, she needed to become comfortable with the tour content—or *products*, as they say in the industry—and assist visitors with planning their time. She relished the new learning curve and jumped into these roles quickly. There was little down time, as she ramped up her knowledge on local tour destinations, scheduling, and travel logistics.

At some point a light dawned in her head. "Wow, the company is actually paying me to learn here," she realized. While moving from job to job within the agency, Cathy's set of skills continued to expand. This was the quintessential "snowball effect." Each new skill built on her previous ones as she gradually assumed greater responsibilities. With her previously comfortable role as a student suddenly concluded at age 16, her awareness of how companies trained their employees became all the more important. And now her travel agency was providing this very opportunity.

Aside from the valuable benefits of learning, the ever-present need to secure a stable income remained Cathy's foremost concern. She was sometimes called upon to support various family members as well, living from one paycheck to the next. Assisting her aging Mama became an ever-greater priority. She explains, "Every five cents, ten cents, a dollar, it all made a lot of difference in my life. For every one dollar I spent, I was trying to save two dollars. This was a very Chinese mentality—and don't forget that I'm 99.9 percent Chinese," she quips—conveniently avoiding the thought of her father's own Scottish lineage.

Each success provided steppingstones to others. After

turning nineteen, she was introduced to a competing travel agency by yet another friend. This agency was searching for a full-time tour assistant, and Cathy was encouraged to interview. Given her previous weekend office experience, she was offered the job, and Cathy did not need to think twice about it. She had just landed her first stable, full-time job in Singapore's budding tourism industry.

Rather than hopscotching from hotel to hotel, this was solely an office job where she enjoyed her own workstation. She quickly assumed the role of an inbound travel agent, focused on planning and coordinating all the daily excursions. During those years the so-called *pickup tours* were popular. Travelers staying at local hotels took shuttle buses to a designated pickup spot in the city, where they were ushered into groups to begin the actual tour.

Always a quick study, Cathy gained enough confidence to earn the attention of her supervisors once again. She was eventually put in charge of coordinating and organizing all the tours. During these heady years of early tourism development, Singapore had not yet become flooded with travel companies—nor with well-trained employees. Though Cathy may not have realized the bigger picture, practically anyone with drive and initiative could get in on the ground floor. To say it another way, this was Cathy's time to shine.

What happened next was perhaps inevitable. Continued shortages of licensed tour guides eventually led to Cathy's first opportunity to lead private tours herself. At that time leading tours without a license was still legal, but only in certain situations. The principal requirement for becoming a tour guide was a university degree. The only alternative for non-degree holders was to gain at least three years of experience working for a travel agency. Consequently, office coordinators like Cathy had an opportunity to be trained as tour guides, but only to lead small groups of four people or less. Fortunate for her, Cathy's manager had already begun to train her as a tour guide even while she still worked as an office coordinator. She explains more about this standard. "To be a tour guide, you needed A-level grades in college and proficiency in two languages. This is why I always emphasize education when I speak to young people. Back then, it took a lot of confidence and proficiency in English to be able to qualify for the tour guide interview."

What she did have was the perseverance to work around the degree requirement. She consistently jumped on opportunities and gained more practical experience. Upon reaching the three-year mark with her latest employer, Cathy's boss encouraged her to enroll in the official tour guiding course. This would be a huge leap, even for Cathy's own self-initiative. Guiding is not a profession for which one can simply jump on the bus, grab the microphone, and say "Here we go." Even after meeting the minimum qualifications, there is a formal, six month-long course to pass. A tour guide license needs to be earned and in hand well before interacting with larger tour groups.

These were boom times. The number of visitors to Singapore continued to surge, with little planning to direct the growth. As such, her travel agency was regularly shorthanded and understaffed. Cathy thus unwittingly found herself joining her country's latest economic venture—that of selling Singapore to foreigners. Prior to the 1980s, Singapore's leaders paid little attention to tourism as a potential growth industry. And perhaps for good reason. Since its independence, the young nation had been knee-deep in problem-solving mode. The primary focus was on building high-rise flats at break-neck speed during the 1970s and 1980s to effectively house a vastly overcrowded population. The thought of entertaining—let alone intently attracting—visitors was just not on the priority list for national leaders at the time.

While Cathy navigated her teenage years, Singapore's private business sector was solely responsible for providing tourism accommodations. The government rarely got involved with tourism development or long-term planning. Responding to the growth in visitor numbers, corporations gradually added new, attractive hotel properties to the urban scene. These included the Singapore Hilton, Shangri-La Hotel, and the Mandarin Hotel, followed later by the likes of the Oriental, the Marina Mandarin, and the Pan Pacific.

What still lacked, according to keen government observers, was an appropriate array of attractions to entertain these newcomers. Aside from cultural tourists who were already enamored with the colorful urban scene, most people needed something to do. Along this vein, only a few minor projects were completed throughout the 1970s. These most notably included the Handicraft Centre, the Rasa Singapore Food Centre, and the Instant Asia Cultural Show.

If there was any conscious effort to promote Singapore at all, early planners rallied around the theme of *Instant Asia*. The idea was for visitors to enjoy the full range of Asian cultural experiences in one convenient stop. This notion took advantage of Singapore's existing multicultural population which ranged from Chinese and Indian to Middle Eastern and Eurasian.

Eventually higher-level government officials took notice. And paradoxically, the existing reasons for visiting Singapore at the time were rapidly disappearing. The pre-modern "charm" of old Singapore was being methodically demolished through continual land clearance, high-rise development, and erasure of historical sites and neighborhoods. The Singapore River was being cleaned up, which also meant the wholesale removal of traditional *lighter* boats and small-scale river trade (see *The Lighters* for more on their story). As would eventually become apparent the world over, these were precisely the types of authentic, culturally rich places that many visitors hoped to experience. Singapore was—according to locals and visitors alike—becoming a city without a soul.

Understandably, Cathy held little awareness of these larger-scale trends, entrenched as she was in her first tourism jobs. Important decisions on what to save from the wrecking ball occurred in the presence of consultants in corporate and government board rooms. Meanwhile, the tourism agencies on the ground were desperately trying to serve throngs of visitors who managed to find their way into the country. In this respect, Cathy found herself once again in the right place at the right time. And ready or not, it was time for Cathy to board the bus.

Chapter 19

A Coveted License

Without the official guide license, Cathy was allowed to take only four visitors at a time on any given tour. Only licensed guides were qualified and formally trained to handle full busloads of tourists. Normally the four-person limit would have allowed aspiring guides like Cathy to ease into the profession gradually. But these were no ordinary times, as the supply of available tour guides fell far short of the increasing demand for tours. The shortage was bad enough that her reeling agency made a bold and desperate decision. Some employees without licenses were deployed to lead entire motorcoaches packed with visitors. "It was okay doing that, as long as you didn't get caught," Cathy explained sheepishly, thinking back to the risks. "I ended up leading full bus tours at age 19, for as many as 40 people at a time. That's just craziness, looking back. It was just sheer luck that I didn't get caught," she admits. "But one of my friends *did* get caught, and she was banned for life from taking the tour guide training course."

Fortunately for her friend, being banned from the course was not necessarily the worst outcome. Cathy says, "It turns out that she really wasn't too interested in becoming a tour guide anyway. She ended up going into another industry, and we remained good friends. Then she went up the ranks in her company and even became a supervisor." She then speculates, "So, maybe it was meant to be, and maybe my friend thought, *Thank God, they caught me on the bus, so that I don't have to deal with this.* She has a great life and career. Even those of us who went through the training course were not all necessarily meant for guiding. Some people discover that afterwards," she concludes.

As to why her company took such risks at the time, she explains, "This was my boss' way of making money in the first place, because we always had the problem that there were not enough tour guides. In those days, a lot of people visiting Singapore decided on the spot to do pickup tours during the day, from their hotels. They didn't usually come on private, pre-booked tours like they do now. So, we would offer, say, five or six different tours, and each tour would require maybe four or five buses throughout the day. So, my boss struggled to find enough licensed guides to fill the buses. If possible, the unlicensed guides like us would take the smaller buses with a few people, while the main licensed guides did the bigger ones. That would be fine. But if duty called, we'd need to take a full busload, which was nerve-racking. I couldn't just sit and chit-chat with the guests informally while getting to know them better. I had to lead and entertain the group. And, of course, I was very nervous, and so were the other new guides in the same situation. Unless something's wrong with you, everybody's nervous about speaking in front of 40 people! But the benefit was that we were thrown into the deep end of the bus, so to speak; you either do it or you don't."

As with previous supervisors, Cathy developed a "love-hate relationship" with her boss. He certainly appreciated her spunk and work ethic but also recognized she "had a big mouth," as Cathy readily admits. In this way, not much had changed since her school days. But her schooling had prepared her well for these early jobs. Her writing, reading, and thinking skills—not to mention her professional speaking—allowed her to jump in and accomplish the necessary duties with relative ease.

It was not long after her three-year anniversary with the agency when her boss sent Cathy and her peers to the official tour guide training course. At barely 21, she was among the youngest to ever attend. The irony was not lost on her that, had she been at university instead, she would not yet have graduated. She was therefore trying for her license ahead of schedule. The course itself was rigorous. Students were required to attend two nights per week, from 6:30 to 10:00, for a total of six months. Weekends were reserved for required fieldtrips when class members practiced and honed their skills.

One vital purpose for the weekly field outings was to learn about the very places they would feature on their tours. In one sense, Cathy and her peers were gaining a crash course on Singapore's history, geography, and urban development. They needed to gain and demonstrate full confidence with teaching outdoors, not unlike a college geography course. Speaking of this, Cathy states, "You had better know what you're talking about in each place, or what's the point of guiding?" The course provided copious volumes of material related to each site for the students to quickly digest. Only days later they were expected to expound on such topics in a clear, confident manner. "Either you came into the course a comfortable public speaker, or you had better learn fast," she adds.

Although the tour guiding course has been modified over the years, effective public speaking has always remained vital. During the weekend outings, student guides are expected to lead and conduct their own talks themselves, imitating conditions of an actual tour. They are further expected to talk from various angles with respect to the group, such as from their right and left sides, front and center, or standing on doorsteps along the sidewalk, for instance. Versatility was key to adapt quickly in any given local situation. Voice projection, body language, mannerisms, and clarity of speech are skills that students are expected to develop and demonstrate proficiently. In sum, they are learning how to present themselves appropriately in front of a group, and how to seek out the most opportunistic stopping locations to do so.

As with any challenging course, some students fare better than others. Cathy explains, "For a lot of new guides who don't make it, it's because they don't feel confident holding the microphone and hearing their own voice. Unless they work as a team with smaller groups to gain confidence, the microphone can be unnerving with large groups. The instructors have licensed mentors to help them develop these skills." Now an experienced guide herself, Cathy occasionally has trainees attending her tours. Sometimes she is even hired on the side to lead them on various training exercises.

Legal or otherwise, Cathy's early experiences provided considerable on-the-ground training that many other students did not yet have. She recalls, "It was easier for us in that course at the time because there were only a few of us, and we were already doing it—leading tours and learning by experience. And most of my peers were coming from other jobs, not starting in the tourism industry like I was, so some of them had more difficulties coping with the course. So, I learned from a combination of early experiences, but not from our own in-house Tourism Board. I guess we had our own training by being thrown into the deep end!"

Following the six-month course, each individual student appeared before members of the Tourism Board for formal interviews. "The joke of it all," Cathy adds, "was that our boss was one of the panelists of judges on the Board." This fact certainly did not hurt her own chances. She adds, "My boss knew when we would be ready to complete the course, which is why he sent us when he did. It was strategic on his part, looking back. The company even paid the $1,200 course fee, so I guess he was betting on our success."

With the coveted license now in hand, Cathy faced an important decision. One option was to become bonded with this same company. This meant she would not be allowed to work as a guide for another agency for a minimum of two years. The alternative was to strike out on her own and become an independent tour guide right away. In this latter scenario, any one of Singapore's travel agencies could hire her for various tours—but only if she could convince them to do so. Some of her peers cautioned her from becoming bonded. They believed this would limit Cathy's flexibility and possibly lead to corporate exploitation. Nor could she determine her own hours or decide which tours to accept and reject.

Despite these apparent downsides, Cathy ultimately chose to become bonded. She realized that her youthfulness would provide more flexibility in future years; nothing was preventing her from freelancing after the two-year minimum. She further preferred a welcome sense of stability with the same company. And no surprise, she dove in headfirst. Reflecting on this pivotal choice, she explains, "I had my own theory. If you are bonded, the company is responsible for grooming and training you, so that you learn things and gain more vital experiences. You also gain more exposure in the industry. Then, when you come out on your own, you will be more valuable and can get employment anywhere. It was only for two years, and I was young. What's the problem with two years?" she asks rhetorically, continuing, "It was all good. Sure, we were paid an allowance, not a full guide fee. We were paid like $4.00 for a half-day tour—say, a city tour between 9:00-12:30. A full day tour would pay around $11. Night tours would add another $7.

Yes, it was pathetic in terms of wages, even in those days, but it kept the money coming in."

Even with unparalleled enthusiasm, Cathy soon learned the rigors of a full-time job. She aimed to impress her supervisors as much as she wanted to learn, so she jumped right in. In response, her company threw plenty of work her way. It was ultimately her youth and personal drive that carried her through those first grueling years. Tours were often scheduled back-to-back with little time for breaks, and they were offered on nearly every weekday. Little rest was to be had on the weekends, as they were reserved for longer day tours. This ambitious schedule led to Cathy sometimes leading tours seven days a week, with up to three tours each day. On weekdays, the first morning tour was followed by a short break and then a second afternoon tour. Cathy then caught a bite to eat before setting out again on a night tour until 10:00. This might be followed in turn by, as she admits, "a couple of hours of clubbing to end the day."

For her part, Cathy mainly conducted large group tours until her bonding was concluded. Instead of rushing away when her two-year term ended, however, she took advantage of existing relationships and simply remained with the same agency. The difference was that she now worked as a freelancer. In this role, the comfort of a small salary disappeared because she was no longer a permanent employee. The flipside was that she could earn a larger guiding fee for each tour. Other companies were now free to hire her as well, given her proven experience. By now she felt comfortable with the system, thanks to her first two years as a licensed guide. Her earlier theory had played out well.

Cathy's winning combination of curiosity and self-initiative led her to embrace numerous types of tours over the next few years. She essentially became a *hawker* of her own making.

That is, she bid out her services for various jobs through different agencies. After an agency scheduled an upcoming tour, they would call Cathy to ask if she was interested in leading it. During those early years—as for much of her career—her answer was simple: "Oh, sure, I'll take it." She elaborates, "When you want to be a hawker, you need continuous training. You need to go out and 'niche' yourself in the sense that you go for product knowledge training. You do more research, and you try to integrate into a company devoted to specific types of tours. With this continuous effort, the companies become familiar with you as a tour guide, and so they will be more likely to call when jobs arise."

True to her earlier prediction, Cathy was eventually able to join a pool of reliable tour guides placed on a shortlist to be called first. This steady and determined approach gradually allowed her to escape her constant sense of financial insecurity.

One of Cathy's earliest regular tours was to a curious destination known as Tang Dynasty Village. First opened in 1992, the Village was billed as one of Singapore's leading new attractions. The hype was short-lived, however, as the operation was shuttered only seven years later. From the outset, however, the development was truly ambitious. Its enormous expanse covered 12 hectares—or approximately 18 European football (soccer) pitches. Surrounded by a three-meter-tall replica of the Great Wall of China, the park was designed as a space to produce Chinese films. The grand vision was to establish the park as the launching point for Singapore's own movie industry. The park's design was largely based on its predecessor in Hong Kong, the similarly named Sung Dynasty Village.

Unfortunately, a combination of high entrance fees and an underwhelming collection of exhibits contributed to the park's early demise. The property eventually became a "white elephant" for Singapore, leaving the leadership perplexed about the site's future. Eventually the park fell into disrepair and was abandoned after its closure in 1999. By 2008 any remaining traces had disappeared from the scene. Cathy's timing, however, was once again impeccable. Her earlier tours usually included visits to the ill-fated theme park, but during its earlier and most successful years.

As she passed through the park with her clients in tow, she often took note of a fortune teller, or psychic perched at his own station. During one such visit, temptation won over, and she sat down to hear her fortune. Among other revelations came the shocking knowledge that she would be divorced due to her short temper and would not get remarried. In better news, she would become independently wealthy by the age of 30. Although the man was clearly delusional on both counts, Cathy felt that the first prediction would be more realistic than the second. Not only did she rely on a secondary school education, but she was also the primary income producer for her makeshift household. Wealthy by 30? Not likely.

She did hold onto some lingering hope that tour guiding would land her a fairy-tale marriage to a wealthy foreigner. But even this dreamy scenario did not strike her as particularly appealing. Now many years later she remains a married woman to her original husband. And as for the wealth, she protests: "I still have the same small income, you liar!" She laughs and waves her hand, recalling the absurd prediction.

Even Cathy is not beyond hoping to strike it rich one day. Let's face it, few people are. But on a positive note, she has gradually become more confident with respect to her own family's security. The mortgage for their flat is now fully paid, and their children are making their way with their own lives. These are all markers of "instant wealth," she explains, which together may be more valuable than monetary assets in the bank.

Reflecting on whether she feels she has "made it" financially, she views this more as a gradual process. With her first jobs following secondary school, her focus remained laser sharp. Her main goal was little more than short-term survival, and employment was always necessary. As she says with some sarcasm thrown in, "You don't get a job to become wealthy, which is never." Looking back, she now feels fortunate that one could still find employment during the 1980s without a college degree.

Considering her own adult children, Cathy believes that today's educational system better provides young people with the tools to succeed—that is, if they are fortunate to be college bound. During her years at convent school, she may not have been college material herself. But she nonetheless gained a valuable educational foundation to be employable in the work force. "Then you just start pushing yourself," as she counseled herself during the 1980s. "And eventually the opportunities will come. You need to find early employment, gain some useful skills and experiences, and then start working toward your own independence." This was the model on which Cathy depended, betting less on fortune tellers and more on her own steadfast perseverance. Whether it was the *chiong* factor or true grit, it's what she had to do.

Chapter 20

A Second Reunion

When not diligently working toward her license, Cathy valiantly tried to maintain some semblance of a social life. This included anything from "crashing" the birthday parties of mutual friends, to continuing her weekend activities at church.

Occasionally the universe can provide a nudge when least expected. While walking to church one day, Cathy ran into one of her half-brothers. Having reacquainted, he said something like, "Oh, Mommy would love to see you. I'm sure she'd love it if you visited her." A skeptical Cathy reacted with a raised eyebrow and silent pause—something rare for this otherwise verbose teen.

As the church service progressed, Cathy ruminated more on this back-door invitation to reunite with her mother. She had further learned that Mike, her strange stepfather, had already passed away. This was little surprise, given that he was Mary's senior by three decades. Beyond all of this was Cathy's aging grandmother, who was paying ever-less attention to Cathy's whereabouts. With all these calculations swirling through her head—never mind the church service—she finally relented. *Oh, why not, let's go find Mommy*, she thought. After church she and her half-brother, Joe, headed there together while catching up on the latest family news.

Upon Cathy's unplanned arrival, the rejoicing commenced immediately. Even Cathy had not prepared for the upwelling of joyful emotions that bubbled up after not seeing her mother for years. They both cried "buckets of tears, until mommy's whole estate was flooded," she fondly recalls. She had evidently made a wise choice to reconnect, and they spent some quality time catching up. There was plenty to discuss. Her mother remained at somewhat of a loss due to Mike' passing, while Cathy was focused on a promising new career path.

Moving forward, Cathy found herself on better terms than ever with her mother. Their visits multiplied quickly, behaving like old friends. Even with Cathy's fast-paced lifestyle, she managed to find time for her mother and has continued to do so. Now an active grandmother herself, Mary readily participates in the lives of Cathy's own family. Both mother and daughter are undoubtedly relieved that a third reunion has never been necessary. Under the circumstances, two was quite enough.

Cathy attributes her decision to reunite with her mother to an innately positive outlook on life. She further enjoys a rare ability to forgive prior transgressions. To this day she remains sympathetic to her mother's early challenges, believing Mary had made the wise choice to leave her father. Cathy explains, "I have no animosity because, through the years growing up, life was not as easy for me as it seemingly was for my sister. She had a good life because she was pampered by my grandmother. For me, I was always moving from one place to another, living with all the aunties and uncles. These were people who spent time liking me, being away from Mama."

With her uncanny adeptness to find silver linings, she adds, "But you know what? My mother was the luckiest woman in the whole wide world. She was only with my father for two years. But my stepmother—the second one, Jessie—has been with him, like, forever, with all those years of abuse," she says, trying to suppress some underlying anger. "So that's why my mother always says she is so lucky. Her second husband passed on, since he was old enough to be her father. And they had three boys—my half-brothers—so finally when he died, she was alone with them. This was when I found her again."

During subsequent visits, Cathy gradually learned more about her mother's recent backstory—perhaps more than she had bargained for. Mike's accumulated wealth and properties were legally passed down to Mary. It turns out he had died several years before Cathy reappeared. Her three half-brothers had still been quite young, and Mike had left his family with not one, but two private properties. Mary decided to stay and live in their spacious home while selling off the second one. The proceeds were wisely reserved to secure her boys' future educations and other necessary expenses.

But there was more to Mary's story, as Cathy enjoys telling quietly. She now turns to a whisper, as if gossiping with friends. "After Mike died, there was this ice cream man who used to come around with a motorbike—a hawker who would sell ice cream. She allowed him to park his bike in her house. So, my busybody Mama, she gets wind of this type of news very fast—she's like CNN or BBC, you know," Cathy laughs, then continues. "Mama then started spreading this rumor that my mother was now going out with the ice cream man. But it turns out that it was more complicated. The ice cream man had a friend, Richard, who would stay down the road, and my mother fell in love with him! By then she was a widow with three boys, who were small when Mike passed on. So, Richard would come to visit, and they eventually got married. Before that, he asked my mother how she was going to survive in this big house. He had said, 'You need a smaller house, if I'm going to marry you.' This is how my mother knew he was genuine, because he didn't know that she owned the house! And then she got pregnant, of course. They got married and had the full wedding after that, when she was already a few months pregnant. Her stomach was already big. So, we joke that it was a shotgun marriage. We always tease her daughter—my new half-sister, Melissa—that she's a shotgun baby, and we all laugh."

For those keeping track, this means that Cathy's mother had successfully given birth to seven children through a total of three marriages—first to the twins and Cathy, followed by their three half-brothers with Mike. Then came a new half-sister, Melissa. As of this writing Cathy remains in contact with all her half-siblings in one way or another—most often during holidays and large family events.

It should be noted that none of these relations involve Cathy's husband's side of the family, which is likewise packed with its own lengthy string of relatives. For his part, Tony has six siblings of his own, each with a separate family. When asked if she finds it challenging to keep track of everyone, Cathy provides a quintessentially upbeat response. "No, it's not difficult for me, because I am *headquarters*. I'm the busybody of the estate," she laughs at one of her favorite self-descriptions. "So, some people who are introverts, they don't like this kind of life, being related to so many people, with everyone always having so much to say. But for me and my children, every time there's a family function, it's a meeting of everybody—a reunion. And it's fun! And the cousins get along. And my mother's house is packed to the brim when it's Christmas, because now my four other siblings have their own families and children. So, my mother has about 12 grandchildren, and she's only 77 years old. Think of what I would have missed out on had I not reunited with her."

Chapter 21

Precious Earrings

Just as one might expect from teenagers, Cathy attracted her share of interest from male counterparts. Some were even occasionally elevated to the status of boyfriend. Still, none of these superficial relationships ever transitioned into anything serious or long-lasting. They came and went like friends naturally do at that age. Most of these pseudo-romantic interests emerged from her days of clubbing. Her female friends predictably had their own brothers, to whom the young women would be introduced.

This is how Cathy eventually met her future husband, Tony, though she thought nothing of it at the time. As of this first encounter, Tony was already 21 years old and enlisted in the Army. All young men are conscripted for two years to serve in one of Singapore's Armed Forces (see *Supporting the Troops* for more). At this point Cathy was barely 16, five years younger. Despite the age difference, they went out casually for a while—at least until Tony managed to get on her nerves one too many times. When she broke off the relationship, they both moved on with little regret.

During their brief time together, she had already become acquainted with Tony's immediate family, and vice-versa. During one Chinese New Year she was even invited to meet his parents. This was admittedly a risky move for both of them. Still a smoker, Cathy lit up at the wrong time. Tony's mother valiantly tried to dissuade him from going out with her, primarily because of that very habit. But Tony retorted that his mother smoked as well, instantly calling out the hypocrisy. No matter, Cathy had little interest in impressing his family, as she hardly viewed Tony as a long-term prospect. Having been cleared to smoke by her mystery grandfather, she simply brushed off his mother's disapproval. Many other teens and adults smoked, so why not her?

Only years later did Cathy learn why Tony's mother smoked. Much like Meiling back in the kampong, she had grown up in a less developed rural area with rudimentary services. When finding it necessary to visit the outhouse, the mosquitos and related pests were nearly unbearable. A lit cigarette at least gave her a fighting chance to avoid being eaten alive. This became a common story for many Singaporeans living in similar conditions.

Regardless of how any of them began to smoke, the larger truth was that Tony's mother never seemed to warm up to Cathy. As Cathy perceived things, his mother remained aloof and distant, never particularly welcoming. At the time, however, Cathy disregarded her cold demeanor because, as she retorts, "It was not like I was going to marry the boy!" And for some time, she would be right. After letting him go, other boyfriends cycled through for another three years. More than anything, Cathy became engrossed with her new career. She consequently focused her energies on matters of employment more than on matters of the heart.

At some point between dismissing Tony and jumping headlong into the tourism industry, Cathy celebrated her eighteenth birthday on 9 February 1985. It was a modest affair, as most things were in her life. Still, this seemed to represent a milestone, or turning point. She was clearly transitioning from schoolgirl to more of an independent young woman with a new life to get on with.

As her birthday progressed, Uncle Kellard managed to get her attention at home. He had something special to reveal, motioning her to a drawer in his room. At his prodding, she opened it to find a small yet elegant jewelry-sized box with a hinge. Inside was a pair of gold, heart-shaped earrings gleaming back at her. Not one accustomed to such lavish gifts, Cathy stood there in absolute shock. No doubt, this was the reaction he sought. Trying to hold back tears—perhaps unsuccessfully— she gently hugged her uncle and thanked him profusely. She wanted very much to ask where in the world he had found the pair. But she held back, content to accept this rare gift.

Something else overshadowed her curiosity about the earrings. She was burdened by a nagging concern about his own health. He had been strangely ill for the better part of a year, with little sign of improvement. Only four days after receiving the earrings—and the day before Valentine's Day—Kellard Maine Ross succumbed to throat cancer at age 45. Of course, Cathy was devastated. Even though she and others sensed something was wrong, there was little to prepare her for this sudden loss in her life. Not even all the prayers to the statues at St. Joseph's could help her account for Kellard's early departure from the earth.

His untimely death shook her profoundly. She had always appreciated his kindness and support since she could remember. After his death she wrote in a school essay that he had been the "sweetest of the sweets," most certainly her favorite uncle. Though for different reasons, his role was comparable to her mysterious grandfather who had also looked after her prior to his own untimely death.

Kellard's ensuing autopsy and death report only added to

the sadness. His throat cancer had been caused by a long-term exposure to asbestos, a serious side effect of working in the insulation business. Little awareness existed—at least publicly—about the risks of this hazardous substance. It was more than ironic that the job provided as an act of familial kindness had ultimately led to his early passing.

Compounding this heartache was the unforeseen financial fallout. The flat now passed on to Mama, who was responsible once again for supporting the household. This only intensified Cathy's motivation to make up for Kellard's income. For some time, she jumped from one job to the next as described earlier. Yet another headache emerged with the news that Mama would not be paid the life insurance from Kellard's death for some strange reason. Really, could life become any more unfair?

Aside from his immediate family, Kellard left behind a beloved, if unofficial, partner named Begam. This young Indian woman from the tenth floor of Cathy's estate had tutored the girls in various subjects when they were younger, especially in math and English. At first, Kellard was only mildly smitten with Begam's occasional visits. He then began a pattern of returning from work each day with an afternoon edition of the daily newspaper, intentionally lending it to Begam before she departed for the night. This was his excuse to strike up future conversations, and things progressed from newspapers to full-blown courtship.

In Cathy's mind their budding relationship was just nice to see; there was something enjoyable about the idea of them going out together. At some point, of course, their romance earned the attention of Begam's Muslim family. Her relationship quickly became a subject of contention, as Cathy vividly recalls. "The first problem was that my uncle was almost 20 years older than she was. And there was the fact that she was from an Indian Muslim family—not Hindu. This was rare but not unheard of. Her mother was upset that my uncle was not the same race, or religion. Her own brother wasn't happy about it either. He used to beat her up for continuing to see my uncle. From then on, she had to slip out secretly on her own to see him. He would meet her and go for bicycle rides or to the movies—but quietly. Mama didn't like it, either, but she gave Kellard a pass because he was older and was already a bachelor on his own."

If that were not enough family drama, an even stranger reason prevented the pair from ever marrying. Cathy continues, "Begam's mother went to a fortune teller, who warned her not to marry this man because he was going to die young. But Begam was like, *whatever*. She didn't take it seriously, and after all, they were in love. She also accused her mother of making up the fortune-teller story because she already didn't like Kellard. What really scared her mother was the thought of her daughter converting to Catholicism if they got married. Of course, the fortune turned out to be true, whether a coincidence or not."

Regardless of her family's staunch disapproval, Begam stubbornly remained with Kellard through the rest of his life. The next part of the story could have come straight out of a romantic comedy. Begam's mother regularly tried to set her up with men whom they considered worthwhile suitors. The family dinners accompanied by awkward, single men seemed endless, as were Begam's typical eyerolls. One particular factor actually dissuaded her male admirers—namely, her family's requirement of an unreasonably high dowry. Her mother even worked with family members back in India to find someone suitable, but nothing ever came to pass. Meanwhile Begam continued to enjoy the company of her one true love. When the cancer was diagnosed and continued its unrelenting toll, Begam stuck with him through thick and thin. Even after losing

Kellard, she never married anyone else.

In Cathy's quintessential way, she joyfully remains friends with Begam to this day. She adds happily, "To me she is still very nice, and I keep in touch with her. I always bring her a meal on her birthday. She's like a mother to me—well, like an auntie, since she's only ten years older than I am," she chuckles while correcting herself. "After Ramadan, they hold the celebration of *Hari Raya* and I'll go to her house for the end of Ramadan, and sometimes she will come to visit us for Christmas. We still love each other a lot." No doubt, Begam provides a warm reminder of her cherished uncle who departed from her own life much too soon.

Chapter 22

Four Cultures and a Wedding

Approximately one year after Kellard died, Cathy rekindled her friendship with Tony. She had made the conscious decision to take the tenuous relationship more seriously. It is entirely possible that her return to Tony was driven by the emptiness she felt without her uncle. Even more so, she viewed Tony as an escape from her unpredictable life. She now suspects that both factors likely played into her decision to seek out her old boyfriend.

More important was that Cathy viewed Tony less of a "Romeo" with a gorgeous physique, and more of an all-around decent person. By this time, a more practical Cathy was looking beyond physical appearances. And, no matter, Tony was not entirely lacking on this front, either. What Cathy took most to heart, however, was that her beau was simply a nice young man. Although typically quiet and introverted, he was overall responsible, predictable and safe. Upon introducing him—again—to her own family, he stayed true to character without rubbing them the wrong way.

The exception, once again, was Cathy's tenacious grandmother. She did not like Tony one bit, and she never had anything nice to say about him. For whatever reason, it seemed that Mama would have preferred a more social, outgoing match for Cathy. In stark contrast was her sister, who was also now seriously dating her own future husband. Her boyfriend better fulfilled Mama's desire for sociability, and they even enjoyed bantering with one another, developing a rapport. Such expectations were beyond the reach of a more humble, reserved Tony. He naturally shied away from conversation and stayed to himself. If he was actively trying to endear himself to Mama's good graces, this was not the way to do it.

Once again, Cathy perceived she was being treated unfairly by the household matriarch. Nevertheless, her decision was unwavering, as she saw too much of her father in many of the other boys. They preened themselves to show off their looks and charms, which was now easy enough to see through. Cathy could sniff out their immaturity and potential abusiveness.

As her 21st birthday came and went with little fanfare, Cathy decided it was time to get married. She had recently passed the tour-guiding course and was just beginning to spread her wings as one of Singapore's more dedicated new guides. The decision made good, rational sense, she believed, now that she was more financially secure. It was also fortunate that her feelings for Tony remained persistent as well.

This all culminated in an epiphany that she needed to act soon, thinking, *I had better propose before the man runs away.* It was clear from the outset that he was not going to take the initiative himself. Still, Tony was a decent, caring human being—a fact that was admittedly refreshing. Looking back at her choices, Cathy recalls, "You wouldn't want to marry someone who's such a Casanova and plays the guitar in a band; then you end up having to feed him. In the long run, do you want a life of tears and abuse?"

The first order of business was to visit the Registry of Marriage. In a strictly legal sense, this meant the government considered the couple to be essentially married right on the spot. More practically, this first step could be compared more to an engagement, still awaiting the more formalized wedding ceremony later. What mattered most was that the registered couple was now eligible to purchase a flat of their own.

Not one to sit back and succumb to fate, a now-engaged Cathy drudged up the courage to present an idea to Mama. She said, "How about if we purchase the flat from you and you can keep the money and continue living with us?" To Cathy's absolute shock, Mama thought it was a brilliant idea and gave the go-ahead. Now 21 years old, Cathy met the minimum age to purchase an HDB flat, and with Tony she would meet the requirement of placing two family members on the title. Thinking rationally, Cathy remained content with the flat in which she had lived since age 13, and she had no burning desire to move. Further, she was eager to avoid the hassle of applying for another HDB unit. In turn, Mama would receive the full $45,000 sale price and could thus enjoy the windfall as she desired. It was a win-win situation.

Tony continued to live at home with his parents for three more years, until after their more official wedding ceremony. In the eyes of the Church and their respective families, the couple was not yet fully married as tradition would have it. In the meantime, Cathy enjoyed her new status as homeowner and began some simple updates and renovations. She finally had her own place. Overall, Cathy's strategy had been implemented nearly without a hitch, and none too soon. Mama was showing signs of dementia and was having trouble finding her way back home. Given Cathy's demanding work schedule, she eventually arranged for Mama to live with Auntie Shirley. This worked out sufficiently for some time, and when not running tours, Cathy visited with her grandmother during the day. Because of her numerous late nights at work, however, Cathy was not able to take Mama home with her for the night.

Unfortunately, this arrangement with Shirley proved unsustainable in the long run. Cathy explains, "Things got sour with my auntie, as Mama was getting frailer, and my auntie no longer wanted to look after her. I ended up taking Mama home each night because I could not afford domestic help with earning only $400 per month. To pay for home care would cost at least $500 or $600 on its own." After a "long and mysterious life," as Cathy describes it—including a brutal occupation, World War II, and being widowed early—Mama eventually left this world at the impressive age of 90.

Prior to her grandmother's passing, Cathy's purchase of her flat had been auspicious in its timing. The market value of HDB housing was skyrocketing across the city. To recall, Cathy's uncle had originally purchased their flat for around $14,000. By the time Cathy did likewise, the price had increased to $45,000. To acquire the loan from the HDB, Cathy paid the required 20 percent down payment, which she had already wisely accumulated.

While this process might resemble a mainstream, capitalist real-estate market, the vast majority of residential properties in Singapore are still considered public housing. It was the Housing and Development Board (HDB) that paid her Mama the full $45,000 sale price after Cathy was granted her loan. In this capacity the HDB serves as principal bank lender, not unlike a standard home mortgage lender in other countries.

Somewhat dampening the good fortune with her "new" home, Cathy's expenses continued to multiply. And now there was a full wedding to plan for. Tony had already left the Army and was earning very little money. For her part, Cathy had just started to move into her tour guiding role and was working practically non-stop for low wages and commissions. Still, in what was a rather rare situation for that time, Cathy was earning a much higher proportion of their total income. This also meant that the wedding expenses fell squarely on her shoulders.

Much like her own situation, Tony enjoyed little financial assistance from his family. She found no choice but to pay for the ceremony and the rings, while Tony paid for the photographer. Recalling her decision to fund her own wedding, Cathy explains, "He was already from a low-income family like mine, so whose family was going to pay whom?"

Another option might have been Cathy's birth mother, Mary. The pair had only recently reunited, with Cathy now 19. Unfortunately, Mary had been more of an acquaintance than a full-time mother, so she was not obligated to assist with the wedding costs. This also meant she could not legitimately ask for a dowry or for equivalent contributions from the groom's family. About Singapore families in general, Cathy adds, "Nobody had the capacity to pay for a wedding except yourself back then, as that was the norm. Nobody was obligated to do so."

Once again, Cathy's personal determination and problem-solving skills kicked in to save enough money on her own. Three more years passed before Cathy and Tony could finally enjoy their wedding ceremony surrounded by family and friends. They were married when Cathy was 24 and had squirreled away enough funds to pay for everything. She recalls, "I sewed my own veil, my stepmother, Jessie's sisters sewed my wedding gown for me, and my best friend from primary school, May Sin, did the hand bouquet and floral decorations for the wedding car that drove us there. May Sin worked as a florist in the marketplace, so she helped with all that. As thrifty as I was, the whole wedding was DIY—do it yourself," she laughs.

Originally the couple was scheduled to be wed on 2 June, but this conflicted with a retreat for the priests beginning that same day. The wedding was thus pushed up one day to the First of June, set to step off promptly at 10:00 in the morning. Yet another wedding was scheduled to begin two hours later. This was an admittedly brief time window, leading to an equally brief ceremony.

For Cathy's special day, she had envisioned a fully traditional Catholic wedding, including the service, Eucharist, and High Mass. In this respect a cultural misunderstanding developed between Cathy and the priest, who was helping to organize the event. She explains, "During our conversation, I told him that Tony's family was not Catholic, so he assumed that we did not need the High Mass because of the husband's family. So, they just provided the service, which I was mad about at the time, because I didn't know yet why that happened."

Perhaps as a consolation prize, the church was decked out with gorgeous floral arrangements along the pews that she had not paid for. They were inadvertently benefitting from preparations for the more lavish 12:00 wedding to follow. Of this discovery, she says, "It looked so nice! We were very blessed to have all the free decorations!"

Yet another hoop to jump through involved the Catholic Church itself. Tony and his Chinese family were Teochew and generally practiced Taoism. It was difficult to be ideologically further away from Catholicism. No surprise, Tony was not permitted to hold a wedding ceremony inside a church. The way around this, strangely enough, was for Tony to voluntarily convert to Catholicism. To his credit, he did so willingly, and his mother graciously approved.

For those familiar with the Hollywood feature film, *My Big Fat Greek Wedding* (2002), one might recall a similar scenario. In the film, Toula's fiancé, Ian Miller, was expected to join the Greek Orthodox Church as a central part of this light-hearted storyline. Likewise, Tony took the plunge to support Cathy and moved through the scripted process of "becoming" a Catholic.

Of course, Tony held little genuine interest in Catholicism, let alone any other organized religion. He was fulfilling this obligation solely for the benefit of Cathy and their marriage. To expect an instant shift of one's fundamental, life-long belief system was a tall order, and quite likely impossible. No matter, Tony could now boast of being a Catholic on paper, which conveniently allowed him to attend his own wedding. If Tony ever stepped foot into a Catholic Church again after that special day, Cathy does not know when.

One factor that assisted Tony in his conversion was his own Taoist upbringing. Cathy explains this quirky scenario from her own point of view. "It can be easier for some belief systems or religions to accept conversions than others. With all the Catholic rituals like Communion, it may be difficult for a Catholic to find a way to join another religion. But Taoism is more open, like Tony's family. Taoism is basically worshipped by anyone who wants to worship it, and if Taoists want to try other belief systems, so be it. My mother-in-law didn't have any qualms about it. So, for us it worked out okay; Tony did not feel the need to abandon all his Taoist beliefs. In other cases, the expectations of conversion can lead to marital problems and even divorce. Some Chinese people have converted to Islam or Christianity. I just can't get over the fact that one party in the marriage needs to convert. Not everybody wants to be religious. In multiracial countries like Singapore, it's probably best to be spiritual rather than religious since spiritualists are more likely to accept other belief systems."

If Ian Miller's experience in *Greek Wedding* suggested a fully Orthodox conversion, Cathy's wedding was more of a blending of Chinese and Catholic rituals. This cross-cultural mixture of customs defines the Chinese Catholic Church throughout the region. Though a staunch Catholic back then,

Cathy also identified principally as ethnic Chinese and, more specifically, Cantonese. It was therefore difficult—as with many people on earth—for either her or Tony to fit into neatly stereotypical cultural categories.

Although Tony bore the brunt of responsibility for his conversion, Cathy found the need to learn various Teochew customs in return. All told, their wedding day was a fusion between no less than four distinct cultural traditions—those of Catholicism, Taoism, Cantonese, and Teochew. She explains, "Each Chinese dialect group leaves the house at different times for a wedding. As my luck would have it, the Teochew must leave the earliest, before sunrise! His family thus left before dawn to pick up the bride, me. Also, because they are Taoist, Tony's mother prays to her idols—to various ancestors and deities. As Chinese Catholics you're allowed to carry the joss sticks, with incense, during the service to respect your dead ancestors, but not to honor the idols. For the wedding, I did not carry joss sticks because I was focused on the Catholic beliefs. So, my in-laws carried joss sticks to the altar."

There remained one additional Chinese custom which Cathy could not avoid. As she explains, "We held a tea ceremony, for which I served tea to my in-laws as a form of respect. I had to learn how to do this—how to pass the tea, hold the teapot, and offer the blessing. At our wedding, we had nice, sweet tea and a traditional tea pot with small, pretty teacups."

Along this vein, their wedding reception incorporated the Chinese custom of little red packets, provided by guests at each table. Inside the packets were varying amounts of cash in honor of the wedding couple. From a more practical perspective, a grateful Cathy was able to recoup some of the funds she had laid out for the festivities.

As might be expected, such multicultural affairs can lead to any number of misunderstandings or hurt feelings. From the perspective of Tony's parents, he was marrying a biracial woman with mixed European and Chinese ethnic backgrounds. They consequently presumed that her family had moved away from practicing the more serious Chinese cultural traditions. The fallacy here was that Cathy identified herself and much of her family as nearly 100 percent Chinese as indicated earlier. She had not even seriously considered her father's own Scottish lineage until much later in life. In the case of a wedding, the Chinese custom typically expects the mother-in-law to gift a set of jewelry to the bride. This gift would traditionally consist of four kinds of gold, in the combination of a pair of earrings, a bracelet, a gold chain, and a necklace.

While a humble Cathy would have been perfectly content with inexpensive knockoffs, she ultimately received none of it. Being human, her rational mind could not fully prevent being hurt by this apparent breach of custom. Was she not being fully accepted by Tony's mother? Such an omission could have easily signaled as much. In place of gold, Tony's mother gave Cathy money instead, which Cathy quietly perceived as highly insulting. As tradition would have it, the four kinds of gold held significant meaning. Together, the jewelry indicated that the groom's mother was taking in a new daughter as part of her family. And in any case, Tony's Chinese mother should know better! A simple cash gift—though always appreciated on its own merits—was no substitute. Despite her best effort to shrug it off, Cathy's hurt feelings lingered beneath the surface, along with some serious puzzlement.

Decades later, Cathy found herself in a casual conversation with Tony's sister at a family event. Somehow the topic of the gold jewelry surfaced again. Cathy was stunned to learn more of the backstory, not the least being that her own husband was to blame for the cultural oversight! It was Tony who had dissuaded his mother from giving Cathy any gold jewelry. He had simply believed that Cathy already owned plenty of it and told his mother as much. By Tony's own logic, he had convinced his mother that it was unnecessary to add to Cathy's existing collection. *Oops.*

To this, Cathy now admits, "I *did* have a lot of gold, because in those days, whenever I received tips or commissions, I usually purchased gold as a form of savings." In addition, she explains that Asians in general tend to invest in gold, and during the late twentieth century the precious metal was relatively inexpensive. Cathy therefore purchased chunky gold chains and related jewelry as an alternative savings account for the future.

It turns out that Tony's mother had actually felt badly about not following through with tradition. In a vain attempt to make up for it, she had decided to provide the cash gift instead. Later she also gifted Cathy a small gold chain, though she claimed this was only because it did not properly fit another family member.

Cathy still contends that Tony's mother could have simply explained all of this, as she would have better accepted the situation while chastising Tony for his youthful error. Either way, the story demonstrated how a lack of communication can inadvertently lead to hurt feelings—sometimes for years or decades. Being the rational woman Cathy grew into, she eventually traded the gold chain for a diamond bracelet and was done with it.

Chapter 23

Into the Suburbs

Now finally living together in Kellard's old flat, Cathy and Tony were required to jump through one additional hoop. This was simply to wait things out. Per HDB rules, the newlyweds were forbidden from reselling the property for a minimum of five years. This was to prevent speculators from "flipping" properties at elevated values to realize a quick profit. Three years had already passed before Tony finally moved in after the wedding. For Cathy the next two years could not go by soon enough.

Tony had barely finished moving in when she recognized that Kellard's flat came with a serious sticking point—namely, its location. Cathy became pregnant with their first child, Rachel, at age 24 and continued to work full time as a tour guide. The problematic issue involved geography and distance. Many of her tour jobs required pickups and drop-offs at Singapore's Changi International Airport, located on the extreme eastern side of the island. This meant much of her precious time each day was devoted to lengthy commutes on the bus. She then met her driver to shuttle clients between the airport and hotels. It was not so convenient to have their flat located more than an hour from the airport. Even worse, the trip was repeated late at night if she wanted to come home.

Though certainly thriving in her new job, the commute quickly became unsustainable. Added to that, her first child was on the way. Preparing for the uncertainties and logistics of motherhood only added to her stress.

The determined couple still somehow managed to outlast the five-year occupancy requirement. By then, they were already searching for a new home, this time much closer to the airport on Singapore's east side. Still enjoying the era of relatively inexpensive housing, she and Tony settled on their second—and current—home, located a mere 10-minute subway ride from the airport. In the other direction to the west, she could now access various downtown hotels on the MRT in under 20 minutes. And there was more good news. The new flat was spacious and came with one additional bedroom. This would undoubtedly prove helpful for raising a family.

Cathy and Tony were certainly not alone in wanting to upgrade to a roomier flat. By the late 1980s the HDB was now allowing residents of five years or longer to sell the lease for their flat on the open market, instead of selling it back to the HDB. Upon doing so, they could purchase yet another subsidized HDB flat more to their liking. The government's assumption was—quite in line with Cathy's choice—that residents would eventually wish to upgrade to larger, more modern flats as their families and incomes expanded. This would allow the "filtering down" of the smaller, older flats to accommodate young couples and lower-income residents looking for more modest housing prices.

It turns out the provision was a huge success. In fact, it caused a reshuffling of the urban population in ensuing years. The selling of older, smaller flats—many of them located in the downtown area—became so prevalent throughout the 1980s that the HDB ceased building their traditional, three-room units entirely. These were the smallest models offered at the time and represented the very layout of Kellard's flat.

With this government-issued success, however, came an unintended consequence. The smaller flats were now concentrated in the more convenient downtown core where many people worked. In contrast, more spacious and modern accommodations were now found on the suburban periphery. Residents were faced with an important tradeoff. One choice involved obtaining more space and amenities on the city's periphery, which necessarily came with a lengthy travel distance. The second option was to accept the older, less comfortable housing units located downtown. But these aging units provided walkable access to the downtown urban scene—and a shorter commute for many.

Perhaps predictably, these coveted downtown units fetched higher prices than the newer ones further out. The resale market for such downtown flats went through the roof, so to speak. The HDB found itself in a bind, as skyrocketing prices downtown pushed out potential lower-income residents. This is how the older downtown neighborhoods became the most highly desired—and most expensive—places to live in Singapore. This demographic situation with respect to downtown and the suburbs generally persists to this day.

Given her impeccable timing, Cathy took good advantage after running out the five-year clock. She sold her uncle's flat for an astonishing $103,000, compared to the $45,000 she had paid only five years earlier. This appreciation allowed Cathy and Tony to purchase their larger, more conveniently located home for $320,000. In Singapore, homeowners actually purchase a 99-year lease on the property, though residents typically overlook this technicality. The outcome is essentially the same as owning one's home.

Now some 25 years later with their loan paid off, they own the property outright—that is, their 99-year lease. Cathy estimates the flat to be worth double what they paid. And newer flats priced similarly would be much smaller than the one they currently enjoy. For these reasons, Cathy has no desire to move again, having found their perfect place. This may seem more like a dreamy, free-market real estate story rather than one of government subsidized public housing. But this is how Singapore creatively encourages a higher rate of home ownership among its citizens.

The impressive appreciation on her uncle's flat was worth celebrating on its own. Beyond that, Cathy and her family have benefitted from the best of both worlds. Her own commuting pattern is oriented more to the airport than to downtown. This meant that a peripheral estate provided not only a newer, more spacious flat, but also reduced her commuting time. Nor was it lost on Cathy that her biological mother, Mary, happened to live nearby as well. She was only a few stops away on the bus. Once Cathy and Tony were installed in their latest home, her mother agreed to watch the emerging grandchildren while Cathy worked overtime.

Cathy recalls those early years when they made some substantial changes. She explains, "Tony also worked very long hours, so half the time the kids were at my mother's house. My mother is located quite close, only three bus stops away, and their school was only a seven-minute walk from her house. So, if I had to work, the kids would finish school and walk to their grandparents' place, where they would eat and play. As they got older, they could ride their bicycles around my mother's estate. And my latest stepfather, Uncle Richard—whom she married after Mike had died—loved all of them. It was neat to see my mother watch them grow up from babies. That's why even today they feel very close to my mother."

Up to that time, Cathy had never felt the need to own a car. A blossoming mass transit system was at her full disposal.

Although she remains reliant on public transit to this day—as do many Singaporeans—she eventually relented and sought out her first driver's license at age 30. This was the final piece to the puzzle of making things work between her job, children, husband, and their new home.

She explains the combination of factors that encouraged her to finally learn how to drive. "Russell came along when I was 29, so I had all three children before I turned 30. I decided to take up driving because I realized it was too expensive to put the children on the school bus every day to go to school. The logic was, the school was only a ten-minute drive from our new house, and school started at 7:30. To use the school bus, I had to pay $70 a month per child, and the bus picks them up an hour earlier and then drives around the whole neighborhood before arriving at school. And we would have had to pay three times the amount, for three kids. And then there's the issue of coming home in the afternoon. They don't take the bus home because of after-school activities. And the final joke is that the school was only a five-minute walk from my mother's house." For these reasons, the school bus did not seem like a viable option for Cathy and her young family.

She continues, "So I decided, it's time for me to learn how to drive. And at that time Tony was doing very well, and he could afford to have a company car. He bought a rickety old car for me," she chuckles. "It was easier for me to drive the children to where they needed to go. They had extra lessons in some neighborhood about a few bus stops away, quite a distance. They had to go for their Mandarin classes, and their math. It just made more sense for me to drive them to school and to all their other activities."

She then recalls her first driving adventure. "I passed the driver's test and got my license on the first try! I was so happy," she laughs at her reaction. "The next day I decided to celebrate and bring the whole family to the zoo—all three of them. It took forever to find my way to the zoo! And the kids kept asking me, 'Are we there yet?' They were getting concerned. And I said, 'Just shut up and stay in the car," she laughs, then explains her reaction. "So, we are typical Asian mothers. We don't put up with stuff. When a child says something, we say directly, 'Yah, don't be rude. Shut up and mind your business.' It's like when they start to cry from some petty thing. I would ask them, straight up, are you bleeding? Do you need an ambulance? Call the police? Maybe the fire engine? They hear all this sarcasm, and then say, 'It's okay.' Then they stop crying. And I still got them to where they needed to go—after I found my way."

Perceptions of Public Housing

As Cathy's personal experience might indicate, the idea of public housing in Singapore has little in common from past failures with subsidizing low-income housing elsewhere. In this case the government does not provide fully funded, clustered housing for unemployed persons or others who cannot afford a mortgage or rent. In fact, Singaporean leaders had learned important lessons about what not to do, based on earlier experiments in the United States and elsewhere. Today, the vast majority of Singapore's citizens—about eight out of every ten people—buy into the public housing program here. It is the rule rather than the exception.

As Cathy explains further, "Singapore uses something called the Central Provident Fund (CPF), which compares in some ways with America's Social Security program." She has learned to compare Singapore's system with that of the United States, given that many of her clients originate there. She continues, "Anyone with a job will pay into the fund, and all employers contribute matching funds to the CPF. The funds are then disbursed to pay a percentage of people's home loans. So, this financial help from the CPF serves as the main 'public' component in public housing here."

Like all employed Singaporeans, Cathy and her husband contribute every month to the CPF through their respective jobs. In return, the CPF contributes part of their monthly payment—or did, when they still owed on the loan. On top of that, homeowners also earn some minimal interest on their CPF contributions. These additional funds can be used for medical needs or education. Rather than paying pensions to retirees, therefore, their homes are paid for instead. The home can thus be considered a financial asset as well as a reliable roof over people's heads.

Cathy then explains facetiously, "You have a choice here in Singapore. If you prefer a lump sum of money when you retire, you can sell your house, purchase a tent, and set it up on the beach." Most people see value within the CPF system, however, and prefer to enjoy stability in their own housing—while also remaining asset-rich. Beyond this, the system now allows families to sell part of their mortgage back to the government. This allows older parents to remain in the same property until they die, with the balance of the property then divided among the children. With the CPF substantially reducing monthly payments, it usually makes more financial sense to own rather than rent. If someone is paying rent in Singapore, they lose the long-term benefits of being a homeowner.

When looking back on her own rocky childhood, Cathy still remembers the prevalence of overcrowded housing, dirty streets, clogged drains and dysfunctional sewer systems. "But I was too young to understand the difference," she reflects. "We didn't know the city was dirty until we saw the cleaner, newer housing and streets being built around us."

This is a common conversation with Cathy's foreign guests—many of whom, she notes, come from greater wealth than she has seen in her lifetime. Some guests believe the idea of public housing is repulsive and something to dismiss outright. Cathy describes her thoughts around such conversations, hoping to open people's minds. "A lot of people who take my tours are high-end guests. When I talk about Singapore's public housing, they usually react something like, 'Oh my goodness, I would rather die than be forced to live in a flat or any kind of public housing!' I then say, well, some four million people here live like this, and they're still alive!" Cathy laughs at her own sarcasm. She continues, "For me, I have never lived in a large, separate home, so I just feel blessed to even have a roof over my head. But I ask them, what about staying in a condominium in a big US city? It's still a flat, meaning one house above another. It's a high-rise! What's the difference?"

She then reflects on the more typical views of her American clients. "Often, American tourists who come here don't think about living this way in the US, since it's probably not very common," she says correctly. A clear majority of Americans still prefer their sprawling, low-density lifestyle for raising families within separate, free-standing homes. She continues, "So, our HDB housing becomes a popular topic for visitors. Sometimes they want to know why we dry our laundry by hanging it outside our windows. They're surprised that many of us don't have electric laundry driers inside our flats. I ask them, 'Why should we own a drier when we can just pop it out of the window for free?'"

Continuing with her train of thought, she adds, "People are so amazed when they find out we don't have driers. It's a common perception that when you live in a flat here, you're a person of low-income. After all, it's public housing, right? But then, 80 percent of us live in this kind of housing. Much of it has improved over the years, with more space, laundry facilities, and even amenities like pools and recreation areas."

Cathy admits that the more opulent, high-end HDB developments do require extra fees for various amenities. This is not unlike American residents who often pay additional fees for homeowner's associations (HOAs) or community clubhouses. For her part, Cathy remains content with the standard public facilities with no extra fees. "It's kind of amazing, there are these beautiful condos being built now by the HDB, which shows the higher standard of living and expectations of people who earn more money. But you still have to pay additional expenses for the pool and everything."

She then recalls a past conversation with one of her children. "One day, Rachel says to me, 'Mommy, my friend lives in this beautiful apartment with a swimming pool and da-dee-da,' and I tell her, 'If you like it that much, then you can move in with them. Pack your bags and move out. Then I have one less mouth to feed – ha! We have a great public pool; for two dollars you can swim until the cows come home. We have three Olympic-sized swimming pools. What more do you want?'"

Showing little sympathy for such extravagance, Cathy explains how expectations of Singapore's younger generations have kept pace with its rapid rise in standard of living. "Most of the pools and recreation areas are outside," she explains of today's developments, "and some are being sheltered with covers just like a resort. They're open on all sides so that you don't get that nasty chlorine smell inside the buildings," she scrunches her nose at the thought. Still, given her childhood frugality, Cathy cannot help but consider that, at some point, enough is enough.

Postscript

It would be very easy—and justifiable—for Cathy to remain bitter about her childhood. She could continue to wonder why she was let down so often by a handful of imperfect and sometimes irresponsible adults in her life. An optimist by nature, however, Cathy finds it healthier and wiser to consider the positive lessons that can arise from life's challenges. She prefers to think of herself as more fortunate than those who have enjoyed an easier upbringing and more predictable lifestyle. Had she hailed from a more stable home environment, she would not have gained her cherished and hard-earned "street smarts" which allowed her to jump into a variety of early jobs. It was easier to cope with society's challenges and to solve problems earlier in life. She contemplates, "For us, we didn't have the money, so our one choice to succeed was to find opportunities, work hard, and try to stay on our feet. So, if given the chance to work for many hours and more money, we would do it."

This alternative, if more erratic approach allowed her to "hit the ground running" both during and after her school years. Still, no amount of positive thinking and genuine gratefulness could prevent her from considering what direction in life she might have pursued, had she enjoyed an opportunity to study at university. "If given the choice, and with more family support for higher education," Cathy now considers, "I would certainly have taken up Law. I always wanted to be a barrister, or a judge. But at the end of the day, it is not worth it to blame or begrudge the people who abandoned you."

To better explain her personal belief system, she cites various Buddhist teachings, including one piece of wisdom she once found at a local business. As she tells it, "There was a whole write-up there, a Buddhist saying. It tells you how to live your life and feel better about who you are and what might have happened to you. You at least provide some gratitude to the person who abandoned you, because it makes you stronger, and you don't blame everyone as you move through life, being the victim."

For her part, these words of wisdom have provided a reason to remain positive and to resist becoming bogged down with grudges or judgments about her past. Through this, more grateful perspective she has further developed a strong sense of empathy for children and families resembling her own earlier experiences. Over the years Cathy has met a lot of people who were somehow abandoned by their parents and who experienced unstable, perhaps abusive upbringings, including children raised by foster parents. She always enjoys meeting and conversing with such individuals, as she can closely relate and more deeply understand their own challenges. "You have to keep pushing," she concludes her thoughts, confirming her tireless determination at the time. "I've had faith that, when one door closes, many windows open. I kept looking for those opening windows."

Select Topics

Around Town with Cathy

Select Topics

Guiding Behind the Scenes: An Interview

Well after our own return home from Singapore, I gradually learned more about Cathy's career through our virtual conversations. I was curious about the day-to-day "nuts and bolts" of being a tour guide, especially those little-known aspects that visitors don't see from the bus or van windows. What follows below is a compilation of our various conversations looking behind the scenes of the industry, along with typical outsider perceptions of Singapore.

T. Paradis (TP): Can you describe the "boom times" of the 1990s that you mentioned, and what you recall from that era? How was guiding different back then?

Cathy Ross (CR): Sure, I remember the 1990s. During those years, I had to work like eight days a week. All agencies and guides were super busy. It was like the laws of supply and demand, I suppose. There weren't so many guides back then. Nor were there so many laws and restrictions. Anybody could play a lot of different roles in the industry, without worrying about whether it was right or wrong.

And when I got into it, the attractions were still very basic, like Chinatown, Arab Street, Little India. Chinatown still has a soul today, but it was more soulful in the early days. It was different from Chinatowns in other parts of the world, as it still had character. Little India was not such a big deal as it is today. For the tourists, there would be a few things they wanted to see, but mainly they wanted to shop. And shopping was popular because the currency was cheaper than other countries. On a good day the tourists would go on a city tour, drive through Chinatown, maybe drive through the civic district. And in those days, there was no Marina Bay Sands, it was just the open sea [laughter]. We used to do tours where I hopped on a boat, like a Chinese junk, and then sailed out to the southern Islands. We didn't sail out far or talk much about the port, but it was just to sail out and impress the tourists how busy the port was. And then slowly, there was Sentosa Island, where they had the wax museum. Very basic tours, and we didn't have to learn so much at that time. It was only in the 1990s, in my time, when they slowly added more about the history of Singapore and more background about the country. Even in our time in school, we were learning about history of other countries. We didn't even have to worry about who was the founder of Singapore; it was not our problem [laughter]. We didn't know there was somebody called Raffles until I became a tour guide.

It was all very simple. We loaded people by the masses. I used to run a bird park tour in the morning. We took the tram, gave them free time to see the bird show, and when we finished, we met at their entrance. That was it, and I sent them back to their hotels. Then on the night tour, I brought them to Chinatown, walked around, stopped for a Chinese meal, and that was the night tour. So, it was just basically sitting in coaches, picking up the guests, going to the zoo and having breakfast with the orangutans [laughter]. And dealing with 30 or 40 people, sometimes it was very fun, but people could be challenging. But then, I was not an easy person to work with. If my guests gave me a hard time, I would give them a harder time back. I had a temper then [laughter].

TP: You mentioned that you preferred freelancing after becoming bonded. Could you explain how this works a bit more, and how you are matched to a visiting group?

CR: When an agency gets a call for a tour package—what we call a *job*—the company will call various freelance guides to see who is available. They also consider the potential match between the interests of the client and the expertise of the guide. So, after you make your reservation through a travel agency, the company says, "The Paradises are coming in two months, so we need to find a guide for them." Because I'm on their list as a possible guide, they call me. If I'm available and interested, I'll take the job and put it on my schedule. If I'm not available, then I decline and tell them regretfully that I can't take it. But the problem is, I don't like to say "no" to most of the agents, because being available and successful only helps to build my reputation with them. If it appears that I'm rarely available for tours, they will start calling others instead. I do get greedy, I admit, as I'll take almost anything.

Some guides are very selective about what kind of jobs they are willing to take. They might not like to lead private tours with only two people, for instance, because they claim it's very draining. They might prefer large busloads where they can direct 40 people on and off the bus and organize meeting times when visiting attractions. A lot of guides enjoy working with the larger busloads. I don't. Because I prefer smaller, personalized groups focused on tailormade, or niche topics. But I will also work with big groups occasionally, so that I have a variety of experiences and abilities.

TP: Did you have a long-term strategy to build your reputation, or did that happen more naturally as you gained experience?

CR: Well, after so many years now, my name is on the list of many agents I work with, but only because I was willing to take anything for many years and show I was willing to jump into whatever they needed. Sometimes they prioritize me now because I've earned a reputation for being reliable and resourceful. Or they know how to match me with certain types of interest groups, so they prefer to give it to me. And there are so many guides out there now! It was very different during the boom years. These tours might be very hard work for me—and at terrible times of the day or night—but my goal is to please the agent and gain a reputation for being reliable.

And if something goes wrong and the guests are not happy for some reason, the guides must uphold the good name of the company. But for me, I need to remain in the company's good graces. When a guest is unhappy or something happens, I try to do damage recovery on the spot. The agents are pleased when I take this approach. And the people who are selling tours might have never been on a tour themselves, so it's the guides' responsibility to make sure the tour runs smoothly, to make sure the passengers and happy. So, yes, on an ad-hoc basis as a freelancer, the first agent to call me will usually get my services. That's how you build a positive reputation.

TP: Is there a downside to freelancing, in that you need to compete with other guides for jobs, and does seniority help now?

CR: I really wouldn't know. But if I'm getting jobs every other day, I think I'm safe [laughing]. Quite honestly, I cannot say for sure what conversations are happening behind the scenes at the agency's office. You see, it's the agency's staff who decide which guide to hire for which job. How they decide that from one time to another, I do not know. It's true that sometimes the person harvesting the job becomes my very good friend [laughter]. Most of the agents know me now. Sometimes I'll pop in and have lunch with the ladies and update them on what's going on from my perspective.

You also recall from earlier that I've got experience in offices like theirs. I've done ticketing—close to everything an agency needs to be done, even being in charge of the teams who book the buses and drivers. I've had groups of drivers under my hands, my responsibility. So, it's funny because they might have a problem with something they can't solve easily, and they ask me to help them. They might say, "Cathy, I'm really stuck, what can I do?" And I'll advise them.

TP: It sounds like you've discovered the importance of building relationships and being helpful when called upon.
CR: Sure, it's worked out that way, I guess. Instead of complaining, I must solve the problem first, on the ground. And only later will I tell them what the problem was and how I fixed it. This approach will gain their appreciation, and they'll learn why I am the best person for the job. This is how I want them to think of me.

TP: When things go wrong, how do these relationships help you solve problems or issues that might arise?
CR: Okay, so here's an example of why this is important. One morning I'm sleeping when my phone rings, and I hear this voice: "Cathy, where are you? Your guest has left already!" And I'm thinking, "Oh my God, I'm supposed to be at the hotel at 6:00 a.m., and I overslept!" But these things matter less because I have a very collaborative team around me. I work like a team with them, and we all have mutual respect. My driver, Saleh—you remember him—he knows me well. He's Malay, and we

chat in his dialect. So, when I overslept, he just went there on his own and picked up the guests and took them where they needed to go. But if I did not work well with my driver, and if he hated me for some reason, he would surely have caused hell for me, and the guests would have complained. But this way, the guests didn't know what was going on, and he just loaded up and went about his business like it was a normal morning.

There was also a departure that happened, and I overslept. A lot of my jobs, I work until late, past 11:00 p.m. with groups like this, and sometimes I'm just dead tired. And many times, what happens is, I come home from a happy assignment, I have a good lunch, a shower, and then I fall asleep. And then I wake up and suddenly it's like, "Oh my God, I missed my assignment!" I get a panic attack. But I had actually done the tour and went to sleep afterward [laughter]. So, these are the things that can happen to you. That's why sometimes in life I think I'm very blessed, to have developed these trusting friendships over the years. It's very important to get along well and to respect the people you work with.

TP: Speaking about your support system, can you describe the role of the Singapore Tourism Board and how that group works with agencies and guides?
CR: The whole function of the STB, it's a government body. It's a licensing board. The purpose is to bring tourists into Singapore. So, it started in 1964, before I was born. In those days, as time passed, they were just licensing officers. They were just a governing body that made sure tourist guides were properly trained. But in recent years, maybe 10 years ago, the whole system has changed. Now they help guides to make them more employable by enhancing them with different kinds of courses and product knowledge. They find ways and means for us to explore our abilities, enhance our knowledge, find

courses for us to take. I think they've done a fantastic job; I've benefitted a lot from them. You can actually sit with the CEOs and department heads and talk about issues.

Sometimes the guides bring concerns to the Board, which helps promote a dialogue. The Board offers opportunities to improve yourself so that you can branch out and make yourself more sellable. I have a habit of speaking my mind to the guides [laughter]. I say to them, the reason you're not getting better paid jobs is you do not enhance yourself by taking extra courses and finding ways to make yourself employable. The thing about guiding is, you can be a licensed guide, but you have your own niche, you specialize. So, when you start specializing yourself, you have more variety in your menu. Like an a-la-carte menu, you need to show that you can do five or ten things, so from there you are specialized and can demand a different fee.

TP: What kind of efforts are necessary to earn and keep your tour guiding license?

CR: Okay, the thing about maintaining the license, the rule over here is that every three years you have to renew it. You pay like $75 for three years, which is actually very cheap for a license. And in my early days, the requirement was that you had to do a multiple-choice test, and then you went on a *practical*—you went to a spot, and they make you guide for 10 minutes. As time passed, they did away with the practical test, so now you're required to do a PDC, which stands for *Professional Development Course*. So, you complete 21 hours total, which equates to three 7-hour courses. Each course is like seven hours a day. There are many different types of PDCs, from wine tasting to *feng shui* and other cultural lessons.

So, the thing is, now the government subsidizes the PDCs, so we are only paying a fraction of the actual cost of the courses. Actually, they make it inexpensive, so we spend more time upgrading ourselves by acquiring more knowledge. So now, since Covid, the licensing test is done all online.

TP: What is the Mandatory Refresher Course all about, and how does it help you stay current with all the changes happening here?

CR: The MRC updates us on current events that are happening around Singapore. Before Covid this was done in the classroom, but now it's all online. After going through the whole MRC update, we have to do a mandatory multiple-choice test.

So, the refresher course keeps all of us up to date on what's going on. I mean, if after 30 years I haven't acquired a lot of things, I think I'm not working, you know? So, I guess it's the passion; you really need to want to know more, then you can tell stories. Like my clients, who are more high-end, more knowledgeable people. Some are professors like yourself [laughter]. You want to know certain things I can explain, and I can't be like "I don't know." That would be quite ugly, right? That's why I tried to niche myself into specialized tours. I'm still considered a general guide—so generally I don't know anything [laughter] ... Sometimes I have corporate delegates from different industries who come for technical visits in high-security areas. This enables me to talk about specialized topics that are not like the regular tourist attractions. They hire me to bring them around and explain things in the field.

So, you really need to build your knowledge, take the MRC, do your research. It's more like *edutainment*. It's like, you're giving them all these facts, but then again you are also doing a performance.

TP: Where did you learn the concept of *edutainment*? That's pretty funny.

CR: So, it has to do with the difference between *travelers* and *tourists*. Travelers go to a country, they spend x-amount of time to mainly discover and learn about places. But you also have tourists who go to countries and want to be entertained. So, if you combine the traveler and the tourist, they want to learn while also being entertained. You break up the two words, and you get *edutainment*. And see, if you take a tour as edutainment, you will enjoy it more while learning something. I do a lot of educational tours, with children as little as three years old, and teenagers, so I have to tell my stories in a way that they are entertained while also learning. So, the thing is, when you have young people and they are entertained, they want to know more. If I had made the tour strictly educational—you have to learn this—they're going to hate it. Nothing goes into their heads. You see, being a teacher is not easy, but being an entertainer is easier.

TP: I'm curious about your use of the word, "product." It sounds like it's more related to economics than tourism. Can you explain a bit more about how products relate to tourism?

CR: [laughter] Okay, *products* are just tours, packages, things to see and do—for instance, experiences that visitors can sign up and pay for. It's similar to an item that you purchase, so it relates to economics. In this case, you're purchasing an experience, a tour to see specific places. So, the Mandatory Refresher Course is devoted to updating us on products that are ongoing or available in Singapore, because a lot of things that were there a year or two ago might no longer be there. They are already outdated. We learn about products related to museums, airport arrivals, types of tourists and their home countries, where they tend to spend their money, and the kinds of nitty-gritty things that we can use on our city tours.

Take passenger arrivals for instance. We as tour guides

need to know more about the people coming into Singapore who book our tours. It's more like an insider tourism thing, providing us with useful information about our clients. And other updates are provided, such as the current year's *Michelin* winners, and things like museums—new exhibits at the museums, planned exhibits in the future, and various upcoming events. These are all called *product updates*. Imagine if you have visitors coming and they ask what's happening in a certain museum, or at the Zoo. I could simply tell them to go look on Google. But a knowledgeable tour guide will be able to quickly inform them while inside the van or other places without internet or phone access. People are coming on tours for the experience and dialogue, so simply sending them to Google is not the best idea [laughter]. A tour guide is a part of their overall visitor experience.

TP: So, for these refresher courses, how do you know if you pass the course? Are there any tests or ways to show how much smarter you are as a result? [laughter]

CR: Right, so during the MRC they put you in a classroom for half a day, and they talk-talk-talk to you about these things. And then afterwards they send you to another room for one hour to take a test, which is multiple-choice, like school. You take it on a computer. For the test you can only get five wrong answers. But if you fail six questions, you are required to retake the MRC and exam again. Usually I get, like, 98 percent, maybe one question wrong. So, this is the approach that the Tourism Board takes just to keep everyone's licenses going.

And I'm very happy, as I just had my license renewed, so I have my new badge for the next three years. This is my eleventh renewal cycle! So proud of myself! I told you that I don't hide anything, so I have to boast. But my friends tell me I'm just showing off, so I'm like, "Shut up" [laughter]. I really love doing these things because I get to talk with so many people, and it's very similar to *show biz.* You know, like show business? When you get up in front of a group and sing a song to perform, you feel the audience and their excitement, and they applaud for you. You feel that sensation. That's how I feel in this line of work.

TP: Thirty-three years is amazing! How have you kept your high level of enthusiasm over the years?
CR: I guess it's the passion. You really need to be someone who always wants to know more, to learn, and then share it with others. Then you can tell stories and add your own personal experiences. Some of my clients are well educated and want to learn all sorts of things about Singapore and what's going on here. It's important for me to keep learning and stay up to date so I can explain things.

And by going for these courses, I'm always learning something new and adding that experience to my portfolio of tour options. So, at least I've learned something and have broadened my experience. If an agent calls and asks if I can do a tour on that topic, I usually say "yes," I'm trained for it, so why not? This is how you add value to your own experience. This is how you build your repertoire. It's important to keep in mind that the Tourism Board is a licensing board; they license you so that you can legally go out there and talk to people about Singapore. Once you're licensed, it's your responsibility to build your own portfolio.

TP: That makes great sense! Would you speak about the *portfolio* more, and how it applies to guiding?
CR: Okay, a portfolio is like a restaurant menu. My portfolio includes the tours I can lead and the places or events I'm comfortable talking about and was trained for. I consider

myself to be a hawker; I'm selling my services as a tour guide. So, if I am only specialized and able to do two or three things, for how long can my business survive? I need to have more experience and qualifications to run a variety of tours and talk about a wide array of topics. So, this is why it's necessary to expand your portfolio as a tour guide. It's like an a-la-carte menu. All the different dishes would be the different kinds of tours. This is how you would be able to do so many different types of tours that are required by the agent. I guess I'm a go-getter in that sense. Some guides are careful about what they enroll for. A two-day course, for instance, would prevent a guide from taking jobs on those days, which means they would be deprived of two days' worth of earnings. For me, if I don't get jobs for a couple of days, that's okay. It's worth it. I've learned something, and I've added it onto the a-la-carte menu. The reality is that it takes time to learn new things.

TP: It seems like your can-do attitude has allowed you to lead a lot of specialty tours. Do you depend on those to provide you with enough business?

CR: Sure, that's why it's important to niche yourself. Take the Port Tour, or Sea Tour, for instance. The port is willing to spend money to promote awareness of their operations to Singaporeans. They allow visitors to go on tours and to walk on designated trails to better understand what happens over there. They developed a whole program for visitors. As I mentioned, my networking is very good, so they were recruiting guides to get involved with their new tour program. I was thrilled that they asked me to do that, and so I said, "Why not?" Of course, there was training, and evaluation involved, to select the guides who best met their standards for the tour. Only a few of us passed. So, not many guides are qualified to lead the Sea Tour. I also do my own research beyond the training. I've got stacks of articles and books at my house that are hard to find laying all over the place [laughter].

Naturally, most people don't know anything about ocean vessels or how cargo transport works, so I give them the background on all that. We sail out of the harbor into the open sea—you recall all those ships anchored when you were here, right? After reading my own research, it really becomes fun; I love maritime. When opportunities come along like that, it's important to jump in—you remember the *chiong* factor. I'm a *chiong* person!

TP: Ha! Yes. But even you can't be interested in everything, right? Are there any topics you shy away from for various reasons?

CR: Aviation has never really appealed to me. You could show me a hundred airplanes, and I'd be like, *okay, whatever*. The other thing I really don't want to get involved with is plants—fauna. No fauna, animals, or trees [laughter]. I have a love for nature and plants, but my inability to remember all their names turns me off. I have friends who can talk until the cows come home about which plant or tree this is, but I'm like, *whatever*. Let it go—ha! So, the Gardens by the Bay, for instance, I bring my guests there and encourage them to walk and enjoy the endless variety of plants and species, like I did with you and Linda. And the general idea of it is fine. But I'm not up in my clients' faces about it. They can read the signs and enjoy at their own pace, as you did. One issue is that the Gardens by the Bay is a massive, manufactured terrarium with plant communities from all over the world. But if we go to an island, such as Pulau Ubin, we would be there for a whole day! Because I can bring them through the actual jungle, the swamps, to see nature and how diverse it all is.

TP: Yes, the highlight for me on Pulau Ubin was the mud lobsters! [laughter] I'm going to bring our conversation full circle to ask about your career overall. With all your success in tour guiding, do you feel that you've "made it" financially, as compared with your childhood?

CR: [After some thought] Well, guiding has put bread and butter on my table for many years, making it easier to raise the kids. And my husband is more of a provider now than when he was starting out, like me. Anyway, we are quite blessed. So now I'm taking time to do the types of tours that I really enjoy doing in my work. But at the end of the day, medical care is expensive, and I have no perks working as a freelancer. I depend on a daily wage. No tours, no income. It is definitely safer and easier to go on holidays now, as my hard work has allowed me to save more money. But if I don't save, how am I going to spend money on myself? [laughter]

You see, as a freelancer, they can't really tell you when to quit. You don't get laid off or let go. It's whether you want to work or not, and whether your body can take the punishment. For me, I will probably only stop guiding when they tell me I'm too blind and can't see well enough, or they realize there's no sound coming out of my big mouth [laughter]. Some of my friends have made it to their late 70s and are still guiding. Eventually you might have clients who report to the agent that a guide is getting too old, at which point the agent will not hire them as often. That's the sure way to kill yourself. Some guides have even passed away during their tours! Maybe that's the best way to go, doing what you love to do—though the clients probably won't appreciate it—ha! I mean, who's going to return them to their hotel then? [laughter]

TP: Okay, well, do you feel like you've financially "made it?" Can you put all of your past worries about money behind you?

CR: So, when you talk about "having made it," I think it's a very gradual process for someone who has been in the same career for all their adult life. I haven't been wealthy or poor since I got involved with tourism, but I think we are more well-off than what we were in the past. The only wealth we have right now, however, is this flat—this house, and maybe some savings for holiday or for a rainy day. My husband and I are not likely to hit a target of one million dollars in our savings account [laughter]. So, if you ask whether I've made it, I'd say "no," but I am more contented. We don't owe anyone anything, and our house is fully paid for. The kids are all doing fine. That's our hidden, or instant wealth. The family *is* wealth.

TP: Let's wrap up with some of your thoughts about how visitors perceive your home country, and what types of myths or misunderstandings you frequently hear. For starters, what do you believe is the most common misperception about Singapore from your clients?

CR: That Singapore is communist. That people here are like puppets. There's another word for it—robots. The perception is that people here have no opinions and are scared to talk about the government, like there is no freedom of speech.

TP: So, the most common perception is that Singapore is communist and authoritarian?

CR: Yes, that there's too much government control and that there's no freedom here, like modern communism. But it's not communist, because not everyone is equal. We have a parliamentary system as a holdover from the British. China was suppressed during communism, but it was a great country before then. They aspired to do a lot of things, and they have a deeply rooted culture. Unfortunately, a lot of their culture, beliefs, and religions were suppressed during communism. So,

Singapore is more like China before communism, where culture can still thrive. Prime Minister Lee Kuan Yew was like a typical Chinese father. He didn't tolerate a lot of nonsense, but he always did things for the betterment of the country.

TP: Okay, I understand better. Do you feel that it's a fair tradeoff, then, to have more rules to create a safer society?
CR: Of course, it's easier when people comply and behave. When they tell everyone to stay home and wear your masks, you stay home and wear your masks! [laughter] We don't have very many people loitering or causing problems on the streets; everyone is just so orderly. Not that we don't have feelings, of course. But if you put yourself in my shoes and think about your own country, would you allow your child to take public transit and travel 45 minutes to school? No, not many people in other countries would do that. The parents will drive them back and forth, or they would use the school bus. Here in Singapore, my daughter started to take public transit when she was eight years old—going to school, to extra classes, all on her own. There is a safety network in this country. You don't have to worry about what you're doing, or whether it's safe for your children to be on the street, unlike during my childhood. There are no muggings, things like that, so we live in a very safe zone.

But had this been a country with no discipline, with unruly behaviors and drug addicts, you're going to get robbed. When people visit here, they just feel calm, with nothing to worry about. Because your safety as a guest is my priority also. Really, who wants to rob you? They just don't bother. The prison is very small, and the food is not very good.

TP: Okay, are there any habits that Singaporeans learned from the past, such as from the British?
CR: Sure. Queuing. We have a strange habit of queuing up in

lines, which is rooted in the history of World War II and the Occupation. The Japanese were executing the Chinese, so everyone was required to get in line to be interrogated. I used to make the joke that the habit filtered down from the war, so people got used to it. So now, people queue up just to buy lottery tickets or food goods, or whatever. And with Covid recently the queues got twice as long because of the one-meter social distancing requirement. This is all very good, because queuing up teaches a level of patience and courtesy. And if there's an outbreak of war somehow, we won't have people running around stabbing each other [laughter].

Sometimes when I see a queue somewhere I get excited and jump into the queue myself! Then I ask them, what is this line for? [laughter] So, it's a pastime now, it's a cool thing to do because everybody does it. You don't see people rushing for things, and that's why it's so disciplined in Singapore. They just say, okay, the line starts here, follow the queue. And that's it. There won't be a stampede, and nobody will start a fight. It's all under control.

Select Topics

Supporting the Troops: Cathy and the Armed Forces

The majority of Cathy's guests are predictably whisked to popular destinations—the likes of Little India, Kampong Glam, Chinatown, and to the more recent entertainment venues of Sentosa Island and the breathtaking Marina Bay. Much less often do visitors inquire about Singapore's more somber sites commemorating World War II, including the Changi Chapel and Museum, the Kranji War Memorial and Military Cemetery, and the Old Ford Motor Factory. This latter site is where Singapore ultimately surrendered to the Japanese on 15 February 1942. It is a uniquely and unexpectedly solemn place. When Cathy is not shuffling around with her foreign visitors, she can sometimes be found at these historically meaningful sites leading specialized tours for fellow Singaporeans.

With one eye always reflecting on her own family's war-time experiences, Cathy has further managed to become a valuable friend to Singapore's military branches. She now even plays a distinctive role in their soldiers' national education. Cathy tried to suppress a hearty laugh when I asked naïvely—in standard tourist fashion—whether Singapore has an Air Force or other armed services. At which point, she decided I should know something more about her country's military involvement and obligations.

It is here where she begins my education. "Since the 1960s we have had an Air Force, Navy, and Army—three main branches. More recently, two additional branches have been added, the Military Police Force and the Civil Defense." With that introduction out of the way, she then explains to my greater astonishment that all males aged 18-22 are expected to serve at least two years in one of these five armed services. This means they are *conscripted*. She explains, "Upon our independence, military service was made compulsory, and this remains true through today. Even if you're from the wealthiest family in Singapore, you still must serve. After two years of full service, they are obligated to be on call for an additional ten years, when they serve for two weeks each year."

I then ask whether any loopholes exist, or exceptions that might allow someone to avoid serving. Shaking her head with a grin, she quickly responds, "Do you want a warrant? Do your parents want that hassle? No, there are no exceptions aside from various disabilities." Still, Cathy admits that not all Singaporean parents or teenagers feel generally enthusiastic about the mandatory service requirement. She says, "I have friends who have tried to avoid it. They might view the requirement as a burden to their careers or other plans."

With this news, I try to imagine this otherwise tranquil scene of corporate high-rises, downtown eateries, and river tours somehow ramping up into a threatening war machine. Remind me never to suggest attacking this place. I ask, "Are women allowed to join as well, or just the men?"

"Service is not compulsory for women. A lot of my clients ask me about that. I say that the women are already doing national service by having babies; they are the ones giving birth and starting their families. Isn't that service enough for your country?" She laughs, from her own motherly perspective. "Our leaders realize that women can better serve in the Army after they have delivered their babies," she quips, adding, "and if you can go through the pain of labor, you can certainly fight in any war! But we do have some very high-ranking women in the military, including pilots in the Air Force. Even our Police Force is composed of a certain percentage of women, and there are certain adventurous women who are eager to serve in some capacity."

I ask for Cathy's own thoughts about her country's mandatory service requirement, to which she contemplates aloud, "I think the best way for a child to grow and become resilient and patriotic is to serve in the military. And by more resilient, I mean that when any type of disaster hits, everyone has a role and knows what they're doing. Every grandfather, father, and son have served, so we also have those generational connections. If you spend some social time with my husband and friends, for instance, they will chat about their time serving in the military. They have plenty to talk about because everybody has been there. It's not just about going to war; it's about being prepared for whatever unexpected disaster might happen here."

I respond logically, "That must mean that your two sons have served as well?"

"Sure, although they won't place siblings together in the same branch. When boys in Singapore turn 18 years old, the military starts to filter them into different channels, or paths. I have a pair of nephews, for instance. One went into the Navy, the other into the Army. My youngest, Russ, was in the Army's Special Operations division, where he served as a platoon sergeant for two years. And Wes, he served in the Police Force. He completed three months of basic police training, then decided to join the Coast Guard. After the basic training in the Police Force, you can be channeled into different divisions, and the Coast Guard is one of them. There are a lot of options now, unlike when my husband was serving, when they all basically went out to march." She giggles at the thought of Tony marching through the jungle. "You can go into the cadets, become an officer, or even do overseas education of some kind. There are a lot of opportunities. That's why I told my children, whatever department you want to go into will be exciting. You're going to learn a lot of useful skills, things that the schools don't or can't teach you. These are all survival skills. These skills can come from any number of diverse opportunities. My son, Wes, likes the ocean and now works on a merchant vessel, so the Coast Guard helped him prepare for that type of work."

"Wow, that's incredible. Nobody would know about any of this just coming to visit here. It sounds like an effective approach to national security."

"Yes, the government spends a lot of money on the military, and there is a lot of investment into the military service here." This reminds her of a story of traveling to the United States. "We have fighter jets too, and we even have the Black Knights, Singapore's elite fighter squadron, like the Blue Angels in the US," she says, adding, "I was flying back from San Diego, and I saw this guy, he was wearing a Black Knights jacket. I was like, 'Oh wow, he's from our Air Force,' so I tried to make friends with him because he was so good looking, but it didn't work out." She laughs.

What Cathy refers to as her "military tours" could be interpreted as a form of national service in her own special way. She has visited the nearby countries of Cambodia, Vietnam, and Malaysia to better understand the impacts of the two world wars with the intent of better informing her own tours back home. Her tours are provided for two main groups of service people—namely the younger, two-year conscripts serving now, and the reservists, who continue to satisfy their annual two weeks of service for the ten-year cycle. Given that nobody in Singapore's military has engaged in battle since World War II, Cathy's task remains a tall order. First and foremost, she aims to instill a sense of national pride in the newest soldiers and to provide them with a sense of historical context.

At my prodding she offers some additional perspective. "In 1965 we became an independent country, and one emphasis was to build and maintain a military to prevent anyone from attacking Singapore ever again." Cathy is referring to the nation's fresh memory of the horrific fall of Singapore and the Japanese Occupation during World War II. "Every 15 February, we have Total Defense Day, because that's the anniversary of the fall of Singapore to the Japanese. I need to turn this history into a story to help show them why it's important that they are serving in the Army. Our country has made amazing progress as a peaceful nation since then—as I teach them—building up from a rural fishing village into a British colony, to the modern city we have today. They don't understand the history, that the British didn't have enough military defense here, which kept us defenseless. We were captured and occupied by the Japanese. When older people take my tours, whether they are in the military or not, they know where I'm coming from. They have a very personal connection to their own family histories."

Total Defense Day constitutes one of the more important annual events in Singapore. Cathy explains that the government leaders promote six specific aspects of "total defense," namely *military, civil, economic, social, psychological,* and *digital.* Together these comprise the key aspects of society. The concept of total defense—to pull together different segments of society—was initiated by the Singaporean government in 1984. This is a creative approach to galvanize collective support for a small island nation. For instance, *civil defense* assures the nation is prepared to handle unpredictable disasters and related crises. The *economic defense* is likewise an excellent example of forward thinking, to ensure the national economy can keep functioning in the face of adversity or wartime. In contrast, maintaining racial and ethnic harmony is the charge of *social defense*, while *psychological defense* is designed to encourage sustained commitment and resilience in the face of any major threats and challenges to the country.

One featured and compulsory stop on Cathy's military tour is Singapore's World War II Museum at the Ford Motor factory, now referred to as FFF, or Former Ford Factory. She recognizes all too well that many young people are not especially excited about serving in the military. And as time passes it becomes ever more difficult to relate to Singapore's troubled past.

Cathy is quick to emphasize the abject conditions that plagued the Prisoners of War (POWs) who remained at Changi. Those sent northward were forced to work side-by-side with locals to build a new railroad route to extract raw materials from the region. The proposed route took the railroad through rugged, mountainous terrain. Known officially as the Burma Railway, or the Thai-Burma Railway, the 258-mile route between Bangkok, Thailand and Rangoon, Burma (present-day Myanmar) would provide a vital economic trade route for the Japanese. Cathy explains, "The Japanese wanted to extend the railroad network all the way up to Burma, so they could extract Burma's resources more efficiently and transport them back to Japan. And they naturally expected the Singaporean POWs to build it, since the Japanese knew next to nothing about how to build railroads."

The project became a global demonstration of human cruelty, constructed with an estimated 180,000 to 250,000 Southeast Asian civilians and more than 60,000 captured allied servicemen. An estimated 100,000 or more workers died during the project's three-year construction period. After the war, Railway Bridge 277 gained instant notoriety for inspiring the Pierre Boulle novel of the 1950s, *The Bridge over the River Kwai*, along with a follow-up feature film.

Cathy helps her young servicemen relate better to the abject horrors they faced, explaining to them, "The Japanese expected their prisoners to build the railroad, and there was little interest in keeping them healthy enough to do their work. It was grueling, and many of them were weakened and died from dysentery, malnutrition, and food shortages. The soldiers also labored without the proper tools necessary for railway construction, such as digging out rock cuts or building bridges. They lacked proper provisions and water, and overall, they were treated very poorly." She usually follows up this serious history with some very welcome levity, telling them, "See, you don't know how good you've got it, not having to build a Japanese railroad! I'm sure you can all survive your two weeks of training," she laughs.

One important motive for initiating Total Defense Day is to help instill a sense of Singaporean identity. Results have arguably been mixed on this count. Even for someone who adores her home, Cathy fumbled for words when asked what it means to be a Singaporean. After pausing for longer than usual to think, she began practically with, "Well, it means you live in Singapore. Everyone has some amount of mixed culture or ethnic background, so we can't say that Singapore is associated with any one ethnic group. We have the Eurasians, and there's no country that officially recognizes the concept of Eurasians, so it's not easy for Singapore to have a single identity. It's a very difficult question to answer; in that context, I'm confused already! It's like a mental block. It's too wide a question to ask. I would make a comparison to the diverse racial backgrounds in America, and yet you all call yourselves 'Americans.' That's not true here; there's no straight Singaporean identity. The only way is if you're born here; that's what makes you Singaporean. So, nationality would be 'Singaporean'—such as when we fill out forms or applications. But our race would be Malay, Chinese, Indian or Other. We are all placed into one of these four categories at birth." Since Cathy is a Eurasian, she is therefore an *Other*—that is, mixed-race.

Cathy's difficulty with describing a singular identity is emblematic of the challenge faced by the government since the days of independence. Today's total defense strategy therefore is designed to help foster a sense of social cohesion where none existed previously.

During Total Defense Day, Cathy teaches an array of topics ranging from the island's eclectic mix of religious and spiritual traditions to its diverse ethnic heritage. She speaks of the racial riots and unrest surrounding independence in the 1960s. Describing more of her own approach, she says, "One of the key points I make is that knowledge is the gateway to respect. Some of them brush it off and act as if they don't need to understand the past. I tell them, 'At the end of the day, you live here, and you must understand this history if you are to feel more pride for your country and home. How can you love your country without understanding what your country went through in the past?' And then we talk about the early efforts to encourage racial harmony and the difficult separation from Malaysia during that time. Malaysia was a Muslim state, and Singapore preferred being multiracial. And Malaysia didn't want us either—they kicked us out. Then I mention the legacy of our first Prime Minister, Lee Kuan Yew, and the risks he took to create an independent country. He had said that 'My responsibility is to the people of Singapore,' which I still find amazing, and it's important for our young recruits to know about Lee Kuan Yew's efforts to build our country."

Occasionally Cathy notices mysterious individuals tagging along on these tours. She has come to realize that the "bosses of certain companies" will sometimes join her group, often well dressed and keeping to themselves in the back. Cathy describes them as "hiding between the pillars" to watch her from afar. The corporations they represent often rely heavily on military contracts. She surmises that "they come to listen to me as spies to see if I'm saying anything against their interests," she chuckles. In a more transparent way, Cathy is held responsible for her messaging through more conventional approaches, including feedback surveys completed by her tour participants. "I'm fortunate that I have more than 90 percent favorable feedback, so I'm still in the pool of guides for military tours," she says smiling.

The Kranji War Memorial provides a pivotal stop on Cathy's tour, where she discusses some of Singapore's key role players during World War II. Now generations later, memories of the Occupation and related war efforts and tragedies continue to fade. Cathy seeks to paint a historical picture for Singapore's young servicemen and women. And make no mistake, this tour is no leisurely outing, nor is it considered a day off for the recruits. She explains, "They first spend several days and nights marching through the jungles in simulated warfare, and then they show up for my tour. They are all smelly and tired!" she laughs. Afterwards, they participate in a service at the Kranji War Memorial which includes Singapore's State Cemetery. True to Cathy's sense of humor, she tells them, "You've been marching and suffering through the jungles, and now you've come here, to your graves." This invariably leads to a collective laugh from the recruits.

The laughs continue at her remaining tour destinations. One mandatory stop involves the National Museum of Singapore. There she leads them to a section devoted to the so-called *secret societies*, or the history of gang membership in Singapore. She explains, "I tell them, in those days the gang members would all have these tattoos, to identify with their own secret societies. Back then the tattoos were gang symbols. And nowadays, people are putting tattoos all over their bodies and calling it 'body art,'" she states, gagging in disgust. "So, I tell them, after you've gotten these tattoos in your younger days, try to go into the corporate world and get hired for professional jobs. If you have too many tattoos, certain kinds of places will refuse your application."

Knowing her younger, male audience quite well, she indicates her disdain for tattoo art while making them laugh. "I say to them, 'Young women now have these tattoos all over their bodies. But God has given them beautiful skin, so why must they draw on it permanently? A beautiful rose will become a withered rose as they grow old. A butterfly will become a moth. So, if you have sisters or girlfriends, try to tell them not to destroy their beautiful skin!" At this point she finds her young servicemen rolling in laughter, while also learning about Singapore's rocky past.

She clearly appreciates their discipline as well, something not always witnessed on group tours for the public. Should a serviceman behave out of line in some way, there would certainly be consequences to pay from their superiors. Even so, the senior reservist groups tend to appreciate Cathy's efforts more genuinely, along with her personal stories and anecdotes. Cathy adds, "The commander has spoken to me and said he likes the way I tell stories, sometimes in a rather subtle way. He says that in the military they can't tell stories like this, as the recruits won't listen," she smiles. "So, this is story-telling time! It provides them all with a different outlook. It's fun. When we have a break in our tour, these guys will come up and chat with me. Sometimes later they see me somewhere else in the city and recognize me," she chuckles with a little pride thrown in.

Cathy enjoys recounting her experiences and the fun she enjoys with the soldiers. After first introducing herself on the bus, she determines whether they are the newer recruits or the reservists. She then tailors her material to that specific group. She explains, "I can usually tell right away if they are the new recruits. They are young, typically between age 18 and 22, and their heads are all shaved, so they come in bald," she giggles at the thought. "Then the 'cycle' ones—the reservists—will do a separate tour, and they are usually older. As reservists they hold all sorts of different jobs. They come back for two weeks, and the government pays their salaries. Some of them take my tour, and I can tell they enjoy it. Sometimes they recognize me from when they were younger. It's kind of like a summer camp for them. I tell them how it's so nice to see them coming back to meet up with their friends, as they often went through the two-year service together."

In these ways Cathy has become an active and strategic partner within this ongoing national project—albeit in her own colorful ways. She smiles and reflects on her own modest contributions. "It's always interesting to see their reactions, taking them back to the early days of Singapore's independence. They see that riots in the streets were common, that we had secret societies—other countries call them street gangs. We didn't dare go outside after 7:00 or 8:00 at night, as I told you my own stories earlier. Nowadays it's so peaceful. We can take the bus or subway back home at 1:00 a.m. The young people go clubbing and hang around on the streets, and tourists wander around without a concern for safety. When I was younger, it was a very different place." She then drives home the fundamental point she makes to her young conscripts: "I tell them, this is the reason you're serving in the military—not so much to protect the country, but to protect this wonderful way of life for your families."

Select Topics

The Lighters: Cleansing the Singapore River

Scrunching her face in disgust, Cathy says, "You could smell it from a mile way." This was her most vivid memory of the final years of local trading along the Singapore River. "Even at Raffles Hotel, you could smell it. I used to hang out around the river with all the boats and workers bustling on and offshore. The trading activities occurred on the west side of the river, with the old shophouses lining the bank. That area is called Boat Quay, the commercial side of the river where the bumboats docked. Anything on the other side—to the east—was the Civic District, since that's where the British had their offices, courthouse, and all that."

In similar fashion to her experiences in the kampong, Cathy still holds poignant memories of the sounds, sights and smells of the Singapore River's last decade of mercantile activities. The bustling energy from the river's economic and social vitality was a far cry from the pristine waterway presented to visitors today. Part of her still regrets not taking special notice of the river and its colorful, vibrant trading activities when they still existed. It is easy to forgive such an oversight, of course. As a youngster she could claim any number of more pressing matters than what was happening around the river. Nonetheless, she still appeared on its banks occasionally to forge some lasting memories of what once transpired here.

Only later as a newly minted tour guide did Cathy's attention focus on the changing river scene. "The river was not something I would have taken notice of, until it was gone," she thinks back, adding, "That was the saddest part, I guess." Still, she is fortunate to have retained vivid memories of the human activity that accompanied the river up through the mid-1970s during periodic brushes with the downtown area. That is when the city began its sweeping campaign to relocate all business and trade away from the overcrowded and seriously polluted waterway. In so doing, however, a large part of the city's character arguably disappeared with it.

Upon my asking about her recollections, Cathy used this opportunity to teach me something about the river's history, and its economic and cultural roles in old Singapore. If I didn't know better, she could easily have been holding a microphone, at least in her mind.

Cathy shared part of the river's story, going even further back. "During the 1820s, the commercial side was the first place in the early town to be reclaimed—or filled in with dirt to expand the riverbank so that the boats could dock. This was also where the first Chinese kampong, or village, was located, and became part of Stamford Raffle's first plan for the new town in 1822. Raffles realized that boats could not dock here easily, so he gave the order to fill in the mangrove swamps on both sides of the river to create a more stable site for the boat docks. They used earth taken from small hills around Chinatown and Battery Road."

She continued to explain more of the river's story of human activities: "After reclaiming the banks, boats could deliver cargo and ship supplies and agricultural goods up and down the river, and out to the bay to awaiting ships. Over time Boat Quay and its shophouses would be completely choked with boats. And lots of those goods would spill into the river, along with all the trash. The water was very stagnant there at the wide bend. So, the river became unhealthy and dirty, and it was really like having a dump in the middle of downtown Singapore. And people who lived nearby only added to the river's pollution, including boat repair businesses upstream. That wasn't helping, either. That's why Prime Minister Lee Kuan Yew was determined to clean it up after independence. It may not have been his idea entirely, but he made it happen. During that time, they were building the container port as well, so the river was no longer needed to support the city's trading activities. The government decided to remake the river into a beautiful, clean attraction for the city, which is what people see today."

During her school years, Cathy thereby witnessed the expedited end of Singapore's mercantile era, characterized by local, small-scale trading activities along the river and its surrounding watershed. Visitors to today's downtown Singapore find an expansive, gleaming, and largely empty waterway with little indication of the livelihoods the river once provided. A handful of boats restored to haul tourists is all that remains of this bygone era.

This earlier river trade was known collectively as the lighterage industry, whose boats and merchants played an integral role in Singapore's early economy since 1819. That is when the colonial founder of Singapore, Thomas Stamford Raffles established the river as a British trading hub for the region—essentially a local marketplace along the water. For generations thereafter, hundreds of smaller boats—known simply as *lighters*—dominated the lively mercantile activities of this relatively modest colonial outpost.

At one point I asked about the origin of the term, *lighter*, and how it compared to a *bumboat*. Both terms seemed to describe these small-scale trading vessels. "Lighters and bumboats are the same thing," Cathy immediately began, now warming up to offer more. "The term *bumboat* is derived from the Germans—it's the English form of the German *bumboot*, where *bum* refers to *tree* and *boot* means *boat*," she clarifies, adding, "They used to use old rubber tires on the edges of the boats, so they would not damage each other, kind of like bumper cars at an amusement park."

Cathy further explained that lighter boats are basically small wooden barges that carry cargo and supplies for trade. She adds, "The word *lighter* comes from the Dutch—the Netherlands. It basically means 'to make your boat lighter' in weight after unloading it. More recently the boats have been fitted with motors, but before that they either had to use sails or poles to push their way upstream if that's where they were going. Some of the boats were designed to transport goods from larger ships in the harbor to the warehouses along the river, or vice-versa."

It follows that the *lighterage industry* refers to the business of transporting, loading, and unloading cargo from flat-bottomed, wooden barges known as either *lighters* or *bumboats*. Asian traders over the centuries had essentially adapted their boat styles from earlier European sources, providing an excellent example of *acculturation*—or the blending of European and Asian cultural traits—right here in Singapore. Such cultural globalization, or mixing has been happening for many centuries.

The river and its shores thus served as the colony's economic and social lifeblood during much of the 19th and 20th centuries. This was the colony's veritable highway for trade, with easy access to the ocean. Even when newer, deep-water wharves were installed at Tanjong Pagar to better accommodate large-scale oceanic trade, the lighterage industry remained steadfast. River traders continued to fill a market niche that the new port facilities had not yet subsumed at beginning of the 20th century.

Yet another variation of trading boat is the *Tongkang*, which is the Malay term for bumboat or lighter. These were larger vessels designed more for inter-island trade. Many of these around Singapore were operated by Indian traders or the Hokkien Chinese, one of the prominent dialect groups still well represented in Singapore today. The *Tongkang* thus paid visits to the Singapore River as well and could be seen loading or unloading cargo at Boat Quay. That is, until the British decided to build bridges across the river.

Cathy continued this intriguing story. "There weren't many bridges in those days. The Cavanagh Bridge was opened in 1869, and there were other bridges built upstream. All the boats had to follow the tides so they could enter or exit the river from the bay. The biggest blunder was to build the Cavanagh Bridge, which is just outside the Fullerton Hotel now. It was supposed to be a draw bridge, but they never put in the mechanism to raise the bridge!"

The Cavanagh Bridge was finally downgraded to pedestrian use after 1909 when the stronger Anderson Bridge was built nearby. In addition to blocking river traffic, the Cavanagh span was no longer able to accommodate the city's expanding road traffic. While some advocated for its reconstruction, the alternative plan was to build the new, sturdier Anderson Bridge, named for the then-governor of the Straits Settlements, John Anderson. Naturally, he was on site for the bridge's official dedication and opening for traffic on 12 March, 1910. With the shift of heavy traffic to the new span, a road sign was placed at the entrance to the now-obsolete Cavanagh Bridge which Cathy always enjoys pointing out to her guests. It instructs that traffic is limited to "any vehicle of which the laden weight exceeds 3 cwt. and to all cattle and horses"—a sign of the times.

Cathy explained how the headaches caused by the Cavanagh Bridge only continued. "To make more room for the boats, they tried to dredge the bottom of the river, but that didn't work. The tide still goes up and down, so the boats still could not get in and out of the river at high tide. This meant the merchants had to schedule their entrance and exit through the river mouth as the tide lowered."

It turns out the bridge's name is just as intriguing. Cavanagh was the last governor of the Straits Settlements, which at that time was under the jurisdiction of British India. The bridge is further noted as being the last project completed from the labor of Indian prisoners. This had been a standard British colonial approach to getting things done up until then. At the time of the bridge's completion, Cavanagh's successor had wanted it named Edinburgh Bridge, to commemorate the Duke of Edinburgh's visit the same year. His plan was thwarted by the Singapore Legislative Council, however, which preferred to have the bridge named for the last governor appointed by the British East India Company. Regardless of whose name ended up being honored, the span still cut off river traffic at high tide and eliminated the larger *Tongkang* boats completely; they could no longer access the river at all.

In 2019 the Elgin Bridge, the Cavanagh and its successor, the Anderson bridge were designated collectively as a national monument.

From Livelihood to Tourism

For hundreds of individuals and families who worked the river, this form of local trade had become a way of life. During the day or evenings, the lightermen could sit aboard their boats and socialize with friends and fellow lighters even in rare down times. The protective lower cove of the Boat Quay area further provided a geographical advantage. Their boats and activities were reasonably sheltered from the pounding waves and relentless winds that blew off the open ocean. With so many lighters parked along the wharfs, their adjacent boats formed a virtual blanket across the river's widest expanse.

Historical photos reveal the bustling river scene that Cathy herself experienced as a teenager. Looking from the north during the 1970s, the 19th century lighterage activities were now juxtaposed with, and even framed by, an emerging collection of glass and steel-framed corporate high-rises representing Singapore's march into the global economy. If there was a starker or grander anachronism to be found within the changing urban landscape, it is difficult to imagine what it might be.

The lighters and their bustling trade scene also forged an economic and cultural link with the shoreline. Up through its final decades, food hawkers and vendors clustered around the riverbanks and surrounding streets, just as local farming and meat-packing communities benefitted from the trading activities nearby. Upstream, the lighterage industry supported a wide range of associated occupations, not the least being the boatbuilders themselves. These traditional craftsmen with their numerous smaller boatyards could be found primarily along the banks of shallow tidal inlets and feeder creeks. These yards were strategically located to allow for the construction of new lighters and the ongoing maintenance of existing boats involved in downstream trade. The economic and social networks here were intricate and represented nearly two centuries of relative stability.

This small-scale form of local trade persevered into the 1970s. At the dawn of independence, however, Singapore's leadership envisioned a very different future for the river and its environs. And that future was already encroaching toward the river from its core downtown business district. By the 1960s the writing was already on the wall for the lighterage industry. As critics consistently pointed out, the "new broom" was already sweeping the country.

Cathy shared more about the daunting challenges her new nation faced, just as she was entering the world herself. "When Singapore was expelled from the Federation of Malaysia in 1965, Lee Kwan Yew and others were saying, 'Oh no, how are we going to make it through this?' This is when Singapore started moving in a whole new direction. There were so many problems to deal with, and everyone was so overwhelmed. Poverty and unemployment were really high, population was increasing rapidly, and we had the race riots and political instability. The place was a mess!" she summed up in her own direct way, adding, "And in addition to all of that, now the newly independent country was isolated within the region, no longer part of a larger country, and left to its own devices. That's when the new government decided to take drastic action." Clearly, Cathy's own sympathy for the early government runs deep, as she appreciates the magnitude of what improvements needed to come, and quickly.

The "drastic action" Cathy describes could not have contrasted more from the earlier, lackluster British approaches to managing its island colony. Perhaps to their own credit—or negligence, depending upon one's perspective—the colonial authorities largely stayed out of the economy's way. They basically allowed business and local industry to evolve gradually with little regulation for the common good. This included the lighter boats and related trading activities, which continued to overcrowd and pollute the river.

It is safe to conclude that the combined vision of

Singapore's leadership was to build a new city and country—a city-state—from the ground, up. Only much later during the 1980s and 1990s would these priorities shift somewhat to recognize the need for heritage conservation and preservation of historical landscapes. Until then, it was full speed ahead. Residential high-rises replaced the kampongs, and the sleepy colonial-era city was transformed into a glistening downtown skyline. Finding themselves surrounded by this urban boomtown, those working the river cautiously wondered about their own futures. And rightly so.

It was within this first phase of urban renewal that the lighterage industry eventually got subsumed. But not at first, strangely enough. For some time, the government's large-scale development scheme left the river and its occupants largely to their own devices. The global city was already emerging around them, its corporate towers casting lengthy shadows on Boat Quay. Scholars and other observers asked why the government was pushing hard on its economic development priorities, all the while leaving the polluted and overcrowded river alone. As such, the river became a prime focus of national embarrassment. Critics eventually lashed out at government leaders, including one citizen who described the river as "absolutely black," clogged with rubbish floating in rancid water. Even more important for river trade, this wholesale pollution made navigation further upstream nearly impossible.

True to his paternalistic instincts, Prime Minister Lee Kwan Yew personally ordered scientific studies of the river's water to determine the sources of pollution. The results from tested water samples only confirmed what residents—including young Cathy—had seen and smelled on their own. The river was not only highly contaminated with organic matter, but in some areas allowed absolutely no form of marine life to survive. With reliable data in hand, a comprehensive report was released by several departments in October 1969 which identified the main sources of pollution: a combination of domestic and industrial waste, along with trash and refuse dumped into the river.

At this point the lighterage industry and its hundreds of boats were not being targeted by authorities directly. From the lighters' perspective, however, the writing was on the wall. Not long following the 1969 interim reports, the decision was made to remove the full range of polluting activities from the river and its catchment areas—that is, everything except the lighter boats. The reports pointed to numerous culprits that did not directly involve the boats themselves. These included various cottage industries, latrines, street hawkers, vegetable vendors, backyard trades, boat repair and related riverside activities, and hundreds of pig and duck farms.

One major source of pollution consisted of the overcrowded tenement buildings and squatter settlements that had appropriated the river as their own collective sewer. Many of these areas, even well away from the river, were densely populated with squatters. To deal with their own human wastes, these makeshift communities were still employing night-soil buckets, pits, and overhanging buckets which, for their part, were unsanitary and presented a serious source of smell and water pollution. As Singapore's massive cleanup campaign got underway, more than 11,000 night-soil bucket latrines were identified. Cathy had experienced these rudimentary facilities at her first stepmother's farm in the kampong and had been told stories about them from family members. With some determination, all of them were eventually phased out, with the last ceremonial night-soil bucket succumbing to cleanup in 1987. By this time, all 621 overhanging latrines were likewise phased out, along with nearly 4,000 unsewered premises that had been discharging sullied water into river catchment areas.

Yet another immediate source of pollution received much

attention, in the form of smaller industries, squatter huts, and food vendors that still lined the river. These consisted of more permanent residents and tradespeople, with many families dating back generations to when Stamford Raffles declared Singapore a colony in 1819. Their days were clearly numbered, however, as all this activity was targeted for removal. With the notable exception of the lighterage industry once again, efforts were unleashed to remove all unauthorized structures—including the beloved food stalls and their hawkers—from the riverbanks. In this way, numerous ways of life along the river were summarily uprooted, with their operators compelled rather quickly to relocate and move into newer, authorized facilities.

Cathy was old enough to further recall the scenes and smells of those who worked on the banks of the river. She happened to be just old enough to witness the final years of old Singapore. She recalls, "I was only ten years old in 1977, and that's when they were starting to clean up the river. It took them ten years, until 1987, about the time I was starting to work. In the midst of the river cleanup efforts, there were times when I used to go to the museum on the other side of the Cavanagh Bridge—the yellow building directly opposite the Fullerton Hotel. During that time, there were hawker food stalls outside the museum. It was a food area, a market. They were called hawkers because people used to peddle food on the street; they didn't have permanent stalls or anything. So as the city continued to clean itself up—creating our 'clean and green' Singapore—these hawkers were given a permanent place to sell their food. They used to be called 'hawker centers,' but now that term has been replaced with 'food centers,' where they are provided with individually assigned stalls. One reason was for hygiene, as they finally had fresh water to prepare their food."

Cathy most vividly recalls those initial relocation efforts.

The food hawkers and their makeshift stalls were moved away from the river during the 1970s. This was no simple, two-day effort to evict a few dozen stalls. The massive undertaking continued beyond 1978, when by one count more than 2,500 hawkers still existed in the river's catchment area. Many of them were scattered throughout Chinatown, while others were located along numerous smaller avenues and lanes near the river. By 1977, more than two-thirds of the remaining holdouts had been compelled or forced to move into these designated business locations. Prominent new facilities included the Boat Quay Food Centre and the Empress Place Food Centre, located along the banks of the river just north of Cavanagh Bridge. More than 800 street hawkers had been removed from Chinatown alone.

The topic of hawker centers triggered another memory that Cathy enjoys discussing. She begins, "Before the city created these food centers, the hawkers used to carry their wares in buckets of water from the dirty river, and they would use that water to wash their plates after serving meals. And sometimes when they ran out of gravy, the water from cleaning out the bowls became gravy, too!" Cathy laughs and scrunches her face in disgust. "Yes, I used to tell that to my guests, and they'd be like 'Ewww!' So, the problem was that these hawkers were all lined up along the river, and some stalls were placed directly along the railings near the water. Whatever they cooked and didn't need simply got thrown into the water. You could see flying noodles going into the river, it was so horrible," Cathy shakes her head and laughs at the thought. "And people used to live along the river, and they dumped their trash there. Some worked on the boats and sometimes even lived there. When I was young, we could still see a lot of these boats going back and forth from the riverbank. So, that's my nostalgia. It was really nice for us because food here was so cheap. Noodles were only like five or ten cents a bowl, so we could afford it. Was it healthy or safe? Probably not."

Meanwhile along the river, cleanup efforts continued as did the eviction notices. The boatbuilders were among the first to be informed of their removal. Their small-scale boatyards not only supplied new boats for the industry but also regularly repaired older ones still in service. Their location was strategic, basically occupying the muddy banks of shallow tidal inlets and feeder creeks further upstream. Together with the remaining charcoal dealers along the river, the boatbuilders were pegged as one of the river's principal sources of pollution. Notices were served to all individual properties and businesses, making it clear that the HDB would provide all affected individuals with priority for rehousing and new sites for commercial activities elsewhere. Though many boatbuilders held out and refused to move right away, the upstream tributaries and feeders were rapidly being bulldozed and transformed into concrete drains. Seeing the river essentially "disappearing behind them," the remaining holdouts worked frantically to finish existing projects before their final removal. Many of these individuals were among the most economically and socially disadvantaged people in the country, and they were rightly concerned with what the future held for them.

While the boatbuilders begrudgingly gave up their businesses or moved to the less hospitable port of Pasir Panjang, the lighterage industry was in its death throws. The mid-1970s saw the abandoned hulls of so many lighters that they were strewn all along the river and even blocked other traffic. Various newspaper articles brought this issue to light, declaring the river as a "graveyard for derelict lighters," as Stephen Dobbs has documented. By 1975 only an estimated 40 percent of the river fleet was still actively in service.

The industry did attempt to fight back and save itself, largely between 1977 and 1983. Both the Lighter Owners and the Transport Vessel Workers associations presented a unified front in their collective attempt to persuade the government to somehow save the industry. During ongoing negotiations, however, the response was the same, that their "time was up." They were also arguing to the government that the relocation facilities at Pasir Panjang were too exposed to the sea and inclement weather, and that there was not enough capacity to hold the fleet. They even tried to persuade the government to view the lighters as an "instant tourist attraction" that would be missed if they were to completely leave the river. All told, it was a valiant effort.

Regardless, the government stuck to its final removal date of September 1, 1983. As Dobbs recounts, "From early morning onward, there was a procession of lighters, some towed, streaming out of the river. Altogether, some 270 lighters belonging to 30 companies left the river for the last time." Only adding to their humiliation, the procession was temporarily halted during a high tide, which trapped them all behind the Cavanagh and Anderson bridges. Those caught by the tide were forced to hold back until evening before proceeding finally to Pasir Panjang.

Although a sizable portion of the remaining lighters had relocated to the new port facility, business retracted quickly now that their surrounding environmental circumstances for river-born trade had been ripped away. By 1986, only three years after leaving the river, business for lighters had fallen 80 percent. This was even faster than the lighters had predicted in their most optimistic thinking. More than half the lighterage firms that moved to Pasir Panjang had closed, and the remaining ones continued to struggle. Many of the trade goods that once typically travelled on lighters—such as pepper, rubber, coffee, maize, and copra, were now handled in bulk by the modern port. The transport of animal feed, which accounted for around 30 percent of the business a few years earlier had completely dried up as pig and poultry farms were phased out.

By this time, most lightermen had resigned themselves to the changes and accepted that they would be the last generation of men to earn a living on their boats. Some of those unemployed were able to fall back on assistance from their families, while others were forced to rely on government welfare or on the support of local community or clan associations. Somewhat amazingly, a handful of lighter businesses were still operating out of Pasir Panjang into the mid-1990s, though the only income-producing activities consisted of the transport of rice and the replenishment of supplies to passing ships.

Meanwhile, the continued enlargement of massive container port facilities continued into the mid-1990s. Some of the last remaining lightermen found new opportunities in the upcoming tourism and recreation industry in which Cathy was likewise entering. These workers either secured jobs on the river as water taxi drivers or on refurbished lighters now used as ferries or outdoor dining facilities. With the river now pristine and the warehouses preserved at Boat Quay, Singapore's final transition to the global economy was complete.

Still, long-time residents like Cathy can feel nostalgic for the character, color and local vitality that hung on from centuries before. "In those days there were filthy old shops and overcrowded streets and vendors everywhere," Cathy says of the rampant challenges, "but the city had a soul." This collective soul, or character, has largely been lost as the city has modernized and regulated its urban development in admittedly safer, healthier ways.

As the river was being cleaned up, Cathy was growing up.

Not unlike a small number of remaining lighters, she too would find a path into her country's emerging tourism industry. Just as the final lighters made their way under Cavanagh Bridge for the last time, Cathy would make her own way—somehow—into the new Singapore.

Select Topics

The Hungry Ghost: Cathy and the Paranormal

When the spirit world emerges in conversation, Cathy expresses mixed and sometimes unsettled feelings. Ghosts and spirits hold a special place in various Asian cultural traditions, making this a natural topic to integrate into guided tours. Still, she was genuinely startled when I broached the topic one day, asking casually if Singapore provides ghost tours. She snapped back with, "Why would you ask that question? How did you even think of that?" I quickly explained that, for better or worse, ghost tours are commonly found in America's historic cities, such as Savannah or New Orleans. This surprised her, as the topic is not usually foremost on her mind. She does admit, however, that such tours do exist and are popular in Singapore—though she also admits to wanting little to do with them.

Occasionally she might raise such topics on her own tours, though usually for fun. "There's a fortress on the island of Sentosa," she tells me, referring to the now decommissioned Fort Siloso, constructed during the 1870s to protect Singapore's harbor from invasion. She continues, "The place was called the Island of the Living Dead in those days. There must have been an epidemic that gave the place its nickname, as a lot of the dead were simply left behind. When I do my maritime tours, I tell my groups that people died there and that their spirits still hang around, so I spook them a little bit," she adds fiendishly.

Cathy then recalls one instance when some tour-guiding friends pushed beyond her comfort zone. While catching up and laughing together, one of them asked what makes her the most afraid. Recalling her response, she says, "I told them that I probably don't like jumping off cliffs or doing stupid things like eating something that crawls." Testing her, they prodded to know if that was all Cathy feared. She continues, "It turns out they had been developing this new ghost tour, and after dinner they brought me to some very spooky places, including a cemetery. I was very uneasy. They joked that I shouldn't be afraid of ghosts based on my earlier answer. Thinking about it more, I told them it's not that I'm afraid of ghosts, I just don't feel good in these situations. I guess I'm most afraid of being possessed," she states with little emotion as if this is a normal response. The cemetery to which they brought Cathy was one of Singapore's oldest, with most of the burials dating to the 19th century. By the time of the world wars, nobody was being buried there any longer.

Cathy explains further, "There had been an issue about building a highway through part of the old cemetery, so this dredged up a lot of folk tales about ghost sightings and such. Years ago, there was a paranormal tour that included this cemetery and other older sites. You could go to all the main locations of ghost sightings and hauntings. They went to the Japanese headquarters from World War II, the old Ford Motor factory, which was all run down and derelict at the time. To scare people even more, they played spooky Japanese music and hyped up the stories. You see, I went on this tour to see how it was organized, and I was really afraid! Then we visited the graveyard I just mentioned. They advised us to not look up or down—I don't remember which. In any case, it was dark at night but still bright enough to see once our eyes got adjusted. My main fear was looking down, because I was afraid of stepping on something that would just appear out of nowhere!" The experience clearly left Cathy unsettled, and the return visit with her friends apparently did not help matters.

Cathy has encountered similar unsettling feelings at other cemeteries as well. One of these involved Singapore's designated Japanese cemetery which represents the period surrounding the Occupation. The cemetery's history is connected to the very neighborhood where Cathy had attended convent school. She says, "During the early 1900s, Japanese prostitutes were living in Singapore, and they had formed their own local community. Guess how surprised I was to learn that their brothels were located just two streets from my school!" She laughs while emulating her original surprise. "So, this was where the Japanese immigrant communities generally located and set up their own businesses, including the brothels themselves. By the 1930s, more Japanese people were coming to Singapore, but some arrived as spies for Japan. They spied on our military camps, airfields, and other sites related to Singapore's defensive capabilities. They were also scoping out the Malay peninsula and mapping out the whole country and sending this information back to Japan. This explains why it was so easy for the Japanese to invade and occupy Malaysia and Singapore during the war," Cathy adds as a personalized history lesson.

She then brings her story closer to home. "There is a Japanese cemetery here in Singapore, in today's suburban area. It was built by two Japanese plantation owners, and they had their own brothels as well. And they knew that the poor girls were dying young. Many of them contracted STDs, so these plantation owners made burial plots for them, and these poor young women were joined by a number of Japanese soldiers who had been executed for war crimes after their trials."

She continues, "So, one day my tour-guiding friends and I visited the cemetery, as we were doing some training there. And one of my girlfriends, she claims that she got possessed!" Cathy laughs nervously, continuing, "She had been wearing a jade pendant of the Goddess of Mercy while we walked around. She believes that the jade protects her from ghosts—she's very superstitious. And for some reason the jade pendant broke while we were there in the cemetery, and she claims that she was feeling uneasy and strange, even in daylight. She told us that she suddenly wasn't feeling well, and that's when her pendant broke. When we left the cemetery later that day, she told us more about her sensations. She was feeling off-center, as if something unseen was moving with her."

Cathy and her friends were inclined to believe her story. As a spiritual person herself, Cathy readily accepts that ghost sightings and hauntings do happen. This has led her to avoid the more uncomfortable tour jobs, as she explains more thoroughly—and with a touch of personal defiance: "When I was doing the crematorium tour—and yes, we do that! —I felt heavy-hearted and kind of sick. When I travel, I can feel when the energy in a room isn't good, so I can understand what my friend is talking about. Now my friends are leading the cemetery tours, which are held at night. I refuse to join them. The agent was willing to pay me extra money, too, but I didn't want to deal with that. I cannot guide people if I'm living in fear. Those cemeteries are so spooky, the graves are old, it's nearly pitch dark, and people are holding yellow candles to see. White candles are used for funerals; red candles are for celebrations. But yellow candles, they're spooky and eerie, and I think they're strange. Even though *dark tourism* is becoming more popular with the locals, I don't want to be doing the cemeteries at night!" At this point Cathy's agitation is ramping up, probably adding to her discomfort. She continues, "I can do the crematorium and the graves during the daytime. But, oh my God, don't freak me out by having me walk in there at night! Something might follow me home. People are paying big money to be spooked out on these tours, but they need to leave me out of it."

This topic leads Cathy to reflect more personally. In her belief system, spirits are real. She describes her own beliefs, saying, "When you talk about the spirit world or the being world, there are still a lot of souls that have not yet rested in peace and have not channeled into the other world. So, they still lurk around." She shows her hands like a cat exposing its claws, adding for emphasis, "It's true, I feel this, because sometimes seeing these types of things is not very pleasant. That's why these tours do not give me a nice feeling. My fear is that people can get possessed if they're not careful, and it's possible they don't know they're possessed. And then they have to hire the *Ghost Busters* and all that," she jokes, lightening the mood. She admits that some of her own fears probably originate from popular culture. "I think Hollywood has made so many movies, and even if they're not true, the plots still seem real. Sometimes it's not healthy to have an imagination like mine." Cathy concludes this topic for now, deciding to laugh it off.

More to her liking is the topic of funerals and, more accurately, the cultural traditions that surround them. "I love talking about funerals," Cathy says proudly, thinking of how various traditions and rituals come on full display during these otherwise somber events. "I learn a lot about these traditions by asking questions during funerals we hold for our extended family members." Cathy's curiosity tends to get the better of her as she delicately seeks knowledge at her own family events. Now eager to share, she says, "In traditional Chinese funerals, they would make paper cars and other paper replicas of everyday objects. It takes you back to the Chinese dynasties with their terra cotta soldiers and all of that. At some point, the Chinese transitioned from stone to paper replicas, including paper houses, cars, and lots of other things. The whole funeral fanfare is very colorful and fascinating, and very different from Western-style funerals. I would even talk to the undertakers and funeral directors when I got a chance," she chuckles somewhat bashfully.

This topic leads into my next line of inquiry, about the extent to which spiritualism or beliefs in the paranormal can be found within Singapore's culture. Of course, it remains a challenge to identify a singular "Singaporean culture," given the diverse ethnic and mixed-race makeup of the population. After feeling somewhat uneasy with our discussion of ghosts, possession, and the like, she now pivots to her more comfortable tour-guide mode. "So, Singapore has a variety of popular ghost figures, since there are so many nationalities here. There is the Malay ghost, the Chinese ghost, the Indian ghost—well, not so much the Indian ghost," she laughs while correcting herself. "Still, there is a distinctive ghost figure within practically all the ethnic groups that comprise Singapore."

To offer one specific example, she begins, "When locals talk about ghosts, some believe that by praying to the spirits they can gain wealth, power, and strength. So, during the olden days in the villages, or kampongs, there were many folk tales about ghostly sightings and people playing with or adopting spirits. Today, we have electricity in modern society, and ghosts are said to be afraid of it, so they disappear. They don't want to be electrocuted," Cathy laughs. She adds a personal account that makes me do a double take: "When I was young, I used to see some of these beliefs among people in my neighborhood. Even though there was electricity, there was all sorts of black magic going on, and people would claim to get possessed. For instance, Malays believe that when a woman dies during childbirth, she becomes a female ghost known as *Pontiana*. This ghost roams around with long hair, and her eyeballs are bleeding. This is found in Malay traditional cultural beliefs."

Cathy continues to reflect on her childhood and the spiritual ideas that pervaded her life. "There was this story during my Mama's time, which my children don't take seriously anymore—they think it's all a big joke—but it did enough to scare me and other children when we were young. The legend is that there was once a trishaw rider who was going home late at night, and he spotted a beautiful, young lady. It was close to midnight, and he decided to stop and offer her a ride. She happily hopped on his trishaw, and as he was riding, he was in euphoria because there was a beautiful young lady sitting next to him. And after riding for a while, she asked him to stop because she needed to pee. And when she got off, she left her baby on the seat of the trishaw. And as he waited for her to come back, he noticed that the baby was crying, and suddenly it stopped. He turned around and looked to see a tombstone instead. The trishaw rider was terrified, and he jumped off the trishaw and ran all the way home." Cathy laughs at her own story.

Folk tales like that of *Pontiana* were typically enough to dissuade children from venturing outside at night. Cathy reflects further, "So, grandmothers tell stories, neighbors tell stories, and there are just lots of stories going around, handed down through generations. Then there are the Malay movies, which tell their own stories. It's like watching *Poltergeist* or *Changeling* and films like that, but it's their local versions."

All of Cathy's stories and personal experiences point to a wider imagination of the afterlife shared by many Singaporeans. Perhaps the most visible—and lucrative—cultural event in Singapore is known formally as the Yulon festival in the Buddhist tradition, and the Zhongyuan festival that originates from Taoism. The every-day Chinese populations throughout Asia and elsewhere know it by its more common, vernacular name, the Hungry Ghost festival. Some have described this event as the equivalent to America's Halloween.

Unlike the one-night celebration of Halloween, however, the Hungry Ghost festival persists in its numerous incarnations for an entire month—namely, the seventh lunar month of the year. This typically falls around August. A wide array of smaller festivals and cultural events provide colorful variety throughout the entire month. In this Chinese "imagination of the afterlife," as described by Hong Yin Chan, practitioners believe that the gates of Hell are somehow unlocked during the seventh lunar month. This is said to be a respite from Purgatory which allows souls in the underworld (or netherworld) to venture out to roam the earth among us humans, perhaps on a sort of "tourist visa." It is generally believed that almost everyone's soul will spend some time in this netherworld as a kind of purgatory before once again being reincarnated as humans back on earth. Only the worthiest of souls may ascend to Heaven without being reincarnated. This may all be well and good, though there is a catch. As Terence Heng explains, "because they roam the earth, they also require sustenance, entertainment, and spending money." They are—quite literally—hungry ghosts.

In a valiant effort to appease, and feed, these roaming spirits, individuals and families can practice their own home-grown rituals. Believers typically perform these activities during the seventh month, such as burning paper money or offering paper effigies that represent the modern material world. These effigies often mimic consumable goods, such as automobiles, clothes, houses, computers, or jewelry. After all, who has not wanted to set fire to a computer at some point, even if only made of paper? Food and incense are also offered during these rituals. These gifts are directed foremost to a family's ancestors but are also available to any other wayward spirits who might happen to be in the vicinity. It is common to find tables outside of HDB flats or local businesses piled with any combination of food items. Offerings can consist of small boxes of modest food goods—with pineapples, crackers, and the like—or entire spreads normally reserved for large family dinners. Feasts of fruit, vegetables, cookies, baked goods, and even noodle dishes from fast-food restaurants are all fair game for these wandering spirits. There are no special dietary restrictions of note.

Among the most popular offerings are paper effigies of gold and silver, referred to as *kim zua*, or gold paper, as spoken in the Hokkien dialect. To regulate the burning of *kim zua*, local town councils often provide special burning drums at designated locations. Makeshift altars are then placed nearby where other paper effigies are burnt. The *kim zua* represents the currency spirits use in the netherworld to either purchase their own items or to bribe other entities for an easier afterlife. These rituals can also take the form of small, crudely made altars located on the roadside, or in more obscure places such as residential stairwells or sidewalks. Individuals offer these as sacrifices to the three principal objects of worship in Chinese cosmology—namely, gods, ghosts and ancestors. One serious purpose for these rituals is to demonstrate *filial piety*—or devotion to family, as Cathy described earlier.

This practice of burning joss (incense) sticks, or paper fashioned into money and various three-dimensional objects remains popular to the present day. During the seventh lunar month, the air becomes visibly clouded with smoke through continuous mass burning rituals held throughout Singapore. These conditions are mostly concentrated, not surprisingly, in areas with high proportions of ethnic Chinese residents. One exception involves the Chinese Catholics like Cathy, who do not directly participate in these rituals themselves.

Nonetheless, Cathy explains more about her own memories and family involvement during Hungry Ghost month. She begins, "If we came upon a pile of burning effigies or joss, we were not allowed to kick or step on it, because a ghost might still be sitting there and eating. We were told that it was taboo to touch anything, or else we might fall sick. My mother-in-law still practices, choosing an auspicious day to provide a whole offering of food. She provides five kinds of meat: fish, crab, chicken, duck, and roast pork. This was offered to my father-in-law, after he passed away, because he became a hungry ghost! She also provided him with his favorite drink, *Johnny Walker Red*, and *Camel* Cigarettes without filters," she says nonchalantly as my own eyebrows rise with curiosity.

She continues by recalling a humorous story. "Now in the modern world, the effigies become more complex. One of my auntie's friends had a grandmother who passed away, and so her granddaughter burned a paper VCR machine because she had loved Chinese dramas. One day she had a dream that her grandmother visited and scolded her for not burning the VCR tapes as well, since she still had nothing to watch!" she laughs. "Nowadays, there are even more gadgets like smart phones, tablets, and computer games that are updated all the time. And everyday material goods need to be burned in effigy as well, such as shoes, bags, cars, and everything we live with. It's all made from paper to be used in the netherworld."

As for the leftover food prepared for the ghosts, much of it is either donated to shelters or consumed at home. The HDB housing now has regulations about placing food in hallways, and the Chinese temple only allows vegetarian foods that can be easily preserved and consumed later. The temple staff then remove it all soon thereafter. Cathy recalls, "One year, a Catholic priest came from the Philippines, and he preached that we would get sick from eating the food left out for the ghosts. But I knew he had no clue, since I've been eating the leftover food for thirty years! The Church doesn't practice it, but nobody said I couldn't eat!" She laughs at her practical conclusion to the ritual.

Recycled or not, it is still necessary to wait before consuming food designated for the ghosts. She explains, "After a few hours with the food out, wooden clappers are thrown on the floor to see if the ghosts have actually eaten it. The clappers are like coins, with heads or tails. They are thrown three times. If they land on heads, it means the ghosts have finished their meal. If the clappers are negative, you need to wait 20 minutes and try again. People are not so afraid of the ancestor ghosts—those from the immediate families—because our ancestors are expected to protect and watch out for us. But it's the other wandering ghosts that may not have people here to feed them. Hungry ghosts can be angry ghosts, so they are the ones that need to be appeased."

On a broader scale, a wide array of organized events accompany the festival, encouraging entire communities to participate. During Hungry Ghost month, public performances abound, including traditional Chinese opera known in Singapore by the Malay term *Wayang*. During Cathy's youth, Chinese opera performances were still prolific, and some still perform today during Hungry Ghost. Most opera troops have fallen by the wayside, however, due especially to a lack of enthusiastic younger people to replenish them. Today's opera troops rely almost entirely on their older members. As to why this is, Cathy provides some intriguing background. "The

Chinese opera is still more active in places like Hong Kong and Taiwan, because they have much larger populations to support them. In the old days, families here had a lot of children and were very poor. Some of those families decided to give or even sell one or more of their children to the opera troops, hoping they would be better fed and might learn useful skills. Nowadays it's been a challenge for the troops to recruit young people, since parents no longer so willingly give up their children—though sometimes tempted," she adds with a smirk.

A Spiritual Shift

With Cathy's tour-guide experiences came more nuanced perspectives on spiritualism and organized religion. Her belief system since early childhood had been ambiguous at best, given her blended, mixed-race family. On the one hand, her ethnicity is largely Chinese with a twist of Scottish thrown in—on those occasions she decides to admit to her father's heritage. And yet she and much of her family were Catholics. In one sense she was the epitome of a multicultural Singaporean whose identity is difficult to label. As she transitioned from secondary school to the budding tourism industry, it was perhaps only a matter of time before she would seriously consider the tenets of other faiths.

During one conversation I asked her to talk about this transition and whether she still considered herself as predominantly Catholic. She prefaced her thoughtful response with some additional background for my benefit. "Well, I was born a Catholic, and I went to a Catholic school, so it makes sense that for me Catholicism was the way to go during those years. The religion itself didn't become really important for me in some ways, however, since I was also dealing with all sorts of other issues—when I was going to eat next, who was going to be at home—you get the idea. Then I started learning a lot more about other religions when I became a tour guide. We had to study different cultures, take classes, and visit the temples where we would be leading people. You can't talk about Catholicism in a temple!" She laughs about this otherwise serious expectation, adding, "So, this is when I really started to learn and become more open minded to other faiths including Buddhism, Hinduism, and Taoism. And of course, I needed to learn about Islam and visit the mosque in Kampong Glam."

She then reflects on her current perspective, continuing, "That's the beauty of being a tour guide, that you have to discuss and teach about a wide range of topics, including religion, without being biased. It's all about discussing religions, cultures, history, all sorts of things about different places and societies that have all influenced Singapore. If I do a tour of a temple, for instance, I need to talk about much more than the symbols, the construction dates, architecture and all the figurines. The story is much broader than that. I must be knowledgeable about the history and religious background." Then she realized, "I even married a non-Catholic husband, so I guess it didn't matter much to me. I was more interested in security after my uncle died, and I needed to take care of my aging grandmother. Tony and his family are Taoist. Sometimes I think I know more about Taoism than my mother-in-law! Because I've studied Taoism for my tour guiding, I think that's probably true," she chuckles.

I follow up with, "Has all of this newfound knowledge affected your own faith, and if so, in what ways?"

With a lengthy pause for contemplation, she offers, "I think it's important to be curious, first of all. I've always been curious and interested in learning new things. As you read, you start to ask yourself about the teachings of other religions, and eventually you start to apply certain things to your daily life. I think Taoism is more about folk tales and lores which later turned into folk religion, for instance. That is why they have many deities. But Buddhism is more about teaching people the way of life, like the idea of what you do is what you reap. You reap whatever you sow. Karma ripples down to your family and children. So, after you start learning these ideas you can better understand why people live in certain ways, and the influence it has on their lives."

I raise my eyebrows at her discussion of karma, which seems to take her in a more spiritualist direction. I then ask the big question, "Do you still consider yourself to be a practicing Catholic?"

To this she lets out a chuckle and responds, "I wouldn't say, after all this learning, that I don't want to be a Catholic. I'm still happy being a Catholic, it's still my religion. But then, I guess knowledge is the gateway to respect. Actually, the real value of God is very simple: love your neighbors, love everybody," she says thoughtfully, adding, "So, when you're guiding, you can't be cynical or critical. This is what makes you a good guide, a good person. You can be excellent with your command of history, facts, and figures, but if you don't have humanity, it's difficult to tell the full story. I can tell you this building was built in this year and by whom, but without your humanity you won't have an emotional attachment to your guests at all. When people take a tour, they want to *feel*, not just *know*."

This sounds like impressive advice for anyone in her line of work. I continue to prod further, asking, "Was there a time when you started to question the Catholic faith, or began to lean in a different direction?" It is intriguing that here we have a Singaporean woman of primarily Chinese ethnicity who discovered Buddhism and Taoism only after her years of Catholic schooling.

To this she responds more quickly than expected. "Oh yes,

I started to question things, such as why some people are so mean, even within my religion. And I became less sure about the Catholic theory about sinning against God. The Catholic services I attend are always so focused on the sin we have. It's like, hello, turn the page. How much can a person sin?" Cathy laughs at her own rhetorical question. She is now on a roll, continuing, "And they talk a lot about Adam and Eve, and how they messed up, and so because of that we all have to wear clothes now! I have to keep my sense of humor with all of this. Don't get me wrong, I think God is almighty, God is great. But it's just branding by the Roman Catholic Church. The core thing I started to question, though, was the sinning. In Buddhism, it teaches the value of good deeds and merits. For instance, when you are kind and do positive things, God will bless you with good merits, your children will be healthy, and so forth. It's based on what you do and accomplish. This is the notion of karma. If you do a lot of good things, you attract more positives for you and your family. It's like being generous; the more you give, the more you receive—not monetarily, but in other areas of life."

I naturally follow up with, "So, have you abandoned the Catholic notion of original sin?"

"I have come to the realization that it's all between me and God. I don't have to answer to people or priests. I don't have time to worry about how much I sin against God. I have to think about what kinds of good things I can do for the world. I'm tired of sinning all the time, so I actually have to lie when I go to confession. I lie in my confession that I did something I didn't do. Just how much can I sin in one day? Like bad mouthing someone, or stepping on someone's toe? Or using bad words—will that send me directly to Hell?" We both laugh at her logical questions. She finishes her train of thought with one more rhetorical question: "With everything going on in our lives, it's already so difficult just to go to church, let alone to confession. Why do I need to confess? God can already see me doing everything down here, right? I don't think I have much to worry about."

Select Topics

The Backstory of *Crazy Rich Asians*

Singapore's tourism industry struck gold with the release of the hit romantic comedy, *Crazy Rich Asians* in August 2018. Chen May Yee, writing for *Mumbrella Asia*, commented that the film's inclusion of popular Singaporean tourist sites "amounted to the kind of sweeping product placement most marketers can only dream of." The film quickly became one of the top-earning romantic comedies of all time, earning $26 million during its opening weekend in the US alone. The film's producers had apparently made the right choice to enter a contract with Warner Brothers for the full theatrical release. They had been seriously tempted by a less risky—and less lucrative—offer by Netflix to keep the film out of the theatres.

Within one year of its release, the film earned over $238 million worldwide and was touted as the first mainstream global romantic comedy featuring an all ethnically Chinese cast. Not since *Joy Luck Club* in 1993 had a Hollywood film included such a high representation of ethnically Asian actors. Numerous actors in *Crazy Rich Asians* were biracial as well, notably of Asian American and British Asian backgrounds. This was a strategic casting decision to encourage viewer connections from these English-speaking regions. The film's ultimate success was further marked through numerous prestigious awards, including various Golden Globe nominations for Best Motion Picture, Best Actress for Comedy or Musical, and a Screen Actors Guild Award for the film's outstanding cast.

Prior to the film's release, American tourists had heavily favored other Asian nations such as China, India, and Japan for their travel preferences. Singapore even ranked as low as the tenth popular Asian destination between 2011 and 2014. "Singapore is relatively well known in Asia," explained Lionel Yeo during his interview for the Singapore Management University. As a former CEO of the Singapore Tourism Board (STB), Yeo confirmed it was "still challenging to reach major segments of the North American markets, outside of the gateway cities on the eastern and western coasts."

It was within this context that the producers for a new movie project showed up at the STB offices in 2017. They specifically asked permission to access various planned filming locations within Singapore. Upon further discussions, Yeo and the STB decided that *Crazy Rich Asians* was a worthwhile project to support. After all, it was being produced by Warner Brothers, a respected Hollywood studio. The Singapore Film Commission ended up backing the project financially as well, with grants that would help assure the film would "highlight Singapore talent in credited roles" along with various other local benefits.

It turned out that local Singaporean actors and thespians with roles in the film gained unparalleled global exposure. At the same time, numerous Singaporean landmarks were also featured in the film, not the least being the Marina Bay Sands Resort and SkyPark, Gardens by the Bay, Convent of the Holy Infant Jesus Middle Education School—lovingly referred to as CHIJMES, Newton Hawker (Food) Centre, the Merlion, and related heritage sites. Lynette Pang of the STB further explained in her own interview with Singapore Management University, "As the movie was set in Singapore and showcased Singapore's culture, food, and attractions, it provided a natural conversation opening about the real Singapore and piqued interest in visiting the country."

The STB was understandably aiming to capitalize from the broader trend of *cine-tourism*, referring to tourists who flock to local sites featured in popular films. For instance, tourism in New Zealand skyrocketed following the release of Peter Jackson's *Lord of the Rings* trilogy in 2001, while the hit comedy, *Lost in Thailand* of 2012 led to a tripling of Chinese visitors there. Likewise, visitors to Rome can step into the shoes of the fictional Professor Langdon (played by Tom Hanks) through a tour of local churches and plazas featured in *The Davinci Code* and *Angels and Demons*. For its part, Singapore was more than happy to invest national funding into the film. The government's financial endorsement and additional forms of support allowed the producers to incorporate a wide range of popular local sites and attractions that are visible as prominent backdrops. In turn the STB and related government officials looked to enhance the country's appeal for cine-tourism by expanding its marketing to foreign visitors.

According to the STB, American searches about Singapore on Google increased three-fold following the film's release in August 2018. Similarly, Orbitz, which serves as a travel fare aggregator web site, witnessed a 110 percent increase in searches for Singapore. This online traffic appears to have foretold the actual increase in visitors to the city-state later that year. The annual number of American visitor arrivals increased by fourteen percent in the year 2018, followed by a record surge of visitors—some five million—between July and September alone. While numerous factors contributed to the increase in conferences and tourism that year, the film was cited as a primary one.

Meanwhile, tour companies in Singapore were benefitting from the film's spillover effect. *Monster Day Tours* reported that their *Crazy Rich Asians* private city tour was already attracting 10-15 mostly American guests each week, only two months after the tour's launch. The company's founder, T.Y. Suen, commented for *Mumbrella Asia*, "We even have guests who are fans of the movie and insist on visiting every filming location." Other locations had not yet seen a boost in visitors from the film as of late 2018. As Chen May Yee wrote, stall owners at Newton Food Centre reported "business as usual," though one claimed that "some locals and tourists do ask us about the movie..." Of course, Americans and other far-away populations cannot simply purchase tickets and jump on a plane immediately after seeing a film. It was therefore reasonable to expect a lag of a year or more before witnessing a surge in American or European visitors.

Though tempting to believe otherwise, not all filming locations were in Singapore proper. Certain filming sites in nearby Malaysia were already witnessing increased visitorship by January 2019. The Four Seasons Langkawi, for instance, experienced increased bookings during the previous month, which management attributed to the movie. This luxury beach resort served as the backdrop for the film's bachelorette party which featured everything from conspicuous consumption to dead fish. Likewise, the Cheong Fatt Tze mansion in Penang—the courtyard of which was featured during the story's climactic mahjong game—had already seen an increase in hotel guests and visitors asking for a tour of the premises.

The filming location for the fictional Young family mansion at Tyersall Park was likewise found one country north in Malaysia. The story's secluded estate was filmed in Kuala

Lumpur at *Carcosa Seri Negara*, a pair of British colonial mansions transformed into a luxury hotel. The property was most recently converted into a museum in 2017. In her article for *Condé Nast Traveler*, Meredith Carey shares anecdotes from the film's director, Jon Chu. He explains, "There were certain aspects to Tyersall Park, where Nick's grandmother lives, that you couldn't find in Singapore. That's what makes the fictional Tyersall Park, this sort of Central Park within the tight squeeze of Singapore, such an amazing location in the book, because those properties just don't exist anymore. So we had to go to Malaysia to film that part, and since we were there, there was a lot we could find." He adds that moving numerous sets to Malaysia made good financial sense as well.

Back in Singapore, Cathy has not been immune from the predictable onslaught of visitor questions. Since the film's release, her guests have continuously inquired about specific scenes and where they were filmed. She explains, "The film did very well in America. Probably nine out of ten Americans who come here say they are in Singapore because of that movie. I don't blame them, as movies are very influential. We have a tour called *Crazy Rich Asians* now, but we've had issues with the travel agents not wanting to make adjustment to fixed tour itineraries. Somebody makes decisions about the destinations scheduled into a given tour, and they just tell the guides to lead it. There isn't much flexibility sometimes because the places on the tour are set in stone. So, it's up to us to dig more and figure out how best to tell the story. I really need to watch it again to really build it into my tour. There are quite a few scenes that are not shot in Singapore, such as the scene with the mahjong game. That was shot in Penang. That's because Penang and Malacca still resemble the older Singapore of the 1970s before everything was redeveloped here. Those are historical places in Malaysia. They still have character, and so they worked well for the film's story." I could not help but chuckle in response, contemplating that the producers purposely left Singapore to find more historically appropriate filming locations.

Like countless movies from Hollywood, *Crazy Rich Asians* was adapted from the book of the same title. The novel's author, Kevin Kwan is of Chinese descent and was born in Singapore, where he lived until his family moved to the United States at age eleven. Kwan could personally relate to the story he wrote, as his own family likewise represents so-called old money. In one interview for the online magazine, *Tatler* in 2018, Kwan described his own upbringing as "normal and idyllic," and claims the story was largely inspired by his childhood more so than his family's wealth. As a child he had lived with his paternal grandparents, "who were not ostentatious people," he reflects. He adds that he was "not brought up in a lavish manner—quite the opposite, actually..."

Kwan further described his Singapore experience as a "Huck Finn kind of life," having attended a rather typical Anglo-Chinese school and spending much of his time outdoors, often cycling around the neighborhood with friends. Of course, his family was clearly well off. Kwan's great-grandfather had been a founding director of Oversea-Chinese Banking Corporation (OCBC), Singapore's oldest bank. His maternal grandfather founded the Hinghwa Methodist Church, and his paternal grandfather was the city's first Western-trained ophthalmologist and was commissioner of the St. John Ambulance brigade. He was later knighted by Queen Elizabeth II for his humanitarian services such as treating the poor without charge.

The women in his family were likewise influential, if in different ways. His paternal grandmother is described by writer MJ Jose as an "elegant and imperious lady who was more traditional in the household," while Kwan described her as the "most sought-after debutante of her day, admired for her beauty and distinctive style." Kwan admitted to being largely unaware of his own privilege until he was whisked away to an American suburb near Houston where much of what he had known no longer existed in his life. Notably, the homes were smaller with no hired help. Still, he credits that his American experience allowed him the flexibility to pursue his creative outlets, including the writing of his novels. Had he remained in Singapore, he doubts that he would have enjoyed such opportunities.

In various media interviews, Kwan describes his novel as a reflection of his own cultural experiences as a young boy. Beyond wanting to preserve his own memories with his novels, his broader goal was, as he explained, "to show the rest of the world an aspect of Asia that isn't limited to what we read about in gossip magazines—that isn't just about people dropping millions on weddings or Hermes bags. I wanted to depict the society that I knew well, one of educated families with style and taste that have been quietly going about their lives for generations."

Kwan perhaps relates most to a main character of the story, Nicholas (Nick) Young, who likewise gained a westernized world view after being sent to boarding school in the United Kingdom. Like Nick, Kwan views himself as an Asian outsider looking in. Aside from his novel, Kwan also wrote the script for the film adaptation and worked closely with the film's director, Jon Chu, a Chinese American director born in the US. Kwan was also heavily involved with the cast and crew throughout the production process. He helped scout for filming locations, choose costumes, and even train some actors to improve their accents.

From an Asian-American perspective, the film was a breakthrough success. As Kirsten Han acknowledges, "the release of a major all-Asian film feels like an antidote to the whitewashing that Hollywood is notorious for." The female lead for the film, Constance Wu, has consistently spoken out about race and representation in the movie industry. Asian representation for the film was further promoted through the intentional call on YouTube for an all-Asian cast. As documented by Terrie Siang-Ting Wong, director Jon Chu explained, "We really just want to open up the process because we know how hard it is to get in the door of a movie, especially for all Asian characters of different shapes, sizes, ages and talent." As such, the film was acclaimed by media as a significant milestone for representing Asian and Asian-American actors in a Hollywood film production.

Half a world away, Singapore's own film industry likewise benefitted significantly and extolled the film as one of their own. According to Wong, media reports described *Crazy Rich Asians* as a "made-in-Singapore" production rather than simply a product of Hollywood. Backing up this claim was the fact that more than 300 Singaporean cast and crew members were ultimately employed for the film, constituting more than five percent of Singapore's entire film industry at the time. For this reason, it turns out that Singaporeans represented the majority of non-US Asian characters in the film. Beyond Singapore, the casting was truly an international effort, with the hiring of Asian actors from Australia, Britain, China, Malaysia, Mongolia, the Philippines, and the United States. Because of the impressive international effort to produce, fund, and cast the film, Wong considers *Crazy Rich Asians* to be a transnational film production rather than one merely of Hollywood.

Clearly the film and its producers deserve accolades for elevating the role of Asians in Hollywood and beyond. One additional question might be the extent to which the film portrayed the "real" Singapore and the complex diversity of

Asian communities around the world. According to Kirsten Han, a Singaporean writer of Chinese descent, *Crazy Rich Asians* still falls into the common trap of stereotyping a global Asian population that numbers over four billion. For non-Asian westerners, Asia is often portrayed in specific ways through oversimplified descriptions. Examples include the concept of "rising Asia" with futuristic skyscrapers and modern urban scenes of wealth and glitz, or—at the opposite extreme—impoverished places that serve as inspirational backdrops for films like *Slumdog Millionaire*.

Speaking from her own Singaporean perspective, Han continues to describe such stereotypes: "We are dumplings and kung fu, curry and tech support, wise gurus who talk in riddles for all your 'eat, pray, love' needs. We are obscenely wealthy people throwing lavish parties." Han thus believes the film misrepresents her home island in fundamental ways. Perhaps unintentionally, the effort to heavily involve the Singaporean film industry in the production of *Crazy Rich Asians* still fell short by obscuring her country's incredible degree of cultural and ethnic diversity. Han continues to describe her experiences as a freelance journalist who writes about Singapore for various foreign news outlets: "I've heard the same stories over and over again, solidified into tropes that supposedly define us: wealth, anal levels of micromanagement ('You guys ban chewing gum, right?'), the caning of American teenagers. These are people who think we're in China, and many don't realize we speak English as our first language." She cites how Singapore has been deployed as a "shiny city backdrop" for numerous action films like *Hitman: Agent 47*, and scoffs at one effort by a British television show to digitally alter various scenes to make it look "more like Singapore." For one thing, producers had changed the street signs from English to Chinese.

Han's concerns may not be misplaced. As someone who

visited Singapore for the first time after seeing the movie, I went in with a visual expectation of witnessing a futuristic city replete with bedazzling architecture, luxury resorts, and high-energy nightlife like one might find in Tokyo or New York's Times Square. I expected bustling streets and corporate office towers ablaze with flashy sky signs and all-night parties. I had also gained the impression that Singapore's glitzy filming locations deployed for various party scenes would be exclusive and inaccessible to the average population.

In stark contrast, we often found the opposite. Although we found a bustling, energetic global city within its downtown and surrounding historical neighborhoods, these places exuded a calmer, lower-stress urban scene. Ours was more of a surprisingly comfortable urban experience than a Tokyo or Manhattan might present.

As for specific sites featured in the movie, I was admittedly astonished with the ease of public accessibility for many filming locations. Upon our first daytime arrival with Cathy to Gardens by the Bay, for instance, we exited our vehicle and walked right up to the base of the towering, artificial grove of so-called *supertrees*. Topping out at 50 meters tall, these concrete towers take the shape of giant, tropical tree trunks transitioning into umbrella-like canopies. Appropriately hiding the concrete structures—for the most part—is a carpet of lush tropical vegetation clinging to their edges as originally intended. The vision was for the supertrees to provide shade and serve as a signature feature of Gardens by the Bay, described by some as the botanic gardens of the future. The entire park was built by Singapore's National Parks Board and was designed by the winner of a 2006 international competition.

Gawking up at the supertrees with my mouth hanging open in awe, I naturally asked Cathy whether there was an entry fee for this area. She responded with a puzzled look, indicating that anybody could walk around, free of charge. This was a shock, as these futuristic, multi-colored supertrees provided the film's glitzy setting for Colin and Araminta's off-the-charts wedding reception. The film's impression of this place was that of an exclusive resort or private club. Instead, we were simply wandering around in a public park as many other locals and visitors were doing.

Upon Cathy's prompting, we returned to Gardens by the Bay on the MRT one night—the fare costing around three dollars each—to enjoy the park's dazzling nighttime transformation into a human-made tropical forest. The supertrees were now glowing with luminous, multicolored lights. More astonishing were the crazy-narrow pedestrian bridges that appeared to dangle precariously across their treetops. With ice cream and other snacks in hand, we then joined hundreds—perhaps thousands—of fellow visitors to lay on our backs to watch the dazzling nightly light show choreographed to inspirational classical music. It was a night for the ages, and at no greater cost than a trip to the county fair.

Situated strategically behind the supertrees and light show was the ever-stunning architectural signature of the new Singapore, the Marina Bay Sands resort. I had also presumed that the iconic hotel and its incomparable rooftop "boat" known as the SkyPark would be off limits as well. Again, with a minutes-long subway ride from downtown, we exited from the underground MRT station strategically placed inside the Sands' expansive shopping area. Access was just that easy, allowing for gawking visitors like us to linger and express our collective awe at one of Singapore's most stunning pieces of architecture. Of course, one would need to drop some serious cash to stay a night or two in the hotel rooms perched above us. Still, these accommodations are little different from any other luxury hotel located in the heart of the world's larger entertainment destinations.

Rather than spend money to stay overnight, it was enough to enjoy the lobby space and pay the entrance fee for the SkyPark, perched 56 stories high atop the third tower. This open-air location was the scene for the film's celebratory finale, featuring Nick and Rachel's engagement party complete with obligatory fireworks. Without knowing any better, one might presume that the SkyPark was inaccessible to everyone except the "crazy rich," or at least the guests of the Sands. And certainly, the resort's infinity pool and various high-end restaurants are off limits to visitors. However, the boat-shaped observation deck was all ours, providing incomparable, breathtaking panoramas of Singapore's ever-changing urban scene. Granted, the act alone of traveling to Singapore from the other side of the world requires serious financial wherewithal and logistics to pull off. That said, it was readily apparent how a film like *Crazy Rich Asians* could provide a false sense that this glamorous city was largely off limits to the rest of us.

It follows that the idea of a "crazy rich" Singapore is something of a misconception. Even millionaire and entrepreneur Kane Lim notes that the sprawling mansions and parks featured in the film created an exaggerated sense of wealth and opulence; this aspect was clearly over the top. For instance, the sprawling mansion of Nick's grandmother was not typical for even Singapore's most elite families. Such houses are unrealistically large. Only three or four such places exist in all of Singapore, according to Sue-Ann Cheow writing for the *Straits Times* in 2018. As noted earlier, this is one reason that the Young family mansion was filmed in Malaysia instead.

As a self-professed shopaholic, however, Lim admits that the jet-setting shopping sprees in the film were not far from the truth. Flying in supermodels, caviar, butlers, and international staff for parties is also not uncommon for this very narrow subset of society. What is not portrayed, however, is the remaining 99-plus percent of Singapore's everyday population, some 80-percent of whom live in HDB public housing flats as discussed earlier—with Cathy, of course, being one of them.

Further, the film did not necessarily resonate with non-western Asians such as the Chinese. Box office numbers indicate that *Crazy Rich Asians* was—somewhat ironically—appreciated more thoroughly by non-Asian audiences. English-speaking regions provided the Merlion's share of support for the film, with 73.2 percent of revenues ($174.5 million) coming from the United States alone. Australia brought in more than $17 million, followed by the United Kingdom at $7.6 million. According to the scholars Giana Eckhardt and Finola Kerrigan, one reason the film did not resonate with audiences in communist China was that they could not relate to the excess wealth and ostentation. This is despite the film's story that serves as its own critique of such blatant over-consumption.

From a Singaporean perspective, the casting was critiqued for the same reason it was praised—for featuring a fully Chinese cast. The absence of non-Chinese characters, some observers noted, oversimplified the country's diverse, multiethnic population. For a film whose primary backdrop is Singapore, an opportunity was missed to represent the cultural diversity of the place more accurately. For instance, ethnic Indian Singaporeans were only depicted in the film as service workers—in the few cases they appeared at all. Various local Singaporean artists and activists expressed disappointment with the film being "too Chinese." Their point was that more than 20 percent of Singapore's population is comprised of the Malay and Indian ethnic groups. The few minority actors included in the film were relegated to the roles of security guards and hawker food sellers with no speaking lines.

Alternatively, proponents of the film point to the story's

main purpose, which was not to portray Singaporean life and its diverse population in general. Instead, the aim was to provide a contrast between the experiences of Chinese immigrants around the world. As Ekhardt and Kerrigan demonstrate, the film explores how Chinese immigration is viewed globally and how this perception has changed. For instance, the character of Rachel Chu's mother, Kerry, had emigrated to the United States to seek better opportunities for her and her daughter. She later became a successful real estate agent in New York while Rachel thrived as a professor of economics. Together they are the American dream personified, that of struggling immigrants determined to improve their livelihoods for future generations.

In contrast, the immigration of Nick's family to Singapore provides for quite a different experience. Although not clarified in the film, the family likely preserved its wealth by migrating out of China during the Revolution and placed roots in other Asian cities where they could grow their influence, such as Singapore, Hong Kong, and Taipei. The younger generation then later migrated to western cities including London and New York to advance their own education. Ekhardt and Kerrigan explain, "This form of immigration—moving to global wealth and education centers to become a part of the global elite—is valorized in the film, in comparison to the 'old' model of non-elites immigrating for work and opportunities to improve their socioeconomic status, which is derided."

In the film, Nick's family generally looks down on, and outwardly sneers at, this latter form of immigration that represents nothing less than the American dream. Such independence and rugged individualism as demonstrated by Rachel and her mother are viewed as unworthy of Nick's family's attention. Rather, Nick's mother prefers that he place more value in his own loyalty to family and its financial operations. Even the typical portrayal of America as the land of abundance is turned on its head when Mr. Goh, the father of Rachel's college friend, Peik Lin, encourages the children to eat their chicken nuggets because "there's a lot of children starving in America." Openly critiquing the American dream in a popular romantic comedy is nothing less than radical. This shift may signal that the time-honored trope of American exceptionalism is wearing thin on some global audiences and film producers alike.

As a mixed-race person of Eurasian descent, Cathy does not often speak outwardly about her own experiences with race relations. However, she does admit to occasional encounters with the stereotypes of strangers. Although tempting to think of Singapore as some kind of multicultural utopia, people here can be all-too-human. With respect to her physical appearance, for instance, Cathy's facial complexion sometimes confuses people who may not immediately place her as Chinese. Rather, they might ignorantly presume she is a Filipino or another minority. On occasion people can treat her with instant condescension while making assumptions about her ethnic background. She explains, "People think I look Filipino, but I can also appear to be Hispanic—Latino—but not fully Chinese. They don't know what I am," she laughs.

Then she shares a recent story: "The other day this shop owner was so fascinated with me. He was blabbering about something, so I blabbered back. I was speaking in [Chinese] dialect. He was shocked and laughed, telling me, 'You speak dialect very well!' And I said, well, 'Welcome to my world, I'm Chinese lah!' And he said that I don't look Chinese. His English was broken, and I was annoyed, so I spoke to him in English too. He was so condescending, thinking I was inferior. I get annoyed with how badly they speak to me sometimes, and then I will correct them in their own dialect, and they feel so ashamed! But after that I become good friends with them because I like to talk," she ends on a positive note. Then she adds, "Another store owner thought I was Malay, and she was being rude to me. So, I asked if she thought I was Malay, and why she had to speak to me like that. When I spoke to her in Mandarin she was startled and tried to cover her mistake, saying she has a lot of friends who are Malay. Ya, right. But we're friends now too, like 'hello' friends."

This leads her to explain further, "That's why when I lead national education tours for school children, we visit Little India, Chinatown, and the Malay ethnic neighborhood in Kampong Glam. The students come from different ethnic backgrounds. I start by telling them why they are on a tour like this, and why people are born with very different backgrounds and religions. Then I explain to them that knowledge is the gateway to respect." She adds, "When you have no knowledge of other people's cultures or religions, it is easy to become critical of them. That's because the only knowledge you have is of your own religion, which of course you think is the correct way because your parents have taught it to you. But let's face it, we're in a world of color; a world of different colors, religions, and languages. I believe that the best way to learn racial harmony is when we are young."

Asked whether she gained a healthier respect for diversity when she became a tour guide, she responds, "I guess my acceptance of others began when I was young, and I really didn't care about what race people were. In my early days, people around me didn't seem to be stereotyping everyone based on race or ethnic background. Our neighbors included every race in Singapore, including Malays, Indians, Chinese, Eurasians like me; there was just about every color you could think of in my block of flats. And I was already mixed-race, so I fit in with everybody else. If I'm already mixed-race, why do I need to be prejudiced against others? I was one of them, so that was good enough to get along with everyone. And that was why the government purposely mixed families of different racial backgrounds in the housing flats, to diversify the public housing and encourage racial harmony after the 1960s."

Cathy is referring to the government's radical mandate for ethnic integration within all HDB housing blocks. Always concerned about the return of ethnic strife, Prime Minister Lee Kuan Yew believed the racial tensions and rioting of the 1960s was the direct result of the city's segregation, whereby many of the island's Chinese, Indian, Malay, and Eurasian communities lived within their own isolated ethnic enclaves. In response, the government instituted the Ethnic Integration Policy, or EIP in 1989. On the surface, the approach is elegantly simple. It places quotas on the percentages of each racial group allowed to inhabit a particular housing block. Of course, the ramifications of this law are not so simple and have been hotly debated for decades.

To identify who belongs within which racial group, the government instituted a standard classification approach. At birth, a child is officially assigned to one of four racial categories known collectively as the CMIO scheme (Chinese, Malay, Indian, or Other). Those who do not fall cleanly into the first three are lumped into an ambiguous "Other" category. Cathy chuckles when discussing CMIO, given her own official designation within this vague category. Her birth certificate marks her distinctly as "Other," due to her Eurasian lineage. Though percentages of ethnic affiliation have certainly shifted, in 2020 Cathy joined only 3.2 percent of Singapore's population who fell within this category. And only a portion of those were considered Eurasian.

Aside from her experience living within integrated housing well prior to the EIP, Cathy reflects on her early training as a tour guide and how that process admittedly influenced her perspectives. She adds, "The guiding has brought my own knowledge of different people to another level, because I had needed to start learning more about people's religions and ethnic heritage in Singapore. I guess it was my own desire to learn also. I've also been passionate about what I do, and there is always more to learn. I've noticed that the most effective guides are those who are passionate about learning and sharing their knowledge. Some guides just go through the motions based on what they already know, but it's important to keep learning because Singapore is constantly changing. It's like there's a new building or development every day, and we have to keep up with these changes! It's very exciting to see change happen so quickly here, but it's important for me and other guides to stay on top of things for our guests. I guess that's why my interest in learning has helped me gain a wider perspective for the diversity of people and places here."

To close out our conversation on such topics, I ask Cathy what she thought of the idea of being "crazy rich" as implied in the film. Would that represent a lifestyle to which she would aspire? After some thought, she offers, "Wealth marries wealth. A wealthy family will try to marry you to another wealthy family, so that is accurate. Even if you have a ton of money, you have issues, so it's just best to not have too much money," she laughs at her logical advice. "It's good to be average. What worries do I have? My worry is whether my favorite hair salon is going to be open, or where I can get the best prawns tomorrow. But when you have wealth, it's usually to impress other people within that social class. They look at you and judge every move you make. But without piles of money, what do I care? I'm free!"

Bibliography

Badalge, K.N. "The Country Where Diversity is Enforced by Law." *We Are Not Divided*, 22 October, 2020. https://wearenotdivided.reasonstobecheerful.world/the-country-where-diversity-is-enforced-by-law/

Barr, Michael D., et. al. *Singapore: A Modern History*. I.B. Tauris & Company, Limited, 2018.

"Bilingual Education." *NLS Resource Guides*. National Library Singapore. https://web.archive.org/web/20131002211453/http://libguides.nl.sg/content.php?pid=57257&sid=551371

Bloomberg. "Crazy Rich Asians Craze? 5 Million People Visited Singapore in July-September." *Mint*. Updated 30 November, 2019. https://www.livemint.com/news/world/crazy-rich-asians-craze-5-million-people-visited-singapore-in-july-september-11575087783186.html

Booth, Jessica. "These Are the Places From 'Crazy Rich Asians' You Can Actually Visit in Real Life. *Bustle*, 16 August, 2018. https://www.bustle.com/p/13-crazy-rich-asians-singapore-filming-locations-that-you-can-actually-visit-in-real-life-10137339

"The Catholic Church in Singapore." *Encyclopedia.com*. https://www.encyclopedia.com/religion/encyclopedias-almanacs-transcripts-and-maps/singapore-catholic-church

Carey, Meredith. "Where was 'Crazy Rich Asians' Filmed?" Condé Nast Traveler, 9 August, 2018. https://www.cntraveler.com/gallery/where-was-crazy-rich-asians-filmed

Chan, Hong Yin. "The Hungry Ghost Festival in Singapore: Getai in the Lunar Seventh Month." *Religions* 11 (2020): 356.

Cheow, Sue-Ann. "How Real is Crazy Rich Asians' Portrayal of the Crazy Rich in Singapore?" *The Straits Times*, 27 August, 2018. https://www.straitstimes.com/lifestyle/entertainment/how-real-is-crazy-rich-asians-portrayal-of-the-crazy-rich-in-singapore

Chia, Joshua, et. al. "Bahau Settlement." *Singapore Infopedia*, National Library Board. https://www.nlb.gov.sg/main/article-detail?cmsuuid=c38cb04c-578e-4264-b714-e2686270b84a#:~:text=Bahau%20in%20the%20Malayan%20state,%E2%80%9D%20or%20%E2%80%9Cbeautiful%20village%E2%80%9D

Chua, Alvin. "Marina Bay Sands." *Singapore Infopedia*, National Library Board. https://www.nlb.gov.sg/main/article-detail?cmsuuid=7f0d359a-12e7-4d6b-8015-cf5e7f2bea72

Chua, Beng Huat. "Multiculturalism in Singapore: An Instrument of Social Control." *Race & Class* 44, no. 3 (2003): 58-77.

____. "Navigating Between Limits: The Future of Public Housing in Singapore." *Housing Studies* 29, no. 4 (2014): 520-533.

Cornelius, Vernon. "Cavenagh Bridge." *Singapore Infopedia*, National Library Board. https://www.nlb.gov.sg/main/article-detail?cmsuuid=563a3d5a-6323-49a4-8f38-fccfd2855c6c#:~:text=Singapore%20Infopedia&text=This%20is%20a%20general%20view,Title%20devised%20by%20Library%20staff

____. "Bumboats." *Singapore Infopedia*, National Library Board. https://www.nlb.gov.sg/

"Crazy Rich Asians: Bringing Americans to Singapore." *Perspectives@SMU*. Singapore Management University, 2019. https://ink.library.smu.edu.sg/pers/473

DeWolf, Christopher. "The Tiger Balm Story: How Ointment for Every Ailment was Created, Fell Out of Favour, Then Found New Generations of Users." *South China Morning Post*, 17 February, 2018. https://www.scmp.com/lifestyle/health-beauty/article/2133311/tiger-balm-story-how-ointment-every-ailment-was-created-fell

Dick, H. "A Slow Ride into the Past: The Chinese Trishaw Industry in Singapore," 1942-1983. *Asian Studies Review* 38, no. 1 (2014): 158-159.

Dobbs, Stephen. "Urban Redevelopment and the Forced Eviction of Lighters from the Singapore River." *Singapore Journal of Tropical Geography* 23, no. 3 (2003): 288-310.

Eckhardt, Gina, and Kerrigan, Finola. "Crazy Rich Asians: A Tale of Immigration, Globalization and Consumption in East Asia." *Markets, Globalization & Development Review* 4, no. 3, article 5 (2020).

"From Villages to Flats (Part 1) - The Kampong Days." *Remember Singapore*, 4 April, 2012. https://remembersingapore.org/2012/04/04/from-villages-to-flats-part-1/

Ghosh, Prianka. "A Brief History of Singapore's Peranakan Culture." *Culture Trip*, 28 February, 2017. https://theculturetrip.com/asia/singapore/articles/a-brief-history-of-singapores-peranakan-culture

Goh, Daniel P.S. "Choreographing Singapore's Utopia by the Bay." In *Tourist Utopias: Offshore Islands, Enclave Spaces, and Mobile Imaginaries*, 97-120. Edited by Tim Simpson. Amsterdam University Press, 2017.

Gruber, Aya. "Public Housing in Singapore: The Use of Ends-Based Reasoning in the Quest for a Workable System." *Harvard International Law Journal* 38, no. 1 (Winter 1997): 236-271.

Heng, C.K. (ed). *50 Years of Urban Planning in Singapore*. World Scientific Publishing Co. Pte. Ltd., 2017.

Heng, Terence. "Hungry Ghosts in Urban Spaces: A Visual Study of Aesthetic Markers and Material Anchoring." *Visual Communication* 13, no. 2 (2014): 147-162.

____. "An appropriation of ashes: Transient aesthetic markers and spiritual place-making as performances of alternative ethnic identities." *Sociological Review* 63 (2015): 57-78.

____. "Making 'Unofficial' Sacred Space: Spirit Mediums and House Temples in Singapore. *Geographical Review* 106 (2016): 215-34.

"History of Currency in Singapore." *Monetary Authority of Singapore*. https://www.mas.gov.sg/currency/history-of-currency-in-singapore

"History of Education in Singapore." *K12 Academics*. https://www.k12academics.com/Education%20Worldwide/Education%20in%20Singapore/history-education-singapore

Hong, Lysa. "Singapore and its Tensed Pasts: History and Nation-building." *Asia Research Institute*, Working Paper Series No. 82. Department of History, National University of Singapore, 2007.

Hong, Yin Chan, 2020. "The Hungry Ghost Festival in Singapore: Getai (Songs on Stage) in the Lunar Seventh Month." *Religions* 11, no. 7 (2020): 356.

Jose, M.J. "The Real-Life Story of Kevin Kwan That Inspired 'Crazy Rich Asians.'" *Tatler*, 17 August, 2018. https://www.tatlerasia.com/lifestyle/arts/my-crazy-rich-asians-author-kevin-kwan

Kent, Daniel. "A New Educational Perspective: The Case of Singapore." *Penn GSE Perspectives on Urban Education* 14, no. 1 (2017): n1.

Lee, Kah-Wee. "Planning as State-Effect: Calculation, Historicity and Imagination at Marina Bay, Singapore." *Planning Theory & Practice* 19, no. 4 (2018): 477-495.

Lee, Siew Yeen. "C.K. Tang (Tang Choon Keng)." *Singapore Infopedia*, National Library Board. https://www.nlb.gov.sg/main/article-detail?cmsuuid=db26a362-ea5e-45a1-9424-144b56d87176

Lim, Alvin Eng Hui. "Live Streaming and Digital Stages for the Hungry Ghosts and Deities." *Religions* 11, no. 7 (2020): 367.

Lim, Irene. "Haw Par Villa (Tiger Balm Gardens)." *Singapore Infopedia*, National Library Board. https://www.nlb.gov.sg/main/article-detail?cmsuuid=7809f4c9-d067-455c-8dbb-a511073e4d31

Lim, Linda. "Singapore's Success: The Myth of the Free Market Economy." *Asian Survey* 23 (1983): 752-64.

Low, Wilson. "Whither Conscription in Singapore." Thesis, Master of Military Art and Science. University of Southampton, United Kingdom, 2006.

Sek, Victoria. "How S'pore's Oldest Department Store TANGS Survived 86 Years – Valued at $476M in 2016." *Vulcan Post*, 12 July, 2018. https://vulcanpost.com/643300/tangs-singapore-history/

Seng, Sabrina. "S'pore Had a Tang Dynasty Village in Jurong That Transported Visitors to Ancient China." *MSNews*, 11 December, 2020. https://mustsharenews.com/tang-dynasty-village/

"Singlish." *Singapore Infopedia*, National Library Board. https://www.nlb.gov.sg/main/article-detail?cmsuuid=5d5de338-98c5-4a97-9b51-727e807d6507#:~:text=Singlish%20is%20an%20informal%2C%20colloquial,Colloquial%20English%20or%20Singapore%20English

Szolomicki, Jerzy and Golasz-Szolomicka, Hanna. "The Marina Bay Sands Complex in Singapore: A Modern Marvel of Structure and Technology." *IOP Conference Series: Materials Science and Engineering* 960 (2020).

Tan, Fred Wei-Shi, and Lew, Psalm B.C. "The Role of the Singapore Armed Forces in Forging National Values, Image, and Identity." *Military Review* (March-April 2017): 8-16.

Van der Merwe, Hugo. "Hongbao: The Who, How and What of Chinese red Envelopes." *Chinese Language Institute*, updated 18 September, 2024. https://studycli.org/chinese-culture/hongbao/

Wee, Sui-Lee. "The Architect Who Made Singapore's Public Housing the Envy of the World." *New York Times*, 24 May, 2024. https://www.nytimes.com/2024/05/24/world/asia/singapore-public-housing-urban-planner.html

____. "Where Public Housing Apartments Can Go for More Than $1 Million." *New York Times*, 24 May, 2024. https://www.nytimes.com/2024/05/24/world/asia/singapore-public-housing-program.html

Wong, Terrie Siang-Ting. "Crazy, Rich, When Asian: Yellowface Ambivalence and Mockery in 'Crazy Rich Asians.'" *Journal of International and Intercultural Communication* 15, no. 1 (2022): 57-74.

Yap, Erica. "The Transnational Assembling of Marina Bay, Singapore." *Singapore Journal of Tropical Geography* 34 (2013): 390-406.

Yong, Ced. "The Chinese Ten Courts of Hell: A Visual Introduction." *Owlcation*, updated 16 November, 2023. https://owlcation.com/humanities/The-Horrific-Chinese-Ten-Courts-of-Hell

Yugal, Kishore Joshi, et. al. "Cleaning of the Singapore River and Kallang Basin in Singapore: Economic, Social and Environmental Dimensions." *International Journal of Water Resources Development* 28, no. 4 (December 2012): 647-658.

Acknowledgements

In addition to Cathy's own stories, I relied on a select set of academic literature and media articles to provide background on Singapore's history and culture. The first step in the research process involved a thorough examination of existing publications. For this initial phase I am grateful for the careful and diligent efforts of Adam Thomas-Fennelly, then a student at Butler University. During a year-long independent study, Adam identified relevant literary sources and highlighted substantial information that ultimately informed the historical perspectives within this book. Much of Adam's work is further reflected in the combination of academic and media sources provided in the Bibliography.

Numerous other individuals donated their time and skills as the book draft took shape. I learned a great deal about writing memoirs from Darryl Pebbles, who teaches a seminar on that topic at Butler University. His thoughtful feedback on an earlier draft contributed immensely to the final narrative and writing style. Regarding the book's development, a special round of thanks is owed to Anna Burrous for her skillful design of the book's cover. What makes the front cover particularly outstanding is the creative artwork of Singapore caricaturist, Adam Chua (caricaturist.sg). He generously devoted precious time and energy to design a fun and colorful image which brilliantly represents the theme of the story.

Lastly and most important, it would be a serious oversight to not recognize our respective families for their unwavering and enthusiastic support. Cathy's immediate and extended family members provided the patience and encouragement necessary for her to participate in lengthy interviews, to review numerous drafts, and to seek additional information. Likewise, I further appreciate the unwavering support, feedback, and creativity of my wife, Linda, with whom I shared our initial adventure in Singapore. Always keen to explore, travel, and learn about other people and places, Linda has encouraged this collaboration with Cathy from the idea's inception.

ABOUT THE AUTHOR

Author Tom Paradis (left), our driver, Saleh (center), and tour guide Cathy Ross visiting Pulau Ubin.

Thomas (Tom) Paradis is professor of geography and community planning at Butler University in Indianapolis, Indiana, USA, where he teaches a full slate of courses on urban, cultural, and historical geography, world regional geography, urban design and planning, and architectural history. He has also taught and led study-abroad programs in Siena, Viterbo, and Rome, Italy. His two previous books focus on Appalachian geography and music in the Hunger Games saga, while earlier books highlight the centuries-old horse race in Siena, Italy, the *Palio*.

www.ingramcontent.com/pod-product-compliance
Lightning Source LLC
Chambersburg PA
CBHW030544080526
44585CB00012B/251